Humor in Interaction

Volume 182

Humor in Interaction
Edited by Neal R. Norrick and Delia Chiaro

Humor in Interaction

Edited by

Neal R. Norrick
Saarland University

Delia Chiaro
Alma mater studiorum Università di Bologna

John Benjamins Publishing Company

Amsterdam / Philadelphia

^{TM} The paper used in this publication meets the minimum requirements of
American National Standard for Information Sciences – Permanence of
Paper for Printed Library Materials, ANSI z39.48-1984.

Library of Congress Cataloging-in-Publication Data

Humor in interaction / edited by Neal R. Norrick, Delia Chiaro.
    p. cm. (Pragmatics & Beyond New Series, ISSN 0922-842X ; v. 182)
  Includes bibliographical references and index.
  1. Joking. 2. Plays on words. 3. Conversation analysis. 4. Pragmatics. I. Norrick, Neal R.
    II. Chiaro, Delia, 1953-
P304.H86   2009
302.3'46--dc22   2009016221
ISBN 978 90 272 5427 6 (HB; alk. paper)
ISBN 978 90 272 5616 4 (PB; alk. paper)
ISBN 978 90 272 8933 9 (EB)

John Benjamins Publishing Co. · P.O. Box 36224 · 1020 ME Amsterdam · The Netherlands
John Benjamins North America · P.O. Box 27519 · Philadelphia PA 19118-0519 · USA

For
Petra and Pippo
after all these years

Table of contents

Contributors

Nancy D. Bell is an Associate Professor at Washington State University. Her research interests include L2 language play and humor, cross-cultural interaction, and the development of L2 sociolinguistic competence. Her work has appeared in journals such as *Applied Linguistics*, *Humor*, and *Intercultural Pragmatics*. She is also the author of *A Student's Guide to the M.A. TESOL*.

Claudia Bubel studied English linguistics at Saarland University, Germany. Her doctoral dissertation focused on the linguistic construction of friendship relations in TV drama. She now works as a secondary school teacher and provides in-service teacher training for English teachers.

Delia Chiaro holds the chair of English Language and Translation at the University of Bologna's Advanced School in Modern Languages for Interpreters and Translators at Forlì, Italy. Since publishing *The Language of Jokes: Analyzing Verbal Play* in 1992 (London, Routledge) she has combined her interest in verbally expressed humor with her passion for cinema by examining what exactly occurs when verbal humor in English is transformed into dubbed or subtitled filmic products. As well as considering the transformations which cinematic dialogues undergo, she is a keen observer of audience perception of translated humor and applies methodologies taken from the social sciences to the field of Translation Studies to examine recipients' reactions. Her latest publications include *Translation, Humour and Literature* (Continuum, 2010) and *Translation, Humour and the Media* (Continuum, 2010), a chapter dealing with humor and translation in the *Primer in Humor Studies* (Victor Raskin (ed.) Mouton De Gruyter 2008) and a chapter in *Reading 'Little Britain'* (Sharon Lockyer (ed.)2010 I.B. Taurus). She has been a keynote speaker across Europe, in Asia and New Zealand.

Susan Ervin-Tripp is Professor Emerita of Psychology at the University of California, Berkeley. Her research publications since1952 include studies of bilingual cognition, bilingual code-switching, monolingual style-switching, the development of child grammar, and pragmatics in both children and adults, including requests and the pragmatics of narratives and of humor in the conversation of both child and adult friends. She was president of the International Pragmatics

Association 2000–2006, served on the board of the Social Science Research Council, and during a year at the Center for Advanced Study wrote on the pragmatics of requests in adults and children. The studies of requests and of humor are based on the collection of a corpus of natural interaction of friends and on filming within families. Her papers on humor are referenced in the chapter.

Cornelia Gerhardt teaches linguistics at the English department of Saarland University, Germany (Lehrkraft für besondere Aufgaben). Her interest in the interplay between talk-in-interaction and media discourse is reflected in her current work on a volume about the appropriation of media in everyday life (together with Ruth Ayass). She has published internationally on the television reception situation as well as different multimodal issues such as gaze behaviour and the juncture of talk and pictures. She maintains the ATTAC-corpus, a collection of transcribed interactions of English football fans watching the FIFA men's world cup on television. Dr Gerhardt has presented talks at a number of international conferences like IPrA, the Sociolinguistics Symposium, AILA or ICCA. She is founder and acting editor-in-chief of *SWPL, the Saarland Working Papers in Linguistics.*

Janet Holmes holds a personal Chair in Linguistics at Victoria University of Wellington. She teaches sociolinguistics courses, specialising in workplace discourse, including humour at work, and language and gender. She is Director of the Wellington Language in the Workplace project (see www.victoria.ac.nz/lals/lwp) and a Fellow of the Royal Society of New Zealand. Her books include *Gendered Talk at Work, An Introduction to Sociolinguistics*, now in its third edition, and the *Blackwell Handbook of Language and Gender* (co-edited with Miriam Meyerhoff). Her recent work focuses on leadership discourse and the relevance of gender and ethnicity in the workplace. Humour has also been a focus in this research. She is co-author of *Leadership, Discourse and Ethnicity* to be published by OUP in 2011 which examines effective leadership in Māori and Pākehā organisations. Most recently she has been investigating the discourse of skilled migrants as they enter the New Zealand workplace.

Kristin Kersten is Juniorprofessor of Foreign Language Teaching and Second Language Acquisition at Hildesheim University, Germany. Her research focuses on psycholinguistics and bilingual education. She has recently published *Verbal Inflections in L2 Child Narratives: A Study of Lexical Aspect and Grounding* (2009, Trier: WVT), which analyzes longitudinal data from picture stories in an English immersion elementary school, as well as guidelines on immersion and teaching principles. She has headed an international EU-funded research project in bilingual preschools, ELIAS (Early Language and Intercultural Acquisition Studies):

18 institutions from Germany, Belgium, England and Sweden monitored children's second language acquisition, intercultural communication, bilingual science skills and environmental awareness ("green immersion") in ten bilingual preschools, among them a unique zoo-preschool. Located on the premises of the Magdeburg Zoo in Germany, this preschool provides an ideal learning environment for bilingual nature and science education. She co-edited *Bilingual Preschools: Vol. I: Learning and Development. Vol II: Best Practices* (2010, Trier: WVT), containing co-authored chapters on intercultural communication, green immersion, and best practices in bilingual preschools. She is a member of EUROSLA and has recently been part of its scientific committee.

Martin D. Lampert is a professor of psychology and the chair of the Division of Social Sciences at Holy Names University in Oakland, California, USA. He also serves as the current Executive Secretary for the International Society for Humor Studies. His research interests include child development, gender differences, the cognitive aspects of humor appreciation, and the roles of humor and laughter in social interaction.

Meredith Marra is a member of the Wellington Language in the Workplace Project team and a Senior Lecturer at Victoria University of Wellington where she teaches a range of courses in sociolinguistics from undergraduate to PhD level. Meredith's primary research interest is the language of business meetings, and she has published in the areas of humour and gender in workplace interactions in *Language in Society*, the *Journal of Politeness Research* and *Text & Talk*. Along with the two other core members of the LWP team, she is co-author of *Leadership, Discourse and Ethnicity* (to be published by Oxford University Press) which documents a three-year cross-cultural research project on the language of effective leadership in Maori and Pakeha organisations.

Neal R. Norrick holds the chair of English Linguistics at Saarland University in Saarbrücken, Germany. His research specializations include conversation, narrative, verbal humor and formulaicity. Professor Norrick acts as Co-Editor in Chief of the *Journal of Pragmatics*, and serves on the advisory boards of the journals *Discourse Processes, Humor, International Review of Pragmatics* and *Text & Talk*. His monograph *Conversational narrative* was just re-issued in a paperback edition (Benjamins, 2010). His recent articles include: 'Incorporating listener evaluation into stories' *Narrative Inquiry* 20, 1 (2010): 183–204, 'Listening practices in television interviews' *Journal of Pragmatics* 42 (2010), 525–543 and 'Laughter before the punch line during the performance of narrative jokes in conversation' *Text & Talk* 30 (2010): 75–95.

Béatrice Priego-Valverde is a teacher in Lingustics at the University of Provence (Aix en Provence, France). She is a member of the Laboratoire Parole et Langage. Since her PhD in 1999 and the publication of her book in 2003 *L'humour dans la conversation familière*, she has specialized in conversational humor. More recently, her studies deal with failed humor.

Stephanie Schnurr is Associate Professor at the University of Warwick. Her main research interests are professional discourse and medical communication. Stephanie has published widely on the multiple functions and strategic uses of humour, (im)politeness, and workplace discourse with a particular focus on gender and leadership performance. Her research papers have appeared, for example, in *Language in Society*, *Journal of Pragmatics*, *Journal of Sociolinguistics*, and *Journal of Politeness Research*. Stephanie is also the author of *Leadership Discourse at Work. Interactions of Humour, Gender and Workplace Culture* (Palgrave Macmillan).

Bernadette Vine is a Research Fellow on the Language in the Workplace Project and Corpus Manager for the Archive of New Zealand English, both based at the School of Linguistics and Applied Language Studies, Victoria University of Wellington, New Zealand. Bernadette's research interests include workplace communication, leadership and New Zealand English. She is the author of *Getting Things Done at Work*: *The Discourse of Power in Workplace Interaction* published by John Benjamins in 2004 and is co-author of the forthcoming book *Leadership, Discourse and Ethnicity* (with Janet Holmes and Meredith Marra, Oxford University Press). She has just completed a study of the use of the pragmatic particle *eh* by male managers in New Zealand workplaces (with Sharon Marsden) and is undertaking new research on the way advice is given to skilled migrants in New Zealand workplaces, and how they respond to this advice.

Humor and interaction*

Neal R. Norrick & Delia Chiaro

This volume brings together an international array of scholars representing various theoretical perspectives, but all specifically concerned with interactional aspects of humor. The collection is not an outgrowth of a single conference panel or symposium. The contributors and topics were chosen to represent current research in the interdisciplinary area of humor studies. The authors are all scholars with interests in both humor studies and adjacent disciplines such as linguistic pragmatics, sociolinguistics, discourse analysis, psycholinguistics, gender studies and translation studies. They analyze data of various sorts, ranging from everyday conversation to talk at work to controlled experiments to questionnaires, and they employ a variety of approaches, from Conversation Analysis and Politeness Theory to Community of Practice and the work of Bakhtin. All these approaches contribute to our understanding of humor in interaction.

Whatever sort of data they analyze and whatever theoretical perspective they adopt, the contributors here are all committed to real data involving real people in real interactions of some type. Too long and too often still writers have advanced arguments about humor based on their personal intuitions about what is funny and how jokes work. Parallel to the evidence-less abstract grammar of the generativists, some advocate an account of 'humor competence' underlying real performance and reception. They detail their own appraisal of written joke texts, disregarding the importance of such performance variables as posture, gesture, voice, intonation, hesitations, disfluencies, not to mention the relationship between the teller and the listeners, their genders, ages, relative social status and the physical context (at home, at school, at work). Among other biases, this has led to the assumption that laughter occurs at and only at the punch line of a joke, whereas observation of practically any real narrative joke performance illustrates listeners and tellers laughing at various times from the announcement of the joke to the punch line

*Acknowledgements
The editors owe a great debt to those scholars who reviewed the individual contributions and the entire volume for their insightful comments and constructive suggestions. Gerardine Pereira, Melanie Gros, Claudia Enzweiler and Sylvia Monzon of Saarland University provided invaluable editorial and clerical support. We would also like to thank *Pragmatics & Beyond* editor Anita Fetzer along with Isja Conen and Patricia Leplae of John Benjamins for all their help.

and on afterwards, as the participants comment on the joke text and the joke-telling performance. From the assumption that the punch line alone constitutes its raison d'être follow other postulates like the testing function of the joke (entailing laughter immediately following the punch line) and a failure to appreciate all its other interactive functions such as illustrating a point or simply sharing a laugh even with an old joke known to the listeners. The field requires more research on joking in interaction, its functions and failures—and listener reactions to them, regardless of its theoretical bent. If researchers cannot find enough relevant examples in the growing body of recorded data, then experiments and questionnaires are obvious methods to employ.

The book consists of ten chapters organized into four sections. We considered various ways of organizing the individual papers into sections. What all the contributions have in common is a fundamental interest in humor as a mode of interaction, what people accomplish with humor rather than the form of humor or the bare text. Thus, one obvious possibility was to arrange the articles according to the nature of the data they analyze such as everyday conversation, talk at work and talk in educational settings. Some of the articles are also linked thematically. From a thematic perspective, the two chapters on doing gender (in the workplace) by Schnurr and Holmes (Chapter 5) and Vine, Kell, Marra and Holmes (Chapter 6) clearly fit together, as do the two articles concerning bilingual humor by Chiaro (Chapter 10) and Kersten (Chapter 9) as well as those addressing failed humor by Priego-Valverde (Chapter 8) and Bell (Chapter 7). Moreover, those contributions broadly in the field of conversational analysis such as Ervin-Tripp and Lampert (article 1), Norrick and Bubel (Chapter 2), Kotthoff (Chapter 3) and Gerhardt (Chapter 4) also share an interest in issues of politeness and identity. The notion of impoliteness also plays a role in Bell's chapter. Especially the connection between humor and impoliteness casts new light on the traditional view of humor as aggressive. At the same time, there are methodological connections such as the common reliance on the Bakhtinian notion of dialogism or multiple voicing by both Priego-Valverde and Kotthoff. In employing irony, a speaker frames an utterance in two ways at once, representing two separate voices, that of the speaker and another representing some other perspective. The double voicing analysis of irony fits well with traditional accounts of humor in recognizing a clash of simultaneous incongruous messages or 'bisociated' meanings. We ultimately decided in favour of a mixed approach, grouping those chapters which most obviously resonate together in terms of either theme, theoretical approach or both. The first section comprises studies based on recorded conversation among friends and family; the second section addresses doing gender based on talk recorded in workplace situations; the third section concerns failed humor and its interactional effects; the fourth and final section contains studies of humor in bilingual interactions of different types.

Spontaneous conversation among friends, family members and peers at school or work is the most frequent, most natural mode of interaction for most people. Conversation, or talk-in-interaction, as it is often called, constitutes the object of much research in linguistics and sociology, while humor research has tended to lag behind with its traditional focus on the humorous text. Thus, conversational joking provides a natural point of departure for a volume concerned with humor in interaction. The first article investigates the humor of self-disclosure based on conversations recorded in everyday settings and transcribed for careful study. In 'The occasioning of self-disclosure humor', Susan Ervin-Tripp and Martin Lampert take a look at the different ways in which humor is introduced into conversational self-disclosures. They focus on whether self-disclosure humor is introduced in the form of humorous narratives largely to entertain and build group solidarity, or emerges as part of a more serious discourse to lighten the import of the self-disclosure to the self and others. We are used to laughing at humor about foibles of famous persons or shared acquaintances, and these often are the basis of repeated stories and jokes. These exchanges have the effect not only of entertainment but of marking shared perspectives. Because laughing at oneself implies public self-criticism, we might expect that speakers would be cautious about such self-disclosures, yet such disclosures often emerge in the context of humorous exchanges. For one thing, speakers may tactically introduce humorous self-talk to lighten a conversation and build camaraderie through shared amusing experiences. Second, they may self-disclose a troubling personal experience and in the process recognize that they can use humor to lighten their concerns and gain a more objective perspective. Further, they can use humor to downplay an unintentional and potentially embarrassing self-revelation. Ervin-Tripp and Lampert observe that self-disclosures, like teases of conversational partners, are risky, in the sense that they can be taken as serious comments, jeopardizing social relations and jeopardizing face. To mitigate these risks, speakers exaggerate or embed such talk in a context of humor.

In the second chapter in the section, 'Direct address as a resource for humor', Neal R. Norrick and Claudia Bubel explore the use of direct address to create humor in everyday conversation based on examples from generally available corpora of transcribed conversational English. They take direct address to include any reference to a real or imagined listener with a proper or invented term of address. They show how humorous forms build on, extend and subvert the standard system. Direct address always has both an 'attention, identification' function and a 'contact, expressive' function, with one more prominent in any given context, but both these functions play various roles in the creation of humorous discourse. In particular, Norrick and Bubel demonstrate how stock jocular phrases, canned jokes and spontaneous conversational joking may incorporate an inappropriate form of address to create the incongruity characteristic of verbal humor and introduce a play frame. Direct address with culturally coded terms of address like *sir* provides a serviceable resource for the creation of humor in fantasy sequences as well. Finally, direct address, especially with obscene terms of address adds force to joke punch lines. The system of direct address is surprisingly flexible, and participants in talk-in-interaction take creative advantage of this flexibility for humorous purposes.

In 'An interactional approach to irony development', Helga Kotthoff discusses conversational data from a small project on how pupils come to use irony and related forms of communication. For an understanding of irony, we must take into account that an utterance can have layers of meaning that are in opposition to each other. To make sense of this type of non-literal communication people must infer other speakers' general stances and then use this information as a basis to infer the speakers' present intentions and attitudes. Children usually cannot understand simple forms of irony before the age of six, because they have not yet developed the habit of imagining the intentions and attitudes of others. In her past work, Kotthoff has analyzed ironic interactions between adults using a Bakhtinian and frame analytic approach; in this article, she applies that framework of multiple voices to understand what sorts of irony nine-year-olds can understand and produce by themselves. She differentiates various sub-types within the broad category of irony. Some sub-types correspond to teasing, others more to critical comments or joint fantasy production. One of her main points is that not only the pragmatics of irony (processing the gap between what is said and what is meant) is important, but also the meta-pragmatics (stance management). The children in the study often stage an authoritative, ironic voice directed at the supervising college students. They thereby show their knowledge of official adult stances (for example, with regard to what is considered to be healthy food) and suggest joint distancing in their ironic remarks addressed at the students. The students join in the irony by 'playing along.' Irony helps the students and the children to create an in-group that plays with its knowledge of official and unofficial stances and unites in sharing unofficial perspectives and attitudes.

In a fascinating departure from studies of free conversation, Cornelia Gerhardt investigates talk between friends and family members watching television. In her 'Intertextual and multimodal humor in the media reception situation: the case of watching football on TV', she describes humor in a corpus of conversations recorded while her subjects were watching football in their own homes. The larger context of her work includes both the reception of mass media and everyday face-to-face interaction. Although mass media have acquired an enormous importance in societies and television takes a central place in the households of most people, language and humor in this particular setting have scarcely been addressed. Gerhardt demonstrates that humor as a social practice plays an important part in the appropriation of media texts in the reception situation. She analyzes both reactions to humorous stimuli in the television program and the strategies television viewers use to create humor of their own. She finds that humor helps television viewers identify themselves by turns as sports fans, football experts and as proponents of a specific team. Again we see that participants in talk-in-interaction employ humor as a means of group identity. People watching football on television laugh frequently and for various reasons. Among other things, they laugh about humorous remarks and situations on television, but, more importantly, they create their own humor against the backdrop of the media text. By linking their talk to the pictures, they create humor multimodally, and by tying their words to the talk of the sportscasters on television, intertextual humor is constructed.

The two chapters in the second section consider humor in workplace interaction. Talk at work includes specific goal-oriented interactions such as meetings and reflects certain power relations and organizational policies. Employees have recourse to humor of various kinds to negotiate these structures, to establish individual identities and group affiliations. In their 'Men, Masculinity and Humor in the Workplace' Stephanie Schnurr and Janet Holmes investigate humor and norms of behavior at work. Workplaces constitute sites where individuals 'do gender' while at the same time constructing their professional identities and meeting their organisation's expectations. In most workplaces, a rather narrow range of masculine styles of interaction are considered normative. In other words, discursive strategies associated with stereotypically masculine speech styles, as well as behaviours associated with the enactment of hegemonic masculinity are generally viewed as paradigmatic ways of interacting at work. The investigation focuses on one particularly versatile discursive strategy frequently employed in talk at work, namely humor. As a multi-functional socio-pragmatic device, humor performs a variety of functions in the workplace. As a solidarity strategy, humor typically contributes to the smoother achievement of work objectives. But humor also enables individuals to construct complex social identities, and, by licensing relatively unconventional behaviour, it allows people to challenge and shift the boundaries of normative and expected behaviours. Schnurr and Holmes explore how professional men and women use this versatile discursive strategy in a variety of ways associated with stereotypical masculinity, but also as a means to make fun of and challenge gendered interactional norms prevailing in their workplace.

In a second essay concerned with talk at work, 'Boundary marking humor: institutional, gender and ethnic demarcation', Bernadette Vine, Susan Kell, Meredith Marra and Janet Holmes investigate how humor helps establish and maintain boundaries between groups in interaction. Based on recorded workplace meetings of Māori and Pākehā women in one New Zealand government department, they illustrate some of the complexities of boundary-marking humor. In particular, they analyse examples where the humor illuminates some of the tensions experienced by less powerful groups working within the institutional parameters or frameworks of more dominant groups or sources of influence. The relevant in-group shifts and the humor may correspondingly orient to boundaries dividing different institutional groups, different sexes, and different ethnic groups at different times. The dynamic flux of talk allows distinct aspects of social identity to come to the fore at different moments. In each case, no members of the out-group are present and the humor functions to build solidarity and rapport between in-group members.

The analysis of workplace humor in different groups suggests that multiple aspects of individual identity, in particular simultaneous membership of more than one subordinate group, expands the range of opportunities for individuals to contribute rapport-enhancing, boundary-marking humorous utterances to enliven mundane, primarily transactionally-oriented workplace discourse.

The third section of this volume concerns failed humor and its interactional effects. Failed humor is a example of humor in interaction par excellence. The study of failed humor must necessarily consider context and negotiation between participants in interaction. Failed humor has long been neglected both in linguistic accounts of interaction and in humor studies, but in this volume two chapters approach unsuccessful humor from different perspectives. In the first, Beatrice Priego-Valverde investigates failed humor in everyday conversation, and in the second, Nancy Bell presents her experimental research on failed humor. In 'Failed humor in conversation: a double voicing analysis', Beatrice Priego-Valverde investigates unsuccessful humor in interaction. Attempts at humor in interaction are not always successful at eliciting laughter and a positive response, and attempts at humor may sometimes fail to accomplish the interactional goals of the initiator. Priego-Valverde analyzes in her essay two distinct types of failed humor: cases where humor is simply not perceived and cases where humor is perceived but rejected by the hearer. She seeks to explain failed humor with a double voicing approach, following Bakhtin. She argues that humor involves speaking in a separate voice from one's own: imitating another's speech patterns, citing another person's words, adopting someone else's stance or opinion and so on. When speakers produce humorous utterances, they appeal to two separate enunciators: one saying and one observing what they say, joking about themselves, about the language they use, about the situation or about the object of mockery. This second enunciator signals the switch into non-serious communication, and humor is often unsuccessful when the receiver fails to recognize the second voice for what it is or fails to recognize the difference between the two voices.

Humor in casual conversations is generally based on knowledge shared by the participants, and it can fail when salient information is missing for the recipient. Failure to recognize the presence or the source of a second voice in the humorous performance provides a good example of the shortfall of shared knowledge, and an interesting site for the investigation of humor in interaction.

In her chapter on 'Failed humor', Nancy Bell uses the concepts of rapport management and impoliteness to examine the rude rejoinders collected in reaction to a failed attempt at humor in tests she designed. Bell instructed investigators to tell an intentionally poor joke to interlocutors in a range of natural contexts and to record their responses, along with the recipient's sex, relationship to the investigator and approximate age. Bell observes that interlocutor characteristics, behavioral expectations, identity concerns/face claims, and the disruptive nature of humor all played a part in the hearers' decisions to respond with aggression. Bell concedes that this preliminary investigation raises, perhaps, more questions than it answers. Although it was presented as if it were spontaneous, the humor her subjects used was not only pre-scripted, but could also be classified as children's humor. Do similar interlocutors respond with similar rudeness to failed spontaneous, adult humor? When less disruptive forms of humor such as narratives fail, are they responded to less aggressively? Future research along these lines should also require data collectors to explicitly note their perceptions of the response in order to create a data set based on emic principles.

Although scholars recognize the many serious functions of humor, among lay people humor is generally considered as merely frivolous and fun, and this portrayal is easy to maintain when all goes well. However, as with a great deal of linguistic behavior, it is when expectations are not met that social norms are revealed. The responses Bell collected suggest that, under some conditions, humor is not at all frivolous – if this were the case, its failure would be of little consequence and certainly not worthy of some of the more vehement responses collected. In the preceding analysis by Priego-Valverde as well, it becomes apparent that there is much at stake in terms of face and identity for both conversational participants, making this an area of humor studies that warrants further investigation.

The final section of this book reports on research involving bilinguals. Both chapters in this section find that humor functions as a coping strategy in various ways. The first chapter in this section explores humor use in the bilingual classroom. Research in the field of second language acquisition (SLA) has not yet focused intensely on the phenomenon of humor in relation to the level of linguistic development in the second language (L2). In her article, 'Humor and Interlanguage in a Bilingual Elementary School Setting', Kristin Kersten focuses on the relationship between humor and language acquisition in a bilingual immersion setting. Her data stems from picture story narrations by 18 informants taking part in an

English immersion program in Germany. The analysis concentrates on instances of laughter and smiling as they appear spontaneously during the children's narrations. Kersten argues that young L2 learners have an awareness of the collision between demands that arise in communicative situations and their limited language skills. She suggests that learners use mechanisms of humor to alleviate the communicative problems that arise from their incomplete mastery of the target language. Ten different categories of laughter and smiling are identified in the picture story narrations of the informants. Five of these categories relate to humor according to the criteria of incongruity, an awareness thereof, and the experience of funniness on the part of the child. The categories are Clowning, Narrative/Behavioral Incongruity, Meta-linguistic Incongruity, Self-disparagement and Pictorial Incongruity. Taken together, the humor categories constitute 50% of the laughter and smiles displayed in the narrations. The results point to young language learners' use of humor as a mechanism to cope with the linguistic inadequacies of their interlanguage. The children are aware of the inadequacy of their own interlanguage system with regard to the expectations of a cooperative social interaction and they respond to this incongruity with humor. Kersten suggests that Repair in order to save face is the most important function with regard to the perceived inadequacy of the interlanguage system.

In the final chapter of this volume, 'Cultural divide or unifying factor? Humor and laughter in bilingual, cross-cultural couples', Delia Chiaro considers the role of humor in communication between couples who speak different languages natively. In the romantic view perpetrated by the cinema, relationships between two people who do not share the same language regularly result in a happy ending, despite a series of cross-linguistic comic misunderstandings. By contrast, studies in intercultural communication have focussed on misunderstandings. Chiaro asks just how different real life situations are from what happens on celluloid? Do couples really use gesture to communicate at the start of their relationship? Do cross-linguistic relationships end happily, as we are so often led to believe at the movies?

Chiaro argues that stable intercultural couples must be good communicators, since findings in social psychology show that communication difficulties are the main reason for marital difficulties and failure. In this spirit, Chiaro sets out to explore the following questions: (1) which is the dominant language chosen by the couple; (2) how far is the dominant language gender-dependent; (3) how stable is the dominant language in time; (4) what are the self-reported attitudes towards partner's language; and, most importantly for present purposes, (5) what is the role of humor in their relationship. Chiaro uses two different and complementary methods to investigate interaction in bilingual cross-cultural couples: first, a self-reporting questionnaire to gather quantitative data; and second, face-to-face interviews along with elicitation of reports from cross-cultural, bilingual informants recounting relevant experiences. Chiaro finds that humorous talk does indeed act as a bonding agent in cross-cultural, bilingual couples, with partners often making a special effort to teach their own brand of humor to their mate and vice versa, so that they learn to appreciate and to use the humor of their partner's culture. Furthermore, interviewees themselves made frequent use of humorous talk in their responses.

In this final article, as in several others in this volume, we find humor bringing people together and keeping relationships working. Humor enables people to interact more smoothly and to accomplish goals difficult or impossible to reach otherwise. Humor can license behaviors outside the norm and help challenge normative patterns, for women in the workplace and for pupils at school. This holds for interactions between partners in bilingual relationships, between friends and family members as well as between pupils and teachers and between colleagues at work. At the same time, the humor itself must be appropriate. Attempts at humor can fail in various ways with negative interactional results. Thus, bad jokes can lead to impolite responses and can strain relationships. We laugh during our own self-disclosures, but not about those we receive. In spite of its role as a peace-maker and an enabler, humor retains its power to injure and attack. Like relationships themselves, interactions involving humor are fragile and must be handled with care.

PART I

Conversation among friends and family

Then the conversation might become filled with comparable humorous stories. When they have broached troubling personal experiences, friends may adopt a humorous perspective and in the process lighten their concerns and gain distance on their problems. They may also joke about themselves to downplay unintentional and potentially embarrassing self-revelations. Thus humor may emerge at the start, during, or at the end of a self-disclosure.

In our prior research on humorous discourse, we observed notable differences in the characteristics and timing of men's and women's self-targeted humor (Lampert and Ervin-Tripp 1998, 2006). We found that in all-women's groups, female friends frequently shared funny personal stories. In their narratives, tellers would often talk about embarrassing situations or gaffes, and the events described were often ones that the other group members could have experienced themselves. Branner (2005) characterized this behavior in teenage girls as arising from an egalitarian culture, promoting a narrative presentation of the self as not perfect (p. 119). The high frequency of humorous self-disclosing narratives by women could be related to a well-known difference in talk. Researchers have observed that self-disclosure often serves as a basis of female friendship, and women and girls are more likely to self-disclose in general and are more likely to self-disclose to female than to male friends (Buhrmester and Prager 1995; Dindia and Allen 1992; Rubin 1983; Rose and Rudolph 2006). Research on whether men are more likely to self-disclose to women, though, has been mixed (Hill and Stull 1987). Not surprisingly then, we would expect to find a higher percentage of humorous self-narratives in female groups.

We also observed that women in all-women's groups were more likely as part of serious discourse to reveal embarrassing personal experiences that sparked subsequent laughter. However, these revelations, rather than being a source of put-downs or teasing, often prompted more focused talk. The group constructed a collaborative evaluation of the topic at hand. In a detailed analysis of conversational laughter during troubles talk, Jefferson (1984) observed that "a troubles-teller can, and perhaps should, laugh in the course of a troubles-telling, and thus exhibit that he or she is in a position to take it lightly" (p. 367). A striking feature of Jefferson's analysis was that the conversational partners did not immediately join in the laughter. Rather, what Jefferson repeatedly found was that when troubles-tellers laughed, listeners often declined to laugh and would instead speak seriously to the prior utterance and the source of the trouble (p. 350). In another remarkable paper, Jefferson (2004) noted that although women were usually more likely to join in other's laughter, they were less likely than men to laugh with troubles-tellers. Thus laughter during troubles-telling is not at all like the camaraderie-enhancing tale-telling by women friends. Kotthoff (2000) suggests that the timing of laughter in troubles talk is crucial, and that in Jefferson's examples "the first traces of laughter usually occur in the closing phase of the topic" (p. 66). If the topic is to be treated playfully, rather than as troubles talk, the teller has to make an early strong signal of key.

Finally, we found that men too engaged in humorous self-talk; however, their self-directed remarks often had a entertaining rather than self-revelatory quality. When men joked about themselves, they often made wisecracks that exaggerated or created a whimsical context for personal characteristics and behaviors made salient in the ongoing conversation (i.e., transforming a negative trait into something positive). Such wisecracks could serve to deflect any interpretation that self-disclosures were troubles talk calling for discussion. Like teases of conversational partners, self-disclosures are risky, in the sense that they can be taken as serious comments, jeopardizing social relations and jeopardizing face. In this light, we have argued that speakers—in particular men—often recast their self-disclosures in the form of exaggerations, fantasy, and humor to minimize their significance and potentially negative interpersonal consequences (Lampert and Ervin-Tripp 2006).

In this essay, we take a closer look at how humorous self-disclosures get introduced into peer talk of young children and adults. We ask (1) whether self-disclosure that is accompanied by laughter carries on an earlier topic, (2) whether it is a response to prodding or pragmatic needs, and (3) whether it is sensitive to accidents within the conversation and the immediate context.

2.   Database

The database that we used involved a collection of 102 taped and transcribed conversations of friendship groups of various ages. The 59 adult samples were primarily composed of college-age students in same- and mixed-sex groups, which students had collected and transcribed for conversational analysis classes. These data were recorded with friends in varied contexts from automobiles to cafes, and the students used permission forms so the data collection was known to participants. Our child samples were composed of 39 seven- and ten-year-old best-friend dyads and 4 ten-year-old triads. The children were recorded at lunchtime in a private room at their school in peer talk to avoid observer effects (see details of method in Ervin-Tripp 2000). We identified humor incidents by laughter that appeared to have an identifiable cause.

In our seven- and ten-year-old samples, very little self-targeted humor of any sort emerged; the frequency of self-targeted humor for each child subgroup was no greater than 7% of the laughter incidents (Ervin-Tripp et al. 2004). In contrast, across our adult samples, 22% of the coded cases involved self-directed humor about the speaker (Lampert and Ervin-Tripp 2006). In all, we found 466 instances of humor in our data set with the speaker as target. Of these cases, we judged that 94 instances disclosed valid information about the self not already likely to be known to the hearer. We found instances of self-disclosure humor in 11 mixed-sex (44%), 7 all-men's (37%), and 13 all-women's groups (93%) as well as in 8 girls' (36%), and 4 boys' groups (19%). Table 1 summarizes the distribution of self-targeted and self-disclosing humor across the 102 groups in our sample.

Overall, we found that the women in the all-women's groups stood out, with 40% of their self-directed joking appearing to be valid self-disclosure, dropping toward the men's level when they were in mixed-sex interactions. Of the 94 humorous self-disclosures, we found that 46 occurred shortly after prior humorous talk.

Our goal in the analysis to follow is to identify conversational contexts that precede the appearance of self-disclosing humor. We recognize that our samples are not large and that additional groups of older adult friends would have been helpful. Nevertheless, with the data at hand, we were able to derive a taxonomy to describe the occurrences of self-disclosing humor.

Table 1. Number of Child and Adult Groups with Self-Targeted and Self-Disclosing Humor and Number of Instances of Self-Disclosure Overall

	Speakers	Groups	Groups with Self-Targets	Groups with Disclosure	Instances of Disclosure
Seven-Year-Olds					
Males	18	9	6	2	3
Females	20	10	9	5	10
Ten-Year-Olds					
Males	26	12	5	2	4
Females	26	12	7	3	7
Adult Same-Sex					
Males	62	19	19	7	12
Females	41	14	13	13	32
Adult Mixed-Sex					
Male-Female Dyads	16	8	8	5	10
2–3 Females; 1 Male	20	6	6	2	11
2–3 Males; 1 Female	15	5	4	0	0
2+ Males; 2+ Females	34	7	7	4	5
Total	278	102	84	43	94

3.   Taxonomy and analysis

In general, we found self-disclosing humor to surface as (1) a collaborative contribution to an existing topic, (2) an introduction to a change of topic or a response to a specific elicitation, and (3) a response to an incidental environmental event. We have labeled these cases of humor as cases of Topical Continuity, Topic Change, and Incidental Responses, respectively. Of these three types, Topical Continuity was the most frequent, encompassing 69% of the instances of self-disclosing humor in our sample. We observed instances of Topical Continuity in four contexts: Humorous Rounds, Troubles Talk, Complex Narration, and Self-Revelation as Entertainment. Less frequent, but still evident, were Topic Changes, which we noted in three types of situations: Mitigations, Elicited Self-Disclosures, and Elicited Boasts. And finally, we found Incidental Responses that fell into two categories: Response to Contextual Reminders and Responses to Teasing. We now turn to look at each one of these contexts in greater detail.

3.1   Topical continuity

The most common context for introducing self-directed humor is simply topical continuity, normal in cohesive informal conversations. The extreme case is rounds that share topic and viewpoint through the turns of various speakers.

3.1.1   *Humorous rounds*
Rounds occur in larger groups more often, and involve maintenance of topic and stance. In this prototypical example from an older sample that a student recorded at a senior center, the distribution of the self-disclosing topic in the transcript is indicated by the highlighted line numbers. The thematic repetition of embarrassing stories about dresses guaranteed repeated self-disclosure.

(1)   **Senior center women**[1]

	22	Ann:	now, what about styles these days ..
	23		how do we feel about 'em ?
	24		for one thing i think they're very easy to wear.....
...			
	33	Ann:	and we can wear what we want\
	34	Bev:	and =we= can be comfortable and stylish
	35	Clare:	=right=
>36		**Bev:**	**and = .. = me with my little bit of weight**
	37		**[laughter] extra**
	38	Clare:	=um hmm=
	39	Bev:	than most of them .. i can get into clothes
	40		that uh = .. =
	41	Clare:	=sure=
	42	Bev:	that at least look *presentable on me but
	43		they kinda hide *disguise .. my figure
	44		because of the loose sizes\

---

1.   Most transcription notations are from Gumperz and Berenz (1993). Specifically = = brackets overlaps, which are aligned across turns, ==leads latched turns, \ marks final sentence fall, *marks extra stress, {[ff] marks forte or loud segments bounded by }, and other vocal changes are similarly described and bracketed.

Later, Ann talks about making a graduation dress, and being traumatized by being required to sew it herself. Then Bev chimes in with a story about lacking enough fabric for puffed sleeves when she made her graduation dress.

```
    352  Bev:     that dress did up, but uh, what was
   >353           *safe to do about the *sleeves\ so i walked
    354           crooked up the =the stage\=
    355  Diane:              =[laugh ]=
```

UC Disclab: WCON1

Danielle then comments that she made a pattern that came out with the back longer than the front. So while Clare only chimed in with supportive feedback, this was a round of stories about problems in sewing that led to making a fool of oneself in a public ritual situation many decades earlier. This personal history context is prototypical for women's self-directed joking among themselves.

This round of personal stories roughly stayed on a continuous topic. There is humor about the self, but only some of it is self-disclosure of information unlikely to be known to listeners. Line 36 is not a disclosure, though it is a joke about the self, but 353 is a self-disclosure, though it may be exaggerated. Line 36 indicates, however, that talking about one's 'defects' is acceptable in this context of shared concerns and experiences.

There were no self-disclosing joking rounds like this in the men's groups in our samples that involved spontaneous disclosure of separate events by each participant, but we do not have data from older men's groups.

3.1.2 Troubles talk

Troubles talk can be a source of laughter, by the teller and sometimes a listener, though as a troubles report it does not begin in humor. In sequence (2) Elena is sitting between Diane and Ben, discussing Elena's weight problems. Topical continuity appears to be guaranteed by the listeners' commitment to supportive involvement when there is troubles talk.

```
  (2)   Weight discussion with a male and a female friend.
    336  Elena:   {[sigh] [p] i weighed myself and i...i, don't
   >337           feel any *better [laugh]}
    338  Diane:   you've *lost a *lot of weight, though\
    339  Elena:   i *lost a lot of weight and then i gained it
    340           back..and i'm starting to lose it again
    341           which is good\
    342           but..it's kinda sad {[f] *why i
    343           started to lose it\ is because i got my-s- i got so
    344           up*set that i'm, i didn't feel like eating\\
    345           =yeah=}
```

346	Diane:	=upset= over what
347	Elena:	over Larry\\
348	Ben:	a::w\
349	Diane:	mm\
350	Elena:	(xx)\ i *really lost my appetite and it's {[f] weird,
351		*usually when i'm really nervous i *eat a *lot, but i
352		*know that *when things are *really *really wrong i
353		just *stop eating..you know *normal nervousness and
354		everything else is i overeat\}
355	Diane:	=yeah\=
356	**Elena:**	**=and= then..when i when i *change my habits like**
357		**that so drastically...sumpns**
>358		**really {[laughing, f] wr-ha-hong\}**
359	Diane:	{[tongue clicking sound] a::w\
360		Elena =~=)}
361	Elena:	{[f, acc] =i'm= takin ad*vantage of it
362		*now so i'm losing *wei~ght\}
363	Ben:	[laugh]

UCDisclab LCON2

Line 337 includes a laugh over a discussion of a problem, the depression Elena believes accounts for her loss of appetite. She doesn't laugh in discussing the dynamics, not until the punchline in 358. This is not a narrative but a clinical analysis of patterns. Her friends pick up her complex stance and give sympathy in 348 and 360 and laughter in 363. But note that Diane's sympathetic reaction follows Elena's laugh. In both 337 and 358 we see Elena telling sad stories about herself, ending in laughs. Nobody else laughed at that point, indeed they gave solace. This difference supports Jefferson's (1984, 2004) observations; only Ben laughed at the end on the same topic.

3.1.3   *Complex narration*

A topic can get launched in a tellable narrative and then bring humorous disclosures as the story unfolds. In our data there was a long conversation involving two students and the dorm cook, which began with B's narrative about flying a kite, and getting laughed at for trying to talk the kite out of a tree, followed by a series of vignettes and stories about people's reactions to talking to oneself. Eventually Bea talked about another instance in which she talked to an inanimate object.

(3)   **Conversation in a dorm: 2 students, female cook B**

686	Bea:	so i say to the door\ you're not closed\ it isn't
687		six\ it can't, it can't be six\then a passing group\
688		the girl says\ another one of these dormy types
689		even though she's probably older than

690		that\ she says\ [it might be]\ giggle giggle \\(laughs)
691	Cal:	oaoah\\
>692	Bea:	*(laughs) *mind your business\ i'm talking to the door\
693		perfectly good thing to talk to\ i didn't ask you for any
694		comments\
....		
707	Bea:	it upsets me so much because i can't
708		help it i live alone\ i always talk to myself\\
709		every time i walk down the street
>710		going mutter mutter mutter\\ (laughs)
711	Cal:	wow\ [~]
712	Ann:	there are so many people at Berkeley that do\\
713	Bea:	i know we all do
714	Ann:	sure\\ yeah\\
715	Bea:	and\ ok if you can be very witty\

UC Disclab: DIN02

The sequence climaxed with a long narrative by Bea about reading a license plate aloud, with the driver's response. Her laughter could be related to her awareness that talking to oneself is seen as odd, a little crazy, so she is both explaining why she did it in each case and reporting public comment, taking two perspectives. Bea was older than the students, and they were respectful to her. They treated her series of stories somewhat as troubles talk, and did not laugh, though she did.

While the talking to oneself series followed topically from the first kite example, it is also possible for light banter on a theme to turn into a longer narrative about a particular occasion. In the example below a group of male students joked about a woman and teased each other. The basketball topic starts with double entendres about basketball and a woman, like "Carl doesn't want to be the rebound man." "I'm a great passer." Then a switch came with "Ed was impressed with Ashley's basketball acumen. She's quite good." This was a transition line that led to serious basketball talk about a particular game.

(4)   Male students discussing basketball.

213	Ed:	they were scoring more\ i was doing shitty\
>214		i couldn't hit a fucking basket\
215		..=although= i did score the
216	Carl:	=when was this?=
217	Ed:	winning..basket\(the winning goal\)
218		[[fast]=that's my= only claim to fame man]\\
219	Carl:	=[[fast]there's like}=
220		==[[fast]there was like everyone at the other end of
221		the court}and Ed = Ed took eight shots\= and finally=
222	Al:	=[laugh]= =[laugh]=
223	Carl:	sunk a-=[laugh]=

224	Al:	=[laugh]=
>225	Ed:	=[laugh]= it was bad i couldn't fuckin'
226		**sink a basket to save my fucking ass\\

UC Disclab DIN09

While Ed talks about his inability to sink a basket, it becomes not an embarrassment story but in 217 a triumph since he makes the winning shot. In this segment, his self-criticism is set up as a narrative tension in 213, reiterated by Carl and by Ed's summary in 225 when he finally joins the others in laughing. So it is not an embarrassment story in which he initiates the laughter, as in the earlier examples.

3.1.4   Self-revelation as entertainment

In the following text the men are talking about recurring dreams, a topic started by Jim and later picked up and elaborated by him. What seems to happen here is that what began as a self-disclosure exchange about dreams becomes a kind of entertainment narrative modeled on fantasy films.

(5)   **Male roommates discuss dreams**

364	Mike:	{[p] (it's cool)}\ ⟨pause⟩\ i *have to (check that)\ …
365		winter's the time to play basketball too bad
366		there's no snow around here\
367	Jim:	*yeah::\ i think i had a dream about snow\
368	Mike:	i had i *always had dreams about playing basketball in
369		the snow\

....

375	Jim:	hm\ i can't remember why (x) or what i was dreaming of
376		but i know there was snow in it\.*huh?\ …
377		i *love talking about dreams when i remember 'em you know?
378	Mike:	i used to dream my brother used to play for a team, um he
379		went to parochial school,.

......

451	Mike:	i {[f] still have} it\= y'know =still (xxx)= it
452		doesn't pop up
>453	Jim:	=[laughs]=
454	Mike:	very often.. but y'know every like once a year
455		at least it'll pop up\
456	Jim:	==that (what) **yeah y'know that's weird\ recurring dreams
457		are weird\ it's like i have this one.. it's not the exact
458		same one but where i have like toothaches and my teeth
459		are coming out and i can't *stop it\ my =teeth are=
460	Mike:	=**ohh=**god\
461	Jim:	it's really bad it's one of my worst dreams {[dc]and:: i
462		have a lot of dreams where um where like I'm::} I'm like
463		running from something but then i turn around and i realize
464		that i don't have to run from these things and i like and i

465		do something, right? but then they're not the villains that
466		i thought they were then they like they =turn= *no *no they
467	Mike:	=crush you=
468	Jim:	don't crush me or anything but they just *turn into these
469		like o-other things and i can't find 'em so it's like
470		if i run from things and then i turn and then i go to like
471		fight 'em but then but then they're changed.. so
472		i can't fight 'em \..*but i'm still a little nervous
473		about 'em y'know ?
>474	Jim:	**[loud laughter in response to Mike's facial expressions]**
475	Mike:	~o::k Jim:: just keep =(xxxxxxxxxxxxxxx)=
>476	Jim:	**=actually i just w-=**
477	Mike	(I'm gonna) put a bolt on my door\
>478	Jim	**[laughs] ahh:: what would {[hi] *Freud} say?**
479	Mike:	{[imitating child character from movie *the Shining*] red
480		rum red rum red rum}\
481	Jim:	oh heh heh heh\ {[dc] red:: rum..} *murder..
482		yeah that's right\...[laughs]
483	Mike:	got some excellent knives here\ *hm *hm::\
484	Jim:	{[imitating a psychotic]heh heh heh heh}\ ...all =work= and
485	Mike:	=( )=
486	Jim:	no *play::
487	Mike:	makes jack a dull *boy\

UCDisclab: RMT02

This sequence started with a discussion of basketball in the snow, and dreams about it. The topic shifted in 377 to recurring dreams, which leads to an example by Mike, and later Jim laughs and launches an elaborate dream report that became so dramatic that in 474 Mike's audience response reinforced the conversion to entertainment comparable to *The Shining*, and dramatic play in 484. In this episode we see a good case of a migration between self-disclosure, fantasy, and entertainment. In most male groups, self-targeted humor was fantastic, rather than realistic self-disclosure; here dreams provide a transition.

Male self-directed fantasies often provoke intense and creative interaction, as in the spoof of self-disclosure below. This is not actual self-disclosure but a parody. The men had been proposing living off women because women live longer, so the humorous vein carries into a related topic.

(6)   **Dinner of male students in apartment, one British, one bilingual Mexican-American, 2 Euro-Americans**

637	Lopez:	this is a really imbalanced sort of thing
638		here...there's no *female present\
639	Rand:	well\

640		[laughter]
641	Lopez:	it's not racially =like balanced either=
642	Nigel:	=it's white dominated=
643	Lopez:	two *white males
644	Nigel:	do you feel..do you feel (real) Lopez?
645	Lopez:	==no i feel spirited =as a matter of fact=
646	Rand:	=do you feel..do you feel=
647		we're oppressing you?
>648	**Lopez:**	**i feel *threatened{[[ff] i feel threatened right**
649		**now..} i feel like if i say the wrong things y'know**
650		I'll look I'll look dumb and stupid and perpetuate
651		the stereotypes you both believe in\ [laughs]
652	Rand:	it's good you think that 'cause
653		it's most likely true\
654	Lopez:	*true i know..Rand's just sitting there waiting like
655		"what's he gonna say next, what's he gonna say
656		{[f] oh that was *stu:pi:d}"
657		[laughs]
658	Rand:	[playfully chastising L]
659	Lopez:	[pretending to be R] "how very *like him"
660		[laughs]
661	Rand:	(pp)that's so like...Lopez\

Disclab DIN11

The pleasure of these men in creating a fictitious self-disclosure and building on it collaboratively makes it clear that the role in male groups of imaginary humorous revelations about the self, of the sort found in Lampert and Ervin-Tripp (2006) often is performance and entertainment rather than disclosure.

By far the most frequent context for laughter about the self is a disclosure induced by a topic already available in the conversation. Of the 94 laughs based on comments we considered to be new and embarrassing disclosures, 65 were topically continuous with the prior talk. This was the dominant context for all the groups, even though children had somewhat more physical context-based humor than adults. In some groups the self-disclosure could morph into entertainment and fantasy, in others the self-disclosure arose out of protracted narratives. In only a few cases in our data did the laughter occur during troubles-telling, and that was usually laughter only by the teller.

3.2   Topic change

3.2.1   *Mitigation*

The humor may occur after one of the participants introduces the topic. The topic is introduced by the mitigator en route to a request or apology, and can include current or recent impositions or planned ones as in the Example (8). In Example (7) Carol is having a housing problem, and delicately apologizes for staying too long. In this case, the topic change has a pragmatic goal beyond narrative entertainment or troubles telling.

(7)   **Female houseguest**

587	Carol:	in any case though, if i have to um- if i haven't
588		found a place? i don't know if El told you yet, Lee?
589	Lee:	hmm?
590	Carol:	i-i'm gonna stay at my friend Bev's if i don't find
591		a place after this\
592	Lee:	oh\
593	Carol:	==cause she's house-sitting for like a week and a half?
594	Lee:	==uh huh,
595	Carol:	==and she's not even gonna be using her place\
596	Lee:	uh hmm
597	Carol:	==so she said.. she said that just to do it because no
598		one will be there\
599	Lee:	mmm\
600	Carol:	yeah\
601	Lee:	okay\
>602	**Carol:**	**but i: thought i was here for too long\ [laughs]**
603	El and Lee:	[laugh]
604	Lee:	we've enjoyed your company, Carol\
605	El:	=i know\ =
606	Carol:	=[laughs]=

UCDisclab: HOME

The question of 'overstaying one's welcome' is a problematic one for guests, so here there is a long lead-in about moving to Bev's place before Carol comments that she may have been here too long, and gets polite reassurances. The laughter accompanies a kind of apology, which follows a long preface on the same topic and provides a solution before the problem is made overt.

Planning future actions is another possible context for mitigating requests by self-directed humor. It is unclear whether Kay's hitching a ride with her friend Dee is an imposition or not, but Kay protects herself with radical self-categorization as someone who imposes on others.

(8)   **Dee and Kay are Chinese-American roommates.**

382	Kay	==you're going to *drive? are you driving by yourself?
383	Dee:	==umhm\
384	[2 sec.]	
385	Gina:	aren't you going to be tired?
386	Dee:	uh uh\

387	Kay:	can i come too? no =[laugh]=
388	Dee:	=umhm\=
>389	Kay:	==i'm terrible\..oh, I'm such a..a *leech\

UCDisclab DIN08

In this case Kay proposes accompanying her roommate on a trip, laughs at her imposition, then criticizes herself to the others, later using the term twice, even magnifying it even to megaleech.

If a speaker believes a story merits telling in order to allow an explanation of a gaffe, there may be no way to bring it up except by changing the topic. In the following example, the narrator is strongly enough interested in telling her tale to reintroduce it later after diversion, the return marked by "well anyway" in line 132:

(9)   **Dinner party of women**

74	Barb:	i had a *heck of a time getting here
		i'll *tell ya\
......		
131	Barb:	well *anyway\
132		so i tried to *leave\
>133		... first i flooded my *car, right\
134		[laugh] (xxxx)
>135	Barb:	*brilliant guest\ . so then I'm *driving down-

UCDisclab FDIN5

The story continued with details about having to backtrack around a truck. Note that the derogatory information in 133 is followed by a sarcastic self-evaluation. Barb worked hard to get this story heard by her friends even though she had a negative view of flooding her car. She had arrived late for dinner.

Although studies of topic continuity in general have identified men as more often initiators of topic change, in the case of self-directed humor all the instances we found in our sample were by women, at the service of politely mitigating impositions.

3.2.2   *Elicited self-disclosures*

Some self-disclosures were elicited by conversational partners who brought up the topic, rather than by the discloser. In these cases, there can be relatively low topical continuity in the conversation, and the question can simply remind a speaker of a reportable experience and license talking about oneself. Elena's willingness to tell about her problems, which we saw in Example (2), is also revealed in her reaction to a standard elicitation a bit later.

(10)   **Female college student talks with male, female students about spring break**

| 396 | Diane: | whatdju do during spring *break |
| 397 | Elena: | o:h, let's see..i mostly *cried\ |

398		um, i stayed *home, in *Berkeley, um, through
399		*thursday and then i went *home but *um..i s-
400		{[acc] you know, i *always make these plans about
401		doing *all my homework *right}
402	Diane:	mhm\
403	Ben:	yeah\
404	Diane:	[laugh]
405	Elena:	{y'know i don't know *what i did\
406		i didn't do *homework, i stayed *home...i didn't
407		clean *u~p, **i didn't do *anything\ i think i just**
>408		***vegetated\ [laugh]}**

UCDisclab: LCON2

In this case, the topic is created by an open question, but some elicitations are more specific and provide a way of directing the topic. Her self-revelation in 397 was not done with a laugh, which occurred after the more neutral description in 408.

The children in a parochial school were observed in a room used by Catholic sisters, and their curiosity about the room led them to discuss their teacher preferences.

(11)   **Seven-year-old males in a Catholic grade school discussing the Catholic sisters who teach them**

038	Will:	who do you like more, =Sr. Barbara or
039	And:	=Sr. Barbara\
041	Will:	yeah me too\
043		well actually i'm not sure yet\
044		because you know how i figure out
045		how i like them?
046	And:	you go to the principal\
047	Will:	yeah,
048		i go to see them cause
>049		**i did {[laugh]something bad\}**
050		i went to Ms. Thornwald **five times
051		one with Ms...umm.. Thomas\
...		
054	And:	what did you do
055		when you went to Ms. Thornwald
056	Will:	got a DR†\
057	And:	doing what
058	Will:	now you have three really bad things
059		and then you get a DR\
060		3 DRs you get in uhh a major DR
063		and that's one in school suspension\
064		3 major DRs you get kicked out\..
065		expelled\
066		i don't plan on doing that

```
067   And:       expelled from school
068              {[ac]for the rest of the year}
069              or for-
070   Will:      ==for your life\
                 †disciplinary referral
```
UCDisclab T2M1

Notice that the culprit laughs, but not his friend. In this case, the confession about the various detentions and visits to the principal started with a simple question and led to a report of bad behavior, with laughter, followed by serious talk, with no laughter, about the possible consequences. Perhaps this is treated by the friend as troubles talk. Andy asks twice what Will actually did, and gets no specifics, so there is no full disclosure in this exchange.

Three ten-year-old boys in another school were concerned about the tape recorder, a contextual stimulus. They went on at length about using forbidden words, even imagining the police might eavesdrop and punish them. Aaron brings up a likely context to talk about the word *bitch*, but he avoids using it because he is being recorded. He becomes an interviewer as his pronoun switch in 124 implies his may be a shared experience, and his elicitation creates self-disclosure by both other boys and then Aaron too.

```
(12)   Ten-year-old boys discussing bad word
       124   Aaron:     remember when we - did you ever call a girl
                        a *"b" word?
       125              you'd be calling them a female dog\
       126   Jerry:     i don't say it no more though\
       127   Teddy:     =last time i did..
     >128   Jerry:      =know *why..because i got *popped\=
                        [boys chuckle]
       129   Teddy:     =*oh=
       130   Aaron:     =cause it *hurt *too\=
```
UCDisclab L5.22.M4

In this fragment the general fear of retribution led to eliciting specifics so that all three boys disclosed their violation of local rules of speech. They chuckle at their common experience.

3.2.3   *Elicited boasts*

In some cases, elicited reports were not presented as troubles but more as boasts, that is, there is no sense that the self-disclosure is embarrassing or negative.

```
(13)   Male student slow to graduate
       86   Mariko:    ...are you going to graduate... next year?
       87   Eiji:      i wish... yeah... i hope. =....i hope. yeah.=
       88   Mariko:                =[laughter]=
```

89		how many units do you have now?
90	Eiji:	now?
91	Mariko:	UN. [*yeah*]
92	Eiji:	i...'ve barely made it to junior.
93	Mariko:	HOMMA? [*really?*]
94	Eiji:	yeah.
95	Mariko:	un.... SOKKAA. [*is that right*]
>96	**Eiji:**	**UN. MOO ZUTTO ASONDETAKARA. [laughter]**
	e:	[*yeah....because i've been playing a lot*]
97	Mariko:	[laughter]
98	Eiji:	first three years. yeah.
99	Mariko:	[laughter]
100	Eiji:	just like ..just interference =or you know=
101	Mariko:	=UN[*yeah*] [laughter]=
102	Eiji:	whatever. =[laughter]=
103	Mariko:	=[laughter]=
>104	Eiji:	i want to party or either people want to disturb me.
105	Mariko:	[laughter]

UC Disclab TSDI1

In this Japanese bilingual exchange, the male student is unembarrassed that his partying has slowed down his educational progress, and his female friend, who launched the topic, joins him in finding these comments amusing.

In the child texts, more of the talk is stimulated by physical context, but even in the talk of seven-year-olds we see the same processes of topic maintenance, exaggeration, and elicitation that we found in adults, and even more likelihood that there is boasting about naughty behavior.

(14)   **Seven-year-old girls discuss clumsy or malicious acts**

385	Kate :	==hey who broke that?
386	Tess:	what?
387		oh,
388	Kate:	that\
389	Tess:	that\ he breaks stuff..all the time\
390		espe=cially me [laugh]?=
391	Kate:	=i always wanted to talk\=
392		*~o::h *really?
393	Tess:	[laugh]{[ac] *you}\
394	Kate:	now i know\
395		now i know who to blame\
396		for breaking all the stuff\ [*hmph *hmph *hmph]
397	Tess:	nope\
398		i know my mom knows what i broke\
399	Kate:	what?

>400	Tess:	i broke oh a {[laugh] glass ball that was in mom's}..
401		that she got from her great-grandmother?
402	Kate:	**Tess
403	Tess:	that was (dead)\
404		i broke my own dolphin?
405	Kate:	~okay\
>406	Tess:	um...i pulled out the chord on purpose when Jim
407		was on the internet?
408	Tess & Kate:	[laugh]

UC Disclab T2F4

We found a case where there was a shared male history that produced humorous mutual priming of male recall in a mixed group, on the basis of what appeared to be actual shared experience. It is hard to tell when the topic began. There was mention of spores, fungus, and a petri dish, which led to the next memory:

(15)   **Mixed dinner party, two men discussing childhood:**

141	Sid:	i also liked ah...your father's grinder machine
142		[laughter]
143	Jeb:	what did we do with the grinder machine\
144		*we also took aerosol cans and flamed them\
145		often..did you = do that? =\
146	Sid:	= yeah =
147		remember you burned my hair that way!\
148	E, S, J:	[laughter].
149	Jeb:	= actually that was simply= because you were trying
150	Eliza:	= [laughing] =
151	Jeb:	to light something\
>152	**Sid:**	**i was trying to light =a firecracker =.**
153	Jeb:	=a firecracker =..yeah exactly\
154	Sid:	and you came up and went = [pfffffffh]\ =
155	Eliza:	= [laughter] =

UCDisclab PRDPT

In gender-mixed gatherings the priming from conversational partners is changed, so that men produce fewer fantasies, and the women fewer narratives about the past (Lampert and Ervin-Tripp 2006). Because this priming is so important, it may make a difference whether a mixed group is two or more men and two or more women, or is just a couple, in the population we have sampled. These data were student papers from their own friendship groups, so the composition is not controlled. At least, unlike much psychological research, the groups are composed of friends. However, it might be possible to ask for friendship groups varying in gender balance. There were 18 instances in the mixed groups of disclosure by women, and 8 by men. Example 15 was the only disclosure case that occurred in a mixed group with more than one man.

Ten percent of the self-directed humor we found was elicited by a conversational partner, a practice more common in males than in females, who spontaneously produced revelations about themselves. In some cases, it was unclear whether anyone considered the confessions as boasts or as derogatory about the self. This judgment, like the judgments about the validity of the information, would be best obtained from informants themselves in future work.

3.3   Incidental responses

3.3.1   *Responses to contextual reminders*
Contextual stimuli can change the topic. A frequent source of joking is something in the immediate context that creates a topic for talk. In the next conversation, the dining partners had an exchange about how the potatoes were cooked, which led Kath to tell of her embarrassment earlier in the supermarket.

> (16)   **Safeway gaffe. Group of women and one man at apartment dinner.**
> 404   Kath: I didn't get very much sleep last night... i tried to
> >405   **leave the Safeway today without my purchases**
> 406   [laughter]
>
> UC Disclab DIN10

There was no antecedent to this topic except the potatoes, which may have been among the Safeway purchases. So this was an unusual incident that got elaborated in the telling. It turned into a longer story, since one of her dinner companions had been with her, and the others were curious about the outcome.

In another mixed eating group, the contextual stimulus is cutting a bagel. What happens next is safety instructions, and a narrative that becomes more dramatic as it builds.

> (17)   **Bagels at Dave and Ruth's house**
> As Helga starts to cut a bagel, Dave says "watch out" and does a demonstration of how to cut.
> 387   Dave: (don't cut it like that\)
> 388   Dave: =(here let me show you\)=
> >389   **Helga: (xxx) since i whacked my finger off**
> 390   Dave: =like this,=
> 391   =[all laugh]=
> 392   you do it like this\
> 393   Helga: n*o n*o\
> 394   Dave: ==just keep turning it\
> 395   Helga: =no=
> 396   Mel: =no\=
> 397   Helga: no that's not it\ you put it down on its flat side\

398		there yeah\
399		**[all laugh]**
400		**bagels and bread knifes are like, like**
401		**scariest=(thoughts)for me=**
402	Mel:	=Helga cut her finger,=
403	Helga:	==on a bagel and bread knife a few years ago
404		really bad\
405	Ruth:	mmh\
406	Mel:	yeah when i came home all the blood was in the bathtub
407		and she was holding her finger over the tub like this\
408	Dave:	==you know i did that recently when dad was here,
409		i was really tired and he always =tells us watch out=
410	Sue:	=he always goes
411		"don't do it that way\"=
412	Helga:	the bagel, you did it on a bagel?
413	Dave:	==yeah i cut myself\
414	Helga:	==hmm*\
415	Dave:	==just a little cut not bad\
416	Helga:	==i was holding it like this,
417	Dave:	=i was just tired\=
418	Helga:	=it was a stale bagel= and it was a brand new
419		serrated knife,
420	Ruth:	uh huh\
421	Dave:	=and it slid off\=
422	Helga:	=(not only) did it slide= and then,
423	Ruth:	oh yuck\
424	**Helga:**	**it was s*o awful and i'm like standing in the kitchen**
>425		**by myself going.[laughter] shit i'm going to have to**
426		**go to the hospital,** you're like,
427		it's just such a =weird=thing =that=
428	Ruth:	=uh huh\=:
429	Dave:	=right\=
430	Helga:	you come to, you go oh my god this isn't very
431		this is bad and =i'm = by myself,
432	Dave:	=and it's=
433	Helga:	and i went in the tub and held it over that and then
434		i couldn't find Mel and i couldn't find anybody
435		to take me to the hospital, i finally found somebody\
436		and it was like hours before i got home and back
437		i came and my apartment was all bloody*\
438	Ruth:	ooh\
>439	**Helga:**	**ooh\ [laughter] it was so {[laughing]awful}**
440	Sue:	==oh my god\

441	Helga:	==it was pretty icky\
>442	**Helga:**	**so i never cut bagels alone after that**
443	Dave:	you always bring someone in\
444	Helga:	(always) make sure somebody's there\

UC Disclab ATT01

After the story became more vivid and detailed, Helga makes a joking moral in 442, in the fashion of a danger-of-death story. So what started as a contextual reminder became two elaborated narratives. Dave's interpolated narrative in 408 helped launch Helga's elaboration in 416.

Children talk mostly about the present context, so context, rather than long topical continuity, is a common antecedent for their humor (Ervin-Tripp et al. 2004). In exchange 18, the girls are eating lunch, and in the process of drinking chocolate milk, Kay spills some milk on her clothes. The two best friends are in an observation room by themselves. The researcher, who had been listening, came in to help clean her up. Kay continues to be upset about her mess.

(18)   **Seven-year-old girls discuss a mess one has made**

229	Kate:	here i'll just smear it\
230	**Tess:**	**{[laughing] actually that's (funny)}?**
>231	**Kate:**	**Tess. it..does it look like i went pee**
232	Tess:	[laugh]
233	**Kate:**	**i'm glad i'm an idiot**
234	Tess:	oh god\
235	**Kate:**	**{[whisper] i'm so dumb**
236		i am\
237		oh good it's coming off\
238		what a miracle\
239		my mom doesn't have to commit suicide?
240	Res:	nah we wouldn't want that\
>241	**Tess:**	**um and one time i spilled spaghetti on myself**
242		**[laugh] and boy my mom was not happy**
243		nope\
244	Kate:	that my mom was not going to be happy
245		when she =sees ( ) stain=
246	Tess:	=it's not like= she's going to go
247		whoopee it spilled
248		but.. once my mom goes-
>249	**Kate:**	**==oh my god Tess look**
250	**Tess & Kay :**	**[laugh]**
251	**Kate:**	**it looks like i'm a baby**
252		ga-ga-ga
253		[whisper] (don't say anything)
254		**i'm practically gonna kill myself**

255		**i am so dumb**
256	Res:	no it's just chocolate milk that's dumb\
257	Tess:	yep\

UC Disclab T2F4

In the last two examples, the conversational partners give cases where they too made mistakes, Dave in 17–408, Tess in 18–241. These enhance the solidarity aspects of the self-disclosing humor. The emotional weight of the mistake is made clear by Kay repeatedly. Nonetheless there is laughter.

Features of a context can change the topic, so that the topic shifts to humorous self-disclosure. Children rely on context more than adults for shaping their talk, but we found that among women twelve percent of the disclosure humor was contextually primed.

3.3.2   Responses to teases

Cases of self-disclosure humor occurred in our data also when an accidental gaffe by one participant led to teasing by another. In teasing between friends, the mood of the interaction is typically already witty, and there is an expectation that participants will make funny criticisms of each other. What is interesting about teasing contexts is that the retort can either be a counter-tease or accepting of the premise of the teaser. It is in the latter type of reply that we see self-directed humor. In such cases, the disparagement was started by the partner as friendly teasing humor with a laugh.

In Example (19), two friends discuss recording, and how as psych majors they might have to read the transcript. This topic leads to a self-disparagement; the laughter in such a case can come from either the target or the others:

(19)		**Women students tease about word choice**
332	C:	and we could *sue her for plagery\
333	J:	plagiarism =[laughs]=
334	C:	=plagery= [laughs]
>335		...okay so my *grammar's going down
336		the tubes lately\ it must be my *mom's influence\
337	J:	==[laughs]

UCDisclab: GDIN1

We can expect teasing to be especially common between siblings. In Example (20), the younger sister knows the problems of an older sister in pronouncing English and joshes her about them. This permits the older sister to make a confession about her most embarrassing gaffe. The prior context had involved a lot of teasing about painting mistakes. Speakers of some Chinese languages have problems differentiating **sh-** and **s-**.

(20)   **Chinese-American sisters S and D and friend N paint an apartment:**

119	Dee:	she **washed *all the stuff\
120	Sara:	and i **lined e::verything\
121	Nancy:	[tsk] with what? spit?
122	Sara:	{[chuckle] yeah that too\} mostly um *shell *paper,
123		adhesive-paper= whatever
124	Nancy:	=**she::ll?=
125	**Sara:**	**it's shell colored\[laugh]**
127	Dee:	it's shell {[laugh] colored} =right?..= Sara
128	Sara:	=yeah, it's shell= colored
129		[laugh]
130	Dee:	**poshishu::n. she can't say the word position\
131	Sara:	o::h, my *sabbatical\
132	Nancy:	excuse me?
133	Dee:	she can't say sabbatical\
134	Nancy:	sabbatical?* what's wrong with sabbatical\
>**135**	**Sara:**	**well there's nothing wrong with sabbatical *now**
136		**but there was a problem with sabbatical**
137		**when i was talking to some um.. people**
138	Nancy:	ABC †[xxx(Chinese phrase}}
139	Sara:	*what?
140	Dee:	the FOB's†† are no better
141		[Nancy laughs]...**poshishun\
142	Nancy:	**poshishun, position, aiyah. i- i want to
143		maintain my poshishun in duh the community\
144	Sara:	what an embarrassment\

†American Born Chinese. †† Fresh Off Boat

UC Disclab: PAINT

In this case, the discussion of "shell" in the context of "shelf" evokes Dee's recall of Sara's problems pronouncing "sabbatical" and "position." Sara is provoked by her sister's teasing into admitting she had mispronounced "sabbatical." The topic seems to have come out of the shelf\shell paper exchange, and turned into teasing and then an admission with laughter. But while Sara volunteers a laughable in 135, she does not herself laugh.

The next example is also from a bilingual speaker, in this case involving problems with spelling. He becomes vulnerable to teasing by asking for help in spelling.

(21)   **Male roommate dinner: D African-American, S Mexican-American,**
   C Indian-American roommates

69	Sergio:	**motivated..is that *m*o*t*i*v*a*e*e*d?
70	Dean:	Sergio, you're in the fifth year of college and don't

71		know how to spell motivated?
72	Sergio:	**fifth..this is my *fourth [laughs]
73	Dean:	*fourth year in college and don't know how to spell motivated\
74	Sergio	==but technically it's my *third [laughs]
75	Dean:	*third year in college and don't know how to spell motivated\
76	Sergio:	** *m*o*t*i*v*a*d*a*t\

……..

91	Sergio:	*o.k. thank you \
92	Dean:	[murmur]
93	Sergio:	*no..because i put..*m*o**v\
94	Chan:	==even a **black man could've spelled that one\
95		#all participants laugh#
96	Sergio:	*no cause..cause when i typed it up i caught it..and
97		i spelled it *m*o**v\

……..

177	Dean:	we'll have *loads of fun on *that tape\
178	Chan:	you *are taping huh?
179	Sergio:	yeah..he's *been taping it\
180	Chan:	you've had *a lot of swears on there\
181	Sergio:	==you know it baby\
182	Dean:	==but that's o.k. ..no actually, Sergio
183	Sergio:	oh my *god..you *got me taping *motivated\
184		#all participants laugh#
>185		**i feel molded [stupid]**
186		#all participants laugh#
187		**[laugh] oh my god**...oh my g::od\ you're
188		so..uhhh..*stop that *tape *now\

UC Disclab: FCON7

Here we see a student of Mexican-American background stumbling over the spelling of "motivated." He accepts help from his friends, who tease him about his spelling problems, until he discovers that there is a permanent record of his embarrassing mistake, which he says makes him feel stupid. He laughs at this disclosure.

Teasing can be a stimulus to disclosure by the victim, but it turned out to be a relatively infrequent form of priming for self-disclosing humor, so it is likely that indeed most friendly teasing receives a retort in kind.

4.   Conclusions

In our small exploratory data set, Topical Continuity was by far the most frequent source of self-disclosing humor. Even though children's humor is usually based on context more than adult humor, in the case of self-disclosure humor, topical continuity dominates for children as it does for adults. Some of the time, the background of the topically continuous humor was troubles talk, but in other cases a tellable narrative led into a complex series of narratives involving self-disclosure by the speaker. In the case of larger groups there could be rounds of such parallel disclosures. Most of the time, humor is an accidental product of the conversational topic, in our data.

In half of these cases, the humor key already existed before the self-disclosure. The antecedent humor was of similar frequency for Topical Continuity and Topic Change, but was less frequent for Incidental Responses. Sometimes what started as self-disclosure veered off into fantasy and entertainment, especially in male groups. Another source of disclosure was topic change by a participant, sometimes to deal with a problem such as mitigation of a request by accounting for the need or making an apology, so that the teller introduces the topic. We also found elicitation of private information by friends, sometimes leading to disclosures, and sometimes to boasts.

However, disclosures sometimes are, like other topics, suggested by incidental stimuli, like something in the context, or by mistakes that lead to teasing by friends, and self-disclosing by the participant whose weakness has been exposed by the gaffe.

Troubles talk was not a major feature of our data, which often came from groups rather than dyads, so it may take a different data source to sample more troubles talk.

A variety of interactional contexts can lead to laughing at oneself, including levity arising from teasing exchanges, faux pas, mitigation in cases of requests, boasting, entertaining tales, and narrative rounds. The sharing of experience can lead to shared laughter and camaraderie. In some cases, talking about troubles can lead speakers to make light of the problem by laughing, or mask embarrassment by laughing.

Since this analysis was based on a limited range of age and culture, future work might extend the sampling. There were indications in our earlier analyses, for example, that whether men are willing to target themselves in humor varies culturally, and the presence of rounds in the senior women makes one hope that such rounds might be found in older men. It would also be useful to examine systematically the effect of numbers of men and women in the conversational group on the willingness of speakers to self-disclose. However, we believe that self-disclosure depends so strongly on friendship that artificially composing groups would change the results. It is of course the case that stage humor can be based on an analogue of this private self-disclosure humor, and it also varies culturally.

References

Branner, Rebecca. 2005. "Humourous disaster and success stories among female adolescents in Germany." In *Narrative interaction*, U.M. Quasthoff & T. Becker (Eds), 113–147. Amsterdam: Benjamins.

Buhrmester, Duane & Prager, Karen. 1995. "Patterns and functions of self-disclosure during childhood and adolescence." In *Disclosure Processes in Children and Adolescents*, K. Rotenberg (Ed.), 10–56. Cambridge: Cambridge University Press.

Dindia, Kathryn & Allen, Mike. 1992. "Sex differences in self-disclosure: A meta-analysis." *Psychological Bulletin* 112: 106–124.

Ervin-Tripp, Susan, Lampert, Martin, Escalera, Elena & Reyes, Iliana. 2004. "It was hecka funny': Some features of children's conversational development." *Texas Linguistic Forum* 48: 1–16 (Proceedings of the Twelfth Annual symposium about Language and Society – Austin. April 16–18, 2004).

Ervin-Tripp, Susan M. 2000. "Studying conversation: How to get natural peer interaction." In *Methods for Studying Language Production*, L. Menn & N. Bernstein Ratner (Eds), 271–288. Mahwah, NJ: Erlbaum.

Gumperz, John J. & Berenz, Norine. 1993. "Transcribing conversational exchanges." In *Talking Data: Transcription and coding methods for language research*, J.L. Edwards & M. Lampert (Eds), 91–122. Hillsdale, NJ: Erlbaum.

Hill, Charles T. & Stull, Donald E. 1987. "Gender and self-disclosure: Strategies for exploring the issues." In *Self-Disclosure: Theory, Research, and Therapy*, V.J. Derlega & J.H. Berg (Eds), 81–100. New York: Plenum Press,.

Jefferson, Gail. 1984. "On the organization of laughter in talk about troubles." In *Structures of Social Action: Studies in Conversation Analysis*, J.M. Atkinson & J. Heritage (Eds), 346–369. Cambridge: Cambridge University Press.

Jefferson, Gail. 2004. "A note on laughter in 'male-female' interaction." *Discourse Studies* 6(1): 117–133.

Kotthoff, Helga, 2000. "Gender and joking: On the complexities of women's image politics in humorous narratives." *Journal of Pragmatics* 32: 55–80.

Lampert, Martin D. & Ervin-Tripp, Susan M. 2006. "Risky laughter: Teasing and self-directed joking among male and female friends." *Journal of Pragmatics* 38: 51–72.

Rose, Amanda J. & Rudolph, Karen D. 2006. "A review of sex differences in peer relationship processes: Potential trade-offs for the emotional and behavioral development of girls and boys." *Psychological Bulletin* 132: 98–131.

Rubin, Lillian B. 1983. *Intimate strangers: Men and women together*. New York: Harper & Row.

Direct address as a resource for humor

Neal R. Norrick & Claudia Bubel

This chapter explores the use of direct address to create humor in scripted jokes and in everyday conversation based on examples from corpora of transcribed conversational English. We take direct address to include any reference to a real or imagined listener with a proper or invented term of address. We show how forms of address in humor build on, extend and subvert the standard system. Direct address always has both an 'attention, identification' function and a 'contact, expressive' function, with one more prominent in any given context, but both these functions play various roles in the creation of humorous discourse, for instance when reciprocal direct address between friends, partners and family members leads to humorous banter in conversation.

Ah, you sweet little rogue, you! Alas, poor ape, how thou sweat'st!
Come, let me wipe thy face. Come on, you whoreson chops.
Ah, rogue! i' faith, I love thee.

Shakespeare *Henry IV, Part II*
II. 4. 233–236

1. Vocatives

Vocatives or terms of address in English include: Kinship terms like *Mom* and *Aunt Helen*; first names like *Samantha* and *James*; familiarized first names, including short forms like *Sam*, nicknames like *Jim* and *Jimmy*; terms of endearment like *honey*; terms of respect like *madam* or *ma'am*; invectives like *idiot*; nonce names like *Ms Know-it-all*; and title plus last name as in *Professor Jones* (cf. Dunkling 1990; Leech 1999). All generally work the same way as forms of direct address to identify a specific listener, though they may vary greatly in interpersonal significance, as we shall see: Just consider *ma'am, dear colleague, Ms Smith, Judy, honey, bitch* all potentially applicable to a single person.

We were initially impressed with the frequent presence of vocatives in narrative passages we were investigating for other reasons, then became interested in the humorous potential of direct address and vocatives in particular. We proceeded to analyze forms of address in humorous materials and sets of conversational stories, but we also performed corpus searches for names and typical terms of address like first names, terms of endearment and terms of respect. We collected conversational examples from various corpora of transcribed everyday talk, including our own Saarbrücken Corpus of Spoken English (SCoSE), the Santa Barbara Corpus of Spoken American English (SBCSAE) and the Wellington Spoken Corpus of New Zealand English (WSC): see the passage *Data Sources* at the end of the text.

We found that vocatives occur in various forms of direct address as syntactically free units, by contrast with pronominal terms of address, which are generally bound (see, e.g., Zwicky 1974). Direct address with a vocative can occur initially, as in (1), medially, as in (2), or finally, as in (3) in an intonation unit, and it can form an intonation unit of its own, as in (4), often an intonation unit introduced with a discourse marker, as in (5).

(1)   **Dad**, don't leave the butter on.   (SCoSE, MARY AT HOME)
(2)   sure **Keith** I'll work   (SCoSE, ADDIE and BRIANNE)
(3)   are you okay **Mom**?   (SCoSE, MARY AT HOME)
(4)   ... You're so strange,   (SBCSAE)
       honey,
       it m- really makes me wonder.
(5)   oh **Audrey**   (SCoSE, Rites of Passage: Audrey)

Certain combinations of discourse marker plus vocative, like this last one, may be more or less formulaic. Thus, 'oh + term of address' with a characteristic falling intonation curve suggests sympathy or resignation, while 'but + vocative' with a rising contour and strong stress on the term of address often indicates resistance, as in 'but MOM'. Free-floating vocatives with a falling intonation contour often convey a deprecatory attitude, especially when the addressee has been shown to lack relevant knowledge or to have committed a blunder, as we shall see.

2.   Functions of direct address

Zwicky (1974) states that direct address serves at least two functions: firstly, calls, designed to catch the addressee's attention and secondly, addresses, which serve to maintain or emphasize the contact between speaker and addressee. Likewise, Davies (1986) distinguishes an identifying and an expressive function.

More recent work by Leech (1999) yields three pragmatic functions (1) summoning attention, (2) addressee identification, (3) maintaining and reinforcing social relationships. But both (1) summoning attention and (2) addressee identification clearly belong on the 'attention, identification' side vis-à-vis the 'contact, expressive' side. We can multiply functions on both sides of this basic divide without calling it into question.

It is important to stress that both sides are co-present, varying in prominence from one context to the next (cf. Davies 1986; Leech 1999). Vocatives pick out an addressee *and* they signal a relationship between the speaker and hearer, because the speaker must choose between options like kinship term, first name, term of endearment etc. Thus, there's no truly neutral vocative, as Zwicky argues: whatever 'attention, identification' work terms of address do, they also necessarily do 'contact, expressive' work in defining and maintaining relationships, as indicated above in the choice of possible names for a single person. Apparently, the better two people know each other, the wider the variety of viable forms of address they possess for each other (Brown and Ford 1961; Leisi 1978).

Humorists draw on all these discourse properties of direct address, as we shall see. They utilize its functions of identifying and distinguishing addressees and take advantage of its role in signaling relationships. They play with the availability of multiple potential forms of address for the same individual with their different connotations. Since different forms of address evoke various sets of associations or discourse frames, the choice of vocatives provides a ready resource for setting up a joke or creating joint pretense in conversational joking.

3.   Stock jocular expressions and jokes incorporating direct address

To give an initial impression of how direct address is used to create humor, let's consider first some recycled jocular moves built around direct address. The basic strategy is a feigned presupposition that the addressee bears the relevant name; and the basic thrust is generally sarcasm directed at some other participant in everyday talk. Inappropriate application of terms of address generates incongruity of the kind most recent humor theories recognize as the necessary condition of humor perception in both scripted joke texts and spontaneous conversational joking (see e.g., Raskin 1985; Norrick 1993). Individual examples may involve (literary) allusions, as in:

(6)   elementary, **my dear Watson**
(7)   no shit, **Sherlock**

This second is, of course, not a true quote, as the first is, though it does refer to the literary figure Sherlock Holmes. In both cases, however, the form of address alone suffices to identify the relevant joking frame; and in both cases, the formulas usually involve knowledge displays and they express deprecation toward someone who has failed to make a connection and/or get the relevant point (see also Norrick and Bubel 2005). Examples may rest on more general cultural references, as in:

(8)   brilliant, **Einstein**

They may also revolve around puns, as in (9):

(9)   smooth move, **Ex Lax**

Of course, Ex Lax is a brand name for a laxative rather than a personal name or even a potential real personal name. Still its use in direct address goes along with the speaker's pretense that the listener bears this name and is responsible—like a laxative—for a smooth bowel movement, and this, in turn, ironically draws attention to some untoward move by the listener.

A stock jocular move incorporating direct address may also revolve around simple word play, as in:

(10)   no way, **Jose**

Some more or less obscene compounds like *dickhead, jerk-off* and so forth may occur as jocular terms of address as well, though, of course, this requires a special relationship between the participants in the interaction.

We must further explore how scripted jokes typically incorporate direct address. Direct address with a proper name or some form of address identifying the relationship between the speaker and hearer in the text serves to clarify who is speaking to whom, for instance, in the classic one-liner:

(11)   Other than that, **Mrs Lincoln**, how did you enjoy the play?

Here the epithet *Mrs Lincoln* along with the second person pronoun *you* signals that this question is to be understood as a quote, and it identifies the addressee of the question as well. Together this triggers the search for the background information necessary to get the joke, namely that Mrs Lincoln was with then President Lincoln in Ford's Theater the night the president was assassinated (by John Wilkes Booth).

Or consider the way the phrase 'all right, Mom' functions in the punch line of the narrative joke below:

(12)   In ancient Palestina, an angry crowd is gathered to stone a prostitute. Jesus walks between the crowd and their victim, saying, 'Let him who is without sin cast the first stone'. An enormous rock flies from the midst of the crowd and crashes into the wall beside the prostitute. Jesus turns and says angrily, 'All right, **Mom**!'

As in the one-liner above, the form of address here specifies the relationship between the speaker and the addressee and thereby uniquely identifies, on the basis of appropriate background knowledge, the only sinless person available.

In the somewhat more complicated example below, personal names stress the difference and distance between the two characters. Tonto was the faithful Indian sidekick of the Lone Ranger, regularly called Kemosabe by Tonto, in both radio and television versions of the Lone Ranger saga.

(13)   One day when the Lone Ranger and Tonto were riding along, they were suddenly surrounded by an angry war party of Indians. The Lone Ranger says, 'It looks like we're done for, Tonto'. And Tonto replies, 'What you mean *we*, **Kemosabe**'.

The Lone Ranger naively groups Tonto and himself together in the face of Indian attack, apparently forgetting that Tonto ultimately has more in common with the enemy than with him. Tonto puts the Lone Ranger in his ethnic place by denying that *we* is an appropriate designation for them as a dyad, at least under the present circumstances. The final word of the punch-line is a form of address, Kemosabe, allegedly a phrase from a Native American language meaning 'trusty scout'. This form of address simultaneously underlines Tonto's Indian heritage and the difference between him and the Lone Ranger. The incorporation of the name 'Kemosabe' conveys the deprecation characteristic of contexts involving knowledge displays: here Tonto talking down to the Lone Ranger, who has failed to see the implications of the situation. The characteristic fake Indian talk of 'what you mean' further enhances the distance between the two characters.

In a whole series of typical 'sick' jokes, the kinship term *Mommy* appears in direct address to invite the inference that the speaker of the initial utterance is a young child and the addressee is the child's mother. Further inferences help to determine that it is the mother who speaks in response to the child's complaint and to reconstruct the probable context of the exchange and get the joke.

(14)   a.   **Mommy, Mommy**, I don't want to go to America.
              Shut up and keep swimming.

        b.   **Mommy, Mommy**, I don't like my brother.
              Shut up and keep eating.

Clearly this joke technique is much more effective than beginning such jokes by saying, for instance, 'A child says to her mother ...' and effecting the transition to the second line with 'and the mother replies'. The long-standing cycle of jokes about customers in restaurants complaining about their food and beginning with 'waiter, waiter' function similarly. Consider two standard examples.

(15)   a.   **Waiter, waiter**, what's this fly doing in my soup?
              I believe it's the backstroke, sir.

        b.   **Waiter, waiter**, there's a dead fly in my soup.
              Yes, sir, it's the hot water that kills them.

In both jokes, direct address serves to identify the participants and suggest the situation as well, obviating the need for an introduction like: 'A guy in a restaurant says to the waiter'. The formal form of address *sir* in the second line reinforces the restaurant frame and specifies the role of the respondent.

A particular form of address may help identify a whole speech event with its characteristic participants, as in the following joke attributed to Carol Leifer in the *Friar's Club Encyclopedia of Jokes*. Here the epithet *Lord* in direct address after the signal of direct speech with *like* invokes the speech event of praying.

(16)   It's slim pickings out there. When you're first single you're so optimistic. At the beginning you're like: I want to meet a guy who's really smart, really sweet, really good-looking, has a really great career. . . . Six months later you're like: **Lord**, any mammal with a day job.

In the riddle-joke below, a standard phrase with a term of endearment in direct address again suffices to identify a specific speech event along with its characteristic participants and location, namely a spouse coming home after work.

(17)   What are three words you never want to hear when you're making love? '**Honey**, I'm home'.

Consider finally an example of a narrative joke with an abusive vocative in final position as the crux of the punch line.

(18)   A country boy goes to Harvard, ready to start his freshman year and he's kind of intimidated. He goes out into Harvard Yard for the first time. And his instructions are that he's supposed to meet at the library at such and such a time, and he's looking around at all the ivy-covered buildings and they all look the same to him. Then he sees a guy walking the other direction, and he's a slightly older guy with a big Harvard letter sweater on—obviously a Harvard student. So he goes up to the fellow and says, 'Can you tell me where the library's at?' And the fellow looks at him and says, 'I am a Harvard student. We're standing here in Harvard Yard. I assume you're going to be a Harvard student too. And the first thing you should know is that no Harvard student ends his sentences with a preposition. So no I do not know where the library's *at*.' And the kid thinks for a second and he says, 'Okay. Can you tell me where the library's at, **asshole**'.

The effectiveness of the scatological vocative here is exemplary. Not only does the country boy solve the problem of the so-called final preposition, he does so in such a way that it creates a perfect put-down for his antagonist. Unexpected rude words provide an excellent final thrust for a joke punch line.

4.   Humorous uses of direct address

Like any other type of talk, direct address also occurs in non-serious contexts. Wolfson and Manes (1980) contend that terms of address frequently occur in speech events typical of interaction between intimates such as teasing. Straehle (1993) shows that first names and terms of endearment seem to proliferate and to receive extra stress in teasing sequences, and McCarthy and O'Keeffe (2003) see direct address as a characteristic feature of badinage—or what we call 'banter', following Norrick (1993).

4.1   Banter

Reciprocal direct address between friends, partners and family members may serve as contextualization cues for a non-serious key in the turns themselves or for the entire interaction. In passage (19) below, the couple Paula and Ted produce paired final terms of address, apparently at least in part for the amusement of their guest.

(19)   1   Paula: just have another glass of wine
        2   so you can't tell the difference.
        3   Ted: I'll come out and help, **dear**.
        4   Paula: just give me instructions, **Ted**.

Paula and Ted are taking turns preparing saltimbocca for their guest, when Paula pretends her version of the recipe may not match up to Ted's, saying 'just have another glass of wine so you can't tell the difference'. Ted offers to help, appending the term of endearment *dear* to his turn, but Paula demurs immediately, playfully appending the first name *Ted* to her turn and even replicating Ted's intonation pattern, namely with a pronounced rise on the final stressed syllable of the clause and a rapid fall on the vocative. In this context, while the address terms are paired, they are not strictly parallel in feeling—*dear* being (mock) affectionate and *Ted*, especially in contrast to *dear*, apparently involving (mock) distancing.

Consider another exchange in the banter or teasing framework (from the WSC, DPC139), this time involving only two people with no third listener. Here laughter and first name frame a humorous, teasing turn, and the recipient frames his teasing response with laughter and first name as well.

(20)   1   Mal: I might have some more weetbix
        2   Kel: °((laughs)) I think you should **Mallory**.°
        3   Mal: ((laughs)) {microphone noise} ((laughs))
        4   thanks for the advice **Kelly** ((laughs))
        5   Kel: it's a Tuesday.
        6   hang on it's a Wednesday.
        7   you definitely should have some weetbix.
        8   Mal: ((laughs)) I know ((laughs)).

Clearly, paired terms of endearment or first names between partners may take on a bantering tone, as opposed to functioning as serious moves to attenuate face threats.

In the excerpt below (from the WSC, DPC013) we see the use of a jocular vocative to mitigate the potential face threat in a gently mocking jab about the traditionally touchy subject of earnings. The 'eh girl' is particularly interesting, as opposed to the less marked first name, in that it serves to signal a non-serious key.

(21)	1	Sue:	how much money do you ((laughs)) get ((laughs)).
	2		no that's not one of the ((laughs)) questions ((laughs))
	3	Tama:	no, not much.
	4	Renate:	((laughs))
	5	Tama:	not as much as YOU get **eh girl** ((laughs))
	6	Renate:	not as much as I get.
	7		((laughs)) get more than Tama.
	8	Tama:	she's gonna get more than me now.

In the excerpt below from the SBCSAE, we see a deprecating term of endearment *honey* functioning in an obviously ironic way, especially flanked as it is with comments like 'you're so strange'. Far from attenuating a face threat here, the term of endearment marks a humorous attack.

(22)	1	MARCI:	@@ (H)]
	2		@Gad @zooks.
	3	KEVIN:	[(H)]
	4	MARCI:	[(H)] @We @are [2really off the deep2] end,
	5	KEVIN:	[2(Hx) (H)2]
	6		[3⟨FOOD What FOOD⟩3],
	7	MARCI:	[3guy3]s.
	8	WENDY:	... You're so strange,
	9		**Honey,**
	10		it m_ really makes me wonder.
	11	KEN:	.. @[@@][2@@@@2]
	12	MARCI:	[@]
	13	KENDRA:	[<@ Oh really],
	14		[2really.

In response to Marci's laughing and using odd-ball lexical items like *gadzooks* to be silly, Wendy teasingly produces two apparently negative assessments 'you're so strange' and 'it m- really makes me wonder' with an intervening term of endearment *honey*. The term of endearment may serve to attenuate face threats in serious contexts, but it serves to signal mock sympathy or deprecation here, as part of the ongoing merriment—notice that Ken, Marci and Kendra all laugh in response to Wendy's turn.

Similar to banter is mocking an outsider, as in the following excerpt (from the SBCSAE). Here three women in a restaurant laugh about the over-friendly manner of their waitress. When their waitress reminds them of her name, Jamie, one of the women may already be mocking her slightly in using her first name in her statement 'thank you Jamie'. Then as Jamie leaves their table, a second woman, Sherry, laughingly repeats the first name and then she and the third woman laugh together.

(23)	1	Jamie:	.. okay.
	2	Sherry:	... she was just asking us.
	3	Rosemary:	.. yeah,
	4		I was asking them.
	5	Jamie:	... okay I'll run get those,
	6		my name's [Jamie] like I said,
	7	Beth:	[great].
	8	Jamie:	you need anything you let me know.
	9		o[kay]?
	10	Rosemary:	[tha]nk you **Jamie**.
	11	Sherry:	.. h. **Jamie**.
	12		((laughs))
	13	Beth:	((laughs))
	14	Sherry:	((brief laugh))
	15	Rosemary:	[h.]
	16	Sherry:	[((brief laugh)) h.]
	17		((brief laugh))
	18	Rosemary:	.. ((laughing)) shoot.

Whether Rosemary actually intends her 'thank you, Jamie' ironically or not, the other two participants Sherry and Beth clearly find it amusing, and Sherry clearly signals this with her laughing repeat of the first name Jamie.

Conversational humor does not always take the form of light hearted banter, it may have a serious, even bitter edge: Boxer and Cortés-Conde (1997) write in this regard of humor as a 'double-edged sword'. As an example, consider the following passage (from the SBCSAE), where a first name in direct address follows laughter and repetition of a sarcastic comment to signal recognition of humor and agreement.

(24)	1	Dolores:	... your daddy,
	2		remember when he was,
	3		... h.-
	4		... suspended from practice and all that,
	5		Tony never called,
	6		. . ((laughs)) never.
	7	Shane:	... oh really?
	8		I didn't know [that].
	9	Dolores:	[nev]er.
	10		... h. when your daddy was real sick,

11		and getting accused of everything,
12		he never called.
13		.. never.
14		... had to close the office and,
15		... and ask McClaren to help me with a patient,
16	Shane:	... [yeah],
17	Dolores:	[he ne]ver offered to [help us].
18	Shane:	[that's] family.
19	Julia:	... ((laughs))
20		... that's family **Shane**.
21		right the[re].
22	Shane:	[((laughs))]
23	Dolores:	when --
		when we came from Houston,

As mother Dolores explains to her son Shane how his uncle failed to help his father in a time of distress, he remarks sarcastically 'that's family', and this refrain is picked up laughingly by his sister Julia, who marks her alignment with his first name, *Shane*, following her repetition of the phrase.

Let's consider one more example (again from the SBCSAE) in which a vocative responds to an ironic turn. Here Wes instigates the humor at the expense of Nei, a friend of his mother Jo. Her response contains a first name in direct address following the click *tsk* and discourse marker *now*—both signals of mitigation in this context, but laughter follows from listener Cam and joker Wes, before Jo goes on with 'that isn't nice'. The disapproval is mild at best and seems to ratify and even appreciate the humorous remark rather than to reprimand Wes for it.

(25)	1	Jo:	did you know Nei,
	2		is teaching at uh,
	3		.. at the ... college in,
	4	Cam:	... nope.
	5	Jo:	.. Arizona?
	6	Cam:	... Arizona State?
	7	Jo:	.. mhm,
	8		[it's his second year],
	9	Wes:	[what's he teaching,
	10		how to be an] asshole?
	11	Jo:	((tsk)) [h. now **We:s**,]
	12	Cam:	[((laughs))]
	13	Wes:	[.. ((laughs))] ((laughs))
	14	Jo:	that isn't nice.
	15		he i:s teaching,
	16		he's teaching something abou:t business,

The jocular suggestion that someone is teaching 'how to be an asshole', with its clear implication that the teacher is himself quite an asshole, seems too impertinent a formulation for Jo to laugh about, at least in front of the kids, but her response signals a kind of complicity in the opinion expressed.

In all these examples so far in this section, forms of address are applied appropriately but playfully. We turn now to cases where mis-naming establishes a non-serious frame for interaction.

4.2   Inappropriate term of address for humor

Direct address in these initial examples occurs during banter or mocking and contributes to the non-serious context, but the forms of address would not be completely inappropriate even in serious contexts: The forms of address alone are not responsible for the humor of these interactions. By contrast, in the following examples, inappropriate application of vocatives creates the genuine incongruity associated with the perception of humor in jokes: this is the same sort of incongruity discussed with relation to stock jocular expressions built around forms of address above. Here the forms of address help define the non-serious framing of a spate of conversation: their inappropriateness elsewhere takes on a mock appropriateness within this new joking frame. Simply registering that direct address can occur in non-serious contexts differs from recognizing that it may occur in outright inappropriate ways to create humor. Thus, interlocutors on a first name basis may suddenly use title plus last name or kinship term for special effect, as in the next excerpt, involving two friends of roughly the same age:

(26)   1   Anne: make sure you don't forget your cap and scarf.
      2   Bill: yes, **Mother**.

Bill jocularly addresses Anne as *Mother* as a kid of put-down in response to her maternal-sounding reminder to wear his winter accessories. *Mother* is clearly the wrong term of address for Anne: it mis-identifies the addressee and it misrepresents Bill's relationship to her. This truly joking direct address differs from the sort of banter described above, where vocatives have their regular functions of correctly identifying and expressing relationships, even if they tend to exaggerate the latter function. For a similar example see Tannen (1993: 168).

Consider another example of direct address with an inappropriate term of address (from the SBCSAE), this time a nonce epithet, used ironically for humorous effect. Here Kevin first mentions the technical term *gestalt*, which Lisa then repeats in a complete sentence 'He's a gestalt kid'. Both Kevin and Marie laugh about this comment, but Lisa carries on with her attempt to sound professional, and this elicits the ironic title 'psychotherapist Lisa' from Marie. Even then Lisa counters with a series of *no*'s attempting to proceed with her technical explanation, as Marie and Kevin both laugh.

(27) 1 Lisa: .. h. does he talk big long things but you just can't understand em?
      2   ... no,
      3   he's okay then.
      4 Kevin: .. a gestalt kid.
      5 Lisa: h. 'he's a gestalt child'.
      6 Kevin: ((laughs))
      7 Marie: [((laughs))]
      8 Lisa: [no,
      9   there's two] different wa-
      10 Marie: yeah,
      11   **psychotherapist** ((laughing)) **Lisa,**
      12 Lisa: no no no no no no n- no: no: n- no:.
      13 Marie: ((laughs))
      14 Kevin: ((laughs))
      15 Lisa: h. it's just two different ways….

Lisa's persistence in the technical routine is noteworthy, given that both other participants are laughing at her expense, but of central interest here is Marie's creative use of an inappropriate but contextually significant form of direct address for humorous purposes.

Let's look at a second example of inappropriate direct address for humor. In another excerpt from the SCoSE, Ted has expressed reservations about Justine's collocation 'make publicity for', and she agrees that it sounds wrong to her, too. When Ted goes on to voice a particular preference, however, Justine jocularly addresses him with the term of respect *sir* and appends the comic nonce epithet 'Mister Prescriptive'.

(28) 1 Justine: I say that
      2   and I don't think it's good English
      3 Ted: I would prefer that you said 'did'.
      4 Justine: yes **SIR, Mister Prescriptive** ({laughing})
      5 Ted: ({laughing}) I said I would preFER.
      6   you can have preferences,
      7   even if you're Mister DEscriptive.

In addressing Ted inappropriately as *sir* and Mister Prescriptive, Justine signals mock respect as a mild rebuke instead of explicitly rejecting his prescriptive tendencies, as we might expect, since both are trained linguists. Just like the kinship term *Mother* in place of the usual first name Anne in the previous example, the term of respect *sir* in place of the first name Ted mis-identifies the interlocutor, functioning as a put-down and creating the incongruity characteristic of humor. Of course, Mister Prescriptive is again an inappropriate form of address. Moreover, it serves to label Ted as a pre-scriptivist, something most linguists would consider negative. Hence, Ted seeks to defend his statement as a 'preference' by contrast with an actual prescriptive state-ment, suggesting that he is Mister Descriptive. Of course, there is also something of a serious core of interactional meaning here: Ted has been 'caught out' in a prescriptiv-ist stance, and Justine is on some level truly rebuking him for it. We have here, then, a complicated conversational use of vocatives with their typical associations within a particular value system to create patterns of humor.

To this point then, we have reviewed the research on the pragmatics of direct address and vocatives, and made two new observations, namely direct address may generate humor through outright misapplication of vocatives, as opposed to simply accompanying banter. Misapplied forms of address create inferences with complex sets of humorous possibilities.

5.   Direct address in humorous constructed dialogue

Not only in narrative as such, but anywhere speakers construct dialogue, as in the excerpt below, they incorporate forms of address into their productions. In this next excerpt from the SBCSAE (0004), Carolyn and Sharon conspire to create a humorous description of Sharon's experience before a classroom full of children. They use two versions of title plus last name to characterize the voices of the children in the class addressing Sharon, who was supposed to be in charge.

(29)	1	Carol:	h. Sharon standing in front of the class going,
	2		h. ((screams))
	3	Sharon:	aw:.
	4		sometimes I'm like that.
	5	Carol:	while these little kids kinda,
	6		h. **Señorita Fli:nn?**
	7	Sharon:	h. hee hee hee hee hee.
	8	Kathy:	((laughs))
	9	Sharon:	oh,
	10		{thump}
	11		'**Miss Fli:nn,**
	12		**Miss Fli:nn,**
	13		**Mi[ss Fli:nn]',**
	14	Kathy:	[((laughs))]
	15	Sharon:	you know,
	16		towards the last couple of days I'm like,
	17		h. I put up a list of rules.
	18		... and all day long,

First, Carolyn cites the children as saying 'Señorita Flinn', then Sharon herself characterizes their voices with three repetitions of 'Miss Flinn'. This repetition seems especially effective as a resource for humor in conversational storytelling.

In the next passage (from the WSC, DPC070) both participants, James and Cecil, use the term of respect *sir* along with *please* to mark moves within the scope of a fantasy dialogue, suggested by 'custard with water" as something from a Dickens novel.

(30)   1   Cary: custard with water
       2   Jim: ((laughs)).
       3   Cary: that's just really- that's just pure Dickens.
       4   Jim: that's not in New Zealand
       5   Cary: no=
       6   Jim: =mm
       7   Cary: must be the English ((laughs)).
       8   must be Dickens ((laughs)).
       9   Jim: mm.
      10   ((laughs)) **'please sir'**.
      11   Cary: ((tongue click)) **'please sir** can I have some more'.
      12   Jim: ((laughs)) mm=
      13   Cary: =MORE?
      14   Jim: ((laughs)) ()
      15   Cary: what happened to him

Once they have established a framework for a fantasy with references to Dickens and the English ('must be the English . . . must be Dickens'), the two participants have recourse to an appropriate form of address to contribute to the construction of humorous dialogue.

Consider a final function of direct address in constructed dialogue within a humorous narrative, this time to convey an attitude of respect and thereby to enhance a put-down. In the excerpt below (from the SCoSE), a student referee describes a situation in which he got the better of an adult coach during a basket-ball tournament. At the end of a longish story about refereeing a game, the student referee describes how a coach verbally attacked him for a questionable call.

(31)   1   Chad: the exact words were,
       2   he came- he came up to me and said,
       3   **'you motherfucker.**
       4   you're holding a grudge from three weeks ago.'
       5   and I'm just sitting, you know,
       6   and I'm like, 'Oh my god', right?
       7   and my first reaction was to say to him,
       8   you know, something very sarcastic about his mother?

9		considering he brought that into effect?
10	George:	m-hm
11	Wayne:	huh huh huh
12	Chad:	but I thought,
13		this guy paid money to be in this tournament.
14		and I said,
15		'sir, I'm in college,
16		I can't reMEMber three weeks ago',
17		and [I walked away.]
18	Wayne:	[huh huh huh huh]
19	Wayne and George:	((laugh for 2 seconds))
20	Chad:	that's what I said to him,
21		[and I walked away.]
22	Wayne:	[that's funny.]

Especially following the verbal abuse by the coach with an abusive term, 'you motherfucker' in line 3, the student referee's incorporation of the term of respect *sir* demonstrates his self-control and leads to the excellent put-down. The use of *sir* not only marks the student referee's ritual respect for the coach, but also indicts the coach by implying that a person of respect should not talk the way he did to an official in a game, and this amplifies the force of the put-down.

In the excerpt from Shakespeare's *Henry IV, Part II* cited as an epigram at the head of this chapter, and repeated below, one sees some interesting comic uses of direct address in professionally constructed dialogue.

> Ah, you sweet little rogue, you! Alas, poor ape, how thou sweat'st!
> Come, let me wipe thy face. Come on, you whoreson chops.
> Ah, rogue! i' faith, I love thee.
>
> Shakespeare *Henry IV, Part II*
> II, 4: 233–236

Doll Tearsheet speaks these lines to Sir John Falstaff after he valiantly drives Pistol from the room with his rapier. Doll and Falstaff routinely duel verbally, but this passage is particularly humorous because of the quick accumulation of assorted terms of address: *little rogue, poor ape, whoreson chops*, and again *rogue*, all of them ostensibly negative in varying degrees, though mitigated by the adjectives *little* and *poor* as well as Doll's overall tone of mocking praise and concern—not to mention her declaration of love to Falstaff at the end. Moreover, Shakespeare has recourse to a device unavailable in contemporary English: He has Doll switch back and forth between the formal *you* and the familiar *thou* (along with *thee* and *thy*) forms of address. Such switching is not unheard of in Shakespeare's plays, though it does not occur in interaction in modern European languages distinguishing two forms of address, but it is exceptionally prominent in this extract. The incongruity of expressions like *rogue, villain* and even *whoreson chops* as terms of affection along with the reversals of *you* and *thou* serves to render this stretch of dialogue quite comical.

6.   Conclusions

In this paper we have investigated the use of direct address to create humor in scripted, recycled jokes and in everyday talk. We reviewed the research to date on vocatives and direct address, and showed how humorous forms build on, extend and subvert the standard system. In particular, we have seen how both stock jocular phrases and spontaneous conversational joking may incorporate an inappropriate form of address to create the incongruity characteristic of verbal humor. Appropriate forms of address within passages of direct address in dialogue help identify the characters and their relationships in jokes and anecdotes. Initially inappropriate forms of address help establish a play frame and nonce identities within it for the sake of humorous interaction. We have further investigated how reciprocal direct address between friends, partners and family members functions in banter, playing a special role in teasing moves and serving as a contextualization cue for a non-serious key in the interaction as a whole. Direct address with culturally coded vocatives like *sir* provides a serviceable resource for the creation of humor in fantasy sequences as well. Finally, direct address, especially with obscene vocatives adds force to joke punch lines.

We have seen that the system of direct address is surprisingly flexible. Participants in talk-in-interaction are aware of this flexibility and how it may be used for humorous purposes. There are often various standard ways friends and family members use to address each other, and these variants create possibilities for teasing of different kinds. At the same time, participants in interaction are awake to the possibilities of mis-naming each other to position themselves within a play frame. This mis-naming may even include the invention nonce epithets like *Mister Prescriptive*. The humorous deployment of vocatives within patterns of address once again demonstrates the creative energy participants in talk-in-interaction are prepared to invest in the production and comprehension of everyday talk for purposes of entertainment and interpersonal relationships.

Transcription conventions

Each line of transcription represents spoken language as segmented into intonation units. In English, an intonation unit typically consists of about four to five words and expresses one new idea unit. Intonation units are likely to begin with a brief pause and to end in a clause-final intonation contour; they often match grammatical clauses. Each idea unit typically contains a subject, or given information, and a predicate, or new information; this flow from given to new information is characteristic of spoken language (Chafe 1994). Arranging each intonation unit on a separate line displays the greater fragmentation inherent in spoken language (Chafe 1982).

Capitalization is reduced to the pronoun *I* and proper names, and diacritics are used to mark features of prosody rather than grammatical units and non-lexical items, for example pause fillers like *eh* and *um*, affirmative particles like *aha* or surprise markers like *oh*. The specific transcription conventions are as follows.

She's out.	Period shows falling tone in the preceding element.
Oh yeah?	Question mark shows rising tone in the preceding element.
nine, ten	Comma indicates a level, continuing intonation.
DAMN	Capitals show heavy stress or indicate that speech is louder than the surrounding discourse.
°dearest°	Utterances spoken more softly than the surrounding discourse are framed by degree signs.
says 'Oh'	Single quotes mark speech set off by a shift in the speaker's voice.
(2.0)	Numbers in parentheses indicate timed pauses.
..	A truncated ellipsis is used to indicate pauses of one-half second or less.
…	An ellipsis is used to indicate a pause of more than a half-second.
ha:rd	The colon indicates the prolonging of the prior sound or syllable.
⟨no way⟩	Angle brackets pointing outward denote words or phrases that are spoken more slowly than the surrounding discourse.
⟩watch out⟨	Angle brackets pointing inward denote words or phrases spoken more quickly than the surrounding discourse.
bu- but	A single dash indicates a cut-off with a glottal stop.
[and so-]	Square brackets on successive lines mark
[why] her?	beginning and end of overlapping talk.
and=	Equals signs on successive lines show latching
=then	between turns.
H	Clearly audible breath sounds are indicated with a capital *H*.
.h	Inhalations are denoted with a period, followed by a small *h*. Longer inhalations are depicted with multiple *h*s as in *.hhh*
h	Exhalations are denoted with a small *h* (without a preceding period). A longer exhalation is denoted by multiple *h*s.

()	In the case that utterances cannot be
(hard work)	transcribed with certainty, empty parentheses are employed. If there is a likely interpretation, the questionable words appear within the parentheses.
((stage whisper))	Aspects of the utterance, such as whispers, coughing, and laughter are indicated with double parentheses.
{doorbell}	Extraneous sounds.

Data sources

The data used for this paper come from three sources: the Saarbrücken Corpus of Spoken English (SCoSE), the Santa Barbara Corpus of Spoken American English (SBCSAE) and the Wellington Spoken Corpus (WSC). The transcriptions of the SCoSE are available on-line at: http://www.uni-saarland.de/fak4/norrick/scose.html (last access 4 February 2009).

The SBCSAE is available through the Linguistic Data Consortium http://www.ldc.upenn.edu/Projects/SBCSAE (last access 4 February 2009).

The WSC is part of the Wellington Corpora of New Zealand English available from Victoria University http://khnt.hit.uib.no/icame/manuals/wsc/INDEX.HTM (last access 4 February 2009).

Transcriptions from both sources have been partially reformatted according to our conventions, as summarized below.

References

Boxer, Diane & Cortes-Conde, Florencia. 1997. "From bonding to biting: Conversational joking and identity display." *Journal of Pragmatics* 27: 275–294.

Brown, Roger & Ford, Marguerite. 1961. "Address in American English." *Journal of Abnormal and Social Psychology* 62: 375–385.

Brown, Penelope & Levinson, Stephen. 1987. *Politeness: Some Universals in Language Usage*. Cambridge: Cambridge University Press.

Bubel, Claudia. 2005. *The Linguistic Construction of Character Relations in TV Drama: Doing Friendship in Sex and the City*. Doctoral dissertation. Saarland University, Saarbrücken.

Chafe, Wallace. 1982. "Integration and involvement in speaking, writing, and oral literature". In: *Spoken and written language: Advances in discourse processes, vol. 9*, Deborah Tannen (Ed), 35–54. Norwood: Ablex.

Chafe, Wallace. 1994. *Discourse, Consciousness and Time*. Chicago: University of Chicago Press.

Davies, Eirlys E. 1986. "English vocatives: a look at their function and form." *Studia Anglistica Posnaniensia* 19: 91–106.

Dunkling, Leslie. 1990. *A Dictionary of Epithets and Terms of Address*. London: Routledge.

Goffman, Erving. 1972 [1967]. *Interaction Ritual: Essays on Face-to-Face Behaviour.* London: Allen Lane.

Gumperz, John J. 1982. *Discourse Strategies.* Cambridge: Cambridge University Press.

Leech, Geoffrey. 1999. "The distribution and function of vocatives in American and British English conversation." In *Out of Corpora: Studies in Humour of Stig Johansson,* Hilde Hasselgård & Signe Oksefjell (Eds), 107–118. Amsterdam: Rodopi.

Leisi, Ernst. 1978. *Paar und Sprache: Linguistische Aspekte der Zweierbeziehung.* Heidelberg: Quelle und Meyer.

Mayes, Patricia. 1990. "Quotation in spoken English." *Studies in Language* 14: 323–363.

McCarthy, Michael J. & O'Keeffe, Anne. 2003. "'What's in a name?': vocatives in casual conversations and radio phone-in calls." In *Corpus Analysis: Language Structure and Language Use,* Pepi Leistyna & Charles F. Meyer (Eds), 153–185. Amsterdam: Rodopi.

Norrick, Neal R. 1993. *Conversational Joking.* Bloomington: Indiana University Press.

Norrick, Neal R. & Bubel, Claudia. 2005. "On the pragmatics of direct address in conversation." *Lodz Papers in Pragmatics* 1: 159–178.

Raskin, Victor. 1985. *Semantic Mechanisms of Humor.* Dordrecht: Reidel.

Spitz, Alice. 2005. *Power plays: The Representation of Mother-Daughter Disputes in Contemporary Plays by Women: A Study in Discourse Analysis.* Doctoral dissertation. Saarland University, Saarbrücken.

Straehle, Carolyn A. 1993. "'Samuel?' 'Yes, dear?' Teasing and conversational rapport." In *Framing in Discourse,* Deborah Tannen (Ed.), 210–230. Oxford: Oxford University Press.

Tannen, Deborah. 1989. *Talking Voices: Repetition, Dialogue, and Imagery in Conversational Discourse.* Cambridge: Cambridge University Press.

Tannen, Deborah. 1993. "The relativity of linguistic strategies: rethinking power and politeness in gender and dominance." In *Gender and conversational interaction,* Deborah Tannen (Ed.), 165–188. Oxford: Oxford University Press.

Watts, Richard J. 1989. "Relevance and relational work: linguistic politeness as politic behaviour." *Multilingua* 8: 131–166.

Watts, Richard J. 2003. *Politeness.* Cambridge: Cambridge University Press.

Wolfson, Nessa. & John Manes. 1980. "'Don't dear me!'" In *Women and Language in Literature and Society and Nelly Furman,* Sally McConell-Ginet & Ruth Boker (Eds), 79–92. New York: Praeger.

Zwicky, Arnold. 1974. "Hey, whatsyourname!" In *Papers from the tenth regional meeting of the Chicago Linguistic Society,* Michael W. LaGaly, Robert A. Fox & Anthony Bruck (Eds), 787–801. Chicago: Chicago Linguistic Society.

An interactional approach to irony development*

Helga Kotthoff

This article discusses conversational data from a project on how pupils use irony and related forms of communication. It employs a Bakhtinian and frame analytic approach combined with a pragmatics of presumptive meaning to understand what sorts of irony nine-year-olds use. Some types of irony correspond to teasing, others more to critical comments or joint fantasy production. The children in the study often perform an authoritative, ironic voice directed at the supervising university students, thereby showing their knowledge of typical adult voices and stances, and the students join in the irony by "playing along." Irony thus helps the students and children to create an in-group that plays with its knowledge of official and unofficial stances and unites in sharing unofficial perspectives and attitudes.

1. Introduction

Irony is very important in face-to-face, as well as in mediated communication (Hartung 1997; Müller 1995). In this highly inferential way of speaking, the ironist attributes stances to the object of irony and at the same time distances him/herself from these stances (Giora 2003; Kotthoff 2002). Irony is probably primarily used because it allows us to communicate a gap between different evaluations and attitudes (*stances*). Wu (2003) views stance as the indication of the speaker's affective position regarding what is said and/or the addressee(s). It is an emergent product that can gain contours in the course of interaction.

In his famous article "Logic and Conversation," Grice (1975) treats irony, in accord with definitions that go back to Aristotle, as saying one thing and meaning the opposite: "Hence, the speaker flouts the first Maxim of Quality" (p. 27). An initially produced implicature of opposite content must be replaced in a second step of understanding by a further inference in order to grasp the conversational

*Many thanks to James Brice, Uta Eckhoff, Thomas Steuber and Tanja Bajorath for cooperation in this project.

meaning. In "Further Notes on Logic and Conversation," he also includes Plato's idea of irony as simulation (feint, deception) (1978). Like Grice, Cutler (1974) also assumes that irony communicates the opposite of the literal meaning of what is said. Unfortunately, these theories do not clarify the circumstances under which speakers become ironic and what advantages this could have for them.

In recent years[1] more attention has been paid to the level on which the irony-specific opposition is located, and whether both the said and the meant are understood, or only the meant. For Wilson and Sperber's echo and mention theory (1992: 75), ironic speech is "a variety of echoic interpretive use, in which the communicator dissociates herself from the opinion echoed with accompanying ridicule or scorn." Thus, "What a lovely party!" echoes a specific or imagined opinion and simultaneously implies that this opinion is absurd. Ironic utterances are like statements in quotes. In echo and mention theory, the conventional conception of mentioning is clarified, insofar as an expression that is mentioned refers to itself. The message that such an opinion is absurd is presented as the relevant one. In contrast to this view, Giora (1995, 2003), Gibbs (2000), Gibbs and O'Brien (1992) and Kotthoff (2002, 2003) assume that irony does not simply replace the indirectly negated message, but rather that it specifically communicates the difference between dictum and implicatum as the most relevant information. Irony is then a parsimonious communication form that presents contrasting stances. The ironic speaker and the object of irony can be linked in an attitude; the ironist can, however, also join with other people who are present, or even with absent persons in opposition to the object of irony. The evaluative dimensions of both the dictum and the implicatum have to be understood and the difference has to be relevant in the communicative context.

While echo and mention theory states that the attitude toward the expressed thoughts is adopted, Clark and Gerrig's (1984) pretense theory assumes that the attitude is directed against the persons who express or accept such thoughts. Not only Clark and Gerrig, but also Sperber and Wilson claim to go beyond the irony theory of meaning substitution. In the meantime, both theories have been combined as an "allusional pretense theory of verbal irony" (Glucksberg and Brown 1995).

Always important in irony is what attitude could be expected in a particular context (mutually manifest), since irony deviates from this attitude. According to Kihara's (2005)[2] cognitive model, a typical ironic speaker states without any distinct

---

1. Gibbs and Colston (2007) present a brief history of irony and an overview of major works within cognitive science on the nature, function, and understanding of irony.

2. Very similar is Coulson's idea that sarcastic utterances present the listener with a blend that must be unpacked into two counterfactual input spaces, an expected reaction space in

space builders that something is the case in the mental space of expectation, in order to make it mutually manifest that it is not so in the initial reality space. This expectation space theory of irony integrates the power of the echo approach with the view of irony as relevant inappropriateness (Attardo 2007).

Although the named theories are indispensable for understanding irony, we also base our analyses on Bakhtin's theoretical treatment of *voice*. When speaking, we draw on different voices, which reflect past and prospective loyalties and alignments (Bakhtin 1981, 1984). In his dialogic epistemology, language use, including role performance, is always multi-voiced. Children learn very early to differentiate an unmarked real-life voice from a pretend voice. For example, caregiver voices are relevant for children, and they assume them in various contexts, first in pretend play (Garvey 1974), later also in parody (Aronsson and Thorell 2002) and, as we will see, in irony.

Recent theoretical discussions have also addressed the motivation for irony and the specifics of the contrast expressed in irony, its recognizability and thereby also the necessity of irony signals. Most linguistic researchers assume that indications of a prosodic, mimetic or kinetic nature usually suggest ironization, graspable as contextualization procedures in the sense of Cook-Gumperz and Gumperz (1976) and Gumperz (1982). Contemporary irony research emphasizes, however, that there are no signals that point exclusively to irony, but rather there are prosodic or other distancing procedures such as marked wording that can help to identify statements as ironic or humorous (Haiman 1990; Schütte 1991; Hartung 1997; Kotthoff 1998).

The question of motivation is answered in very different ways. Many linguists regard irony as an aggressive form of communication (for an overview, see Lapp 1992). Brown and Levinson (1987) and Barbe (1995), in contrast, argue that ironic critique is less face-threatening than direct critique. They thereby regard politeness as a reason for employing irony. I, however, disagree not only with the general statement that irony is aggressive, but also with the claim that it is polite (Kotthoff 1998). Above all, these assertions do not clarify what achievements are primarily characteristic of irony. There is really no obvious reason why one needs to use irony to be polite, for one can just as well express politeness and aggressiveness with other means. Irony communicates initially that there is an expectation in the situation from which the ironist manifestly deviates or points to others' unexpected forms of behavior. In some circumstances the deviation from a social standard resonates with politeness or impoliteness. The social relationship dimension that irony can communicate ranges from rejection to recognition, from affiliation to distance.

---

which the speaker reacts to the situation in a normal fashion, and a counterfactual trigger space that models the situation that might provoke the speaker's actual utterance.

Previous irony research, and especially irony acquisition research have, with the exception of Hartung (1998), Clift (1999), Gibbs (2000) and Kotthoff (2002, 2003), concentrated on the individual ironic act. In everyday interactions, irony can, however, extend over several sequences. We regard social and situative typification knowledge as an important prerequisite for the production and reception of ironic statements (which fits well with Kihara's expectation space theory). Children between 7 and 10 years of age can produce contra-factual utterances if they have enough knowledge of social and situative expectations regarding utterance formats that they can also impute to their partner. For research on irony the communication-oriented sociology of knowledge is thus also relevant (Berger & Luckmann 1967). This branch of sociology explores structures of common-sense knowledge and "the social construction of reality" on the background of expectations. Very much in line with sociology of knowledge and its highlighting of situative typification, Levinson's pragmatics of presumption (2003) is based on the distinction of unmarked and marked developments (textual as well as situational). Interpreting the quantity, quality, relevance and manner of utterances functions for Levinson (2000) on the basis of knowing what is normal and can accordingly be expected. Deviations from normal discourse (such as humor or irony) orient the listener to something special. Normality assumptions hold for all sorts of institutionalizations (e.g., activity types, genres, styles and culture-specific formulation conventions). In irony and in humor, speakers use implicit meta-communication to make the communicative act comprehensible as something special (Kotthoff 2006). Clark (1996) calls meta-communicative procedures "collateral projects" (p. 243) or "layering" (p. 353) In irony, speakers at the same time violate and rely on normality assumptions. The understanding of the dictum and the implicatum requires typification knowledge.

Irony fulfills very diverse functions. It is quite often integrated into teasing, but speakers can also use it to distance themselves from certain positions or to create ridiculous imaginary scenes. It is always important to know how the irony is interactionally integrated and developed and what role it plays in the social history of the interlocutors' relationships. Irony research has too long restricted itself to the study of single acts in artificial situations (Gibbs and Colston 2007). It also has an aesthetic dimension, because artistic performance (special wording, marked prosody, etc.) is often a focus. The ironic act steers the recipient's attention to form and formulation, a prerequisite of a poetic dimension.[3] The intertextuality of irony is displayed

---

3.   I agree with Gibbs (1994) who claims that there exist cognitive operations once thought to be poetic–their most fabulous products being most easily seen in poetry – that are instead, at least in their central forms, constitutive of everyday thought and language.

to varying degrees. Let's look at an example of echo irony from Kotthoff (2002: 221). Methodically, I combine conversation analysis and a pragmatics of presumption with the analysis of cognition in interaction.

(1)   Annette (A), Bernd (B), Friederike (F), Lars (L), Martin (M)
       (the lines focused on are in italics)

       1   F: hier hats ja nur ein fEnster.
       2   L: is aber doch SCHÖN fürn jungen hErrn. weischt.
       3   A: ja, das REI (hh) CHT fürn jungen mAnn.
       4   L: fürn jungen HERRN, sagt deine mUtter immer.

       1   F: *there is only one window.*
       2   L: *but it is really nice for a young gentleman. you know.*
       3   A: *yes, it suffices for a young man.*
       4   L: *for a young gentleman, your mother always says.*

Bernd is showing his friends around his new flat. Friederike suddenly notes that Bernd's kitchen has only one window and will accordingly be dimly lit during the daytime. Thereupon Lars delivers a phrase from the repertoire of elderly women (*really nice for a young gentleman*). Annette agrees with him in line 3 and raises the level of playful impoliteness (*it suffices for a young man*). Bernd is defined as a *young gentleman* who does not need a brightly illuminated kitchen. This activity integrates dimensions of a mock challenge. In line 4 Lars makes the source of the flowery phrase explicit, Annette's mother. The attribution of domains and objects to gentlemen and ladies is found equally absurd in this circle of academics (whose ages are close to 40 and who are only considered young from the perspective of elderly people). *Really nice for a young gentleman* is a playful compliment on the level of the dictum and a critique on the level of the implicatum. Bernd is a journalist who is very often away on business trips. Lars and Anette, on the one hand, communicate that a rather dark kitchen would not be a problem for him. After line 4, brief joint laughter can be heard on the cassette. On the other hand, through the quotation of a highly typified speech style of a sort of people they all know, they evoke this alternate world. These people of the older generation live up to clear gender patterns, which are criticized by circles to which Friederike, Lars, Annette and Martin belong. But it turns out that their criteria for flat choices are more in line with outdated ways of thinking than they themselves are aware. Of course, stance is involved here; a gap between stances is communicated.

Lars and Annette work together on the formulation. It is obviously important for the performance of irony that the wording is correct. One goal of the performance seems to be to evoke a milieu familiar to all, that of their parents' generation. For many theoreticians of verbal art, the evocation of a play frame and the focus on wording are features typical of artistry (Finnegan 1992). To Turner (1986) humans

count as 'homo performans.' Since performances are reflexive, they manifest themselves in shaping, or designing the material side of communication and are insofar
a precondition of artistry. Performance is often relevant in irony (lexical choices,
prosody, mimicry, gestures), even if it is communicated "dry" (Haiman 1990).

The humorous potential of irony varies: it can be either serious or humorous.
Highly standardized forms of irony are normally not funny. The embedding of
irony in the interaction and the interactional history of a relationship are of interest
(see Hartung 1997). Lars' remark in line 2 "is aber doch schön fürn jungen Herrn.
weischt. (*but it is really nice for a young gentleman. you know.*) can be enjoyed by
those who can process the gap of stances and who share the relevance of these gender and age related stances. Both the dictum and the implicatum make sense in the
example above.

2.   Acquisition of irony competence

Irony, as has been shown, is a communicative competence that children tend to
acquire later than many other skills (Ackermann 1984; Winner 1988).

Understanding and producing irony presupposes the ability to infer:

a.   a contrast between what is said and what is meant,
b.   what the speaker him/herself thinks,
c.   what ways of thinking s/he attributes to the listener ("second order belief attri-
     bution") according to Perner and Wimmer 1985 and Dews and Winner 1997),
d.   what intention the speaker is pursuing by using irony.

Dews and Winner (1997) show that at about the age of six a child can begin to manage "second order belief attribution" and acquires the ability to respond to irony.
Irony research gives us access to "inter-subjective phenomena" (Bruner 1990), but
there is more to understanding the social component of irony.

The comprehension of irony was in the past chiefly studied using reading
tests. Here we discuss only two very influential studies. Their methods are also
found in later studies. In reading experiments, Ackermann (1984) examined how
children draw on contextual discrepancies and intonation in order to understand
irony. Short stories with a certain range of variation were read to first- and third-
graders, and also to university students. The stories had an ironic, a non-ironic
and a neutral ending. In some cases the intonation was strongly marked, in others
it was not. He found two processes involved in irony comprehension: detection
(of the unsuitability of an utterance in the context) and inference (interpretation
of the intention behind the utterance, p. 488). Ackermann writes that children

do not have direct access to what is meant by skipping over the literal meaning. With Giora (2003), I question whether adults really skip over the literal meaning (Kotthoff 2002, 2003). Rather, interlocutors have to process both the said and the meant. In contrast to Ackermann and other irony researchers, I start from the thesis that in prototypical irony what is said and what is meant and especially the gap between them must make sense. Studies of everyday life contexts show the range of children's attempts to make sense of ironic and quasi-ironic scenes.

Winner (1988) discusses the indirectness dimension of metaphoric and ironic communication. Metaphor and irony differ in function and structure. The functional difference is that metaphor serves to clarify, illuminate or explain. Irony is employed to comment and evaluate, usually critically. Children also become adept at grasping unusual metaphors sooner than irony.

Creusere (2007: 410) classifies the acquisition studies into five categories: The first group includes studies of the understanding of non-literal speech (metaphor, hyperbole, deception, irony). This group includes, e.g., Winner (1988). Irony proves to be the most difficult, especially the type of ironic understatements. The second group includes research that pursues the question of the extent to which contextual information is useful in comprehending irony (Ackerman 1984). The third group (to which Perner and Wimmer and Creusere herself belong) focuses on a "second-order theory of mind" (the ability of a person A to infer what a person B knows). The fourth research approach investigates the role of intonation and facial expression. Dews et al. (1997), Creusere (1997) and others have been able to show that a conspicuous intonation facilitates the comprehension of irony. In the fifth group are studies that evaluate the communicative function of irony. These differentiate functions, e.g., whether the ironist wanted to be friendly or nasty. Perlocutionary effects distinguish friendly from sarcastic irony (Hancock, Dunham and Purdy 2007). In laboratory studies (which, however, appear very artificial) children seem to begin to understand ironic critique earlier than ironic compliments.

All the studies were carried out in experimental settings, and all test only the comprehension of irony (not the production, including further co-constructions of the sequences), which is assumed to start at about the age of six years. In the samples of these studies only an isolated speech act is presented as ironic.

I draw on these studies but initially have more interest in the co-construction of ironic episodes; second, I start from a broader spectrum of ironic activities and, third, have no reason to consider critical irony to be the dominant type in everyday life. I place irony in the context of highly inferential, contrastive discourse, because I also want to capture similar activities that likewise work with contrasts between the said and the meant and with "acting as if" (highly inferential communication with performative presentation), e.g., teasing, mocking, playful provocation and fantasy construction. I hope that the interactional linguistic approach will illuminate dimensions of irony that have previously remained in the background in experimental research.

Let's assume:

a. that previous research on irony acquisition has *not* adequately captured the broad spectrum of the ironic,
b. that reading tests for children represent different barriers to comprehension than interactively imbedded utterances,
c. that irony often extends over several sequences, whereby it becomes clear (and for children more understandable), and
d. that we still do not know in what contexts older children themselves produce forms of irony.

Interestingly, findings on the processing of highly-inferential communication that displays a gulf between dictum and implicatum do not entirely accord with research on children's teasing, for which the mentioned characteristic of a discrepancy (but not a full opposition) between dictum and implicatum likewise holds.

Since I place irony in what I call "highly inferential contrastive discourse," I will also examine related phenomena that communicate contrasts and pretenses, such as teasing (Eisenberg 1986; Schieffelin 1986), playful provocation and joint fantasy construction. I hope that an interactional approach to the communication of irony will shed light on dimensions that tend to be neglected by experimental psychological research.

I start from the assumption that the child does not acquire the ability to understand irony overnight, let alone to produce irony on her/his own, but rather that there are activity types (e.g., teasing and fantasy scenes) which teach the child to play with contrasts. In the course of kindergarten and grade school, it becomes increasingly clear to children how complex the relationship can be between the said and the meant (Bermann 2004).

3.   The data

I will introduce a current research project on how nine-year-old children practice irony and related phenomena of contrastive framing. We video- and audio-taped interactions with nine-year-old children in homework settings; we chose this method instead of gathering data in lab situations. In lab studies, the situations where ironic acts take place are contrived, and the irony is transmitted as a monological act in order to isolate certain cognitive features.

In the homework group, we witness irony in talk in interaction. We can trace cognition in interaction, because in some cases the children's reactions to irony and their own ironic initiatives allow us to reconstruct their understanding of what is going on within the conversational context.

Every week for eight months the supervising university students, Tanja Bajorath and Uta Eckhoff, videotaped a homework group consisting, by chance, only of 8 nine-year-old boys. At this age, most children can already understand and express irony, although some still cannot. Prior to each homework session, the students held informal talks with the children. We are mostly interested in these episodes. Spontaneous interactions took place, and the children recognized that the students were not behaving like their classroom teachers. In their irony the boys sometimes mirror to the students their knowledge of typical adult positions.

The project aims to reconstruct how children create sense in highly inferential contexts and is to this extent located in a tradition of "collaborative cognition" (Bearison and Dorval 2002). The children are real creators and addressees of different types of irony and the initiators of related activities. The students and the children practiced ironic or irony-related activities that fitted into the context and shaped it. The richness of the ironic interaction is thus not artificially limited. In experimental research, the addressees simply remain recipients who cannot influence the context. They are not personally affected by the ironic act, and there is little need to choose an appropriate response. In experimental research it remains unclear what motivates children to gradually become competent in more and more aspects of expressing irony and related speech phenomena.

Many studies report an understanding of irony beginning only at the age of 9, whereas other studies show that children are already able to play along in highly inferential communication at about the age of 3. However, there are some inconsistencies in studies about highly inferential discourses. With regard to the ironic subtype of teasing, studies from anthropological sociolinguistics indicate that (a) teasing and making fun of others are culturally significantly distinct, and (b) that children can actively participate in teasing sequences as early as the age of three, insofar as these are repeated in similar form. Teasing can be a form of communication in which critique is expressed in an entertaining way, and differences are negotiated in such a way that they ultimately find recognition in the relationship.

4. Findings of anthropological linguistics on teasing

Teasing, for example, is a humorous activity type related to irony that is also highly inferential, often ironic, but sometimes plays with hyperbole; see Guenthner (1996a), Straehle (1993) and Boxer and Cortés-Conde (1997) for characteristics of this activity type as practiced among adults. Various anthropological and socio-linguistic studies have shown that this type of communication combines the communication of difference and support. Schieffelin (1986: 165) reports for Kaluli society in Papua New Guinea that adults there prefer teasing and shaming children to physical punishment. Teasing helps introduce the society's moral order to children. Schieffelin found some contextualization cues that enable children to differentiate teasing from other verbal activities. Often, mothers asked hyperbolically threatening rhetorical questions, such as: "Where are you climbing?" in order to discourage them from climbing. As in our culture, children learn at a very early age that questions with marked (falling) intonation do not function as informational questions, but rather as indirect orders to desist from something.

In California, Eisenberg (1986) found that two Mexican families influenced their children by teasing them. It is important that the children do not take what was said seriously. Very often an adult says something threatening to a child, e.g., "We are going to throw Marissa into a garbage bag!" This is said with much laughter and a sing-song intonation, whereby smiling also signals a playful modality. Very often emotive threats form the core of the provocation. For example, a mother will say that everyone is now going to visit grandfather, but Nancy will have to stay home. After Nancy expresses disappointment, her parents reassure her that she can, of course, accompany the others. In teasing, the adults first threaten the children, but they then revoke the threat completely, and a possibility is thus created to communicate closeness, security and affection. It is viewed as a great success if a child initially believes a provocation. But the child very early learns to grasp this double-coded form of interaction, which might be easier to process than irony, perhaps because of the stability of the format. It is still not entirely clear why young children are often able to understand teasing at a quite early age and are even able to tease others, yet are still unable to understand irony.

5. Highly inferential contrastive speech activities in the data

In the following we present sequences in which the boys' irony initiatives appear in a thematic context that is very relevant in this age group, namely the negotiation of status and membership within the peer group. At this age and even earlier children are adept at recognizing register differences and are even able to use them (Garvey 1984; Andersen 1996). Sometimes a boy uses a formal style in order to distance himself from another boy.

5.1   Stylistically marked irony

Irony can be framed by a style change; another voice is adopted (in the Bakhtinian sense). Let's look at the first datum. Ruth, a university student, and Felix, a young boy, know each other quite well.

(2)   (Corpus family talk)
       Ruth (university student, 22) talks to Felix (7 years)
       1   R: spielst du eigentlich noch mit JIMMI?
       2   F: erwähne NIE: wieder diesen nAmen. (--)
       3   ich kEnne den jungen nicht.
       4   R: HÄH? was ist denn JETZT kaputt.
       5   F: hehehehe
       6   R: spielst du also NICHT mehr mit jimmi (-)
       7   oder wie darf ich diese wOrte deuten.
       8   F: was IST das fürn junge.
       9   R: du kEnnst jimmi also gar nicht mehr.
       10   F: dO:::ch.

       1   R: do you still play with JIMMI?
       2   F: don't ever mention that name again. (--)
       3   i do not know the boy.
       4   R: HUH? what's wrong now.
       5   F: hehehehe
       6   R: so you don't play with jimmi anymore (-)
       7   or how may i interpret these words.
       8   F: what kind of boy IS he.
       9   R: you don't even know jimmi anymore.
       10   F: I do.

Felix reacts to Ruth's question in a very formal style. The imperative in line 2
(erwähne) is unusual in colloquial speech: in German the informal imperative
normally ends without the schwa represented by 'e' here. Also, in line 3, Felix for-
mulates a syntactically hypercorrect sentence. If Felix really didn't know Jimmi,
he probably would not have said: "ich kenne den jungen nicht," but simply, "kenn
ich nich" (don't know). Here the English translation minimizes the stylistic differences between the formal and informal variants. In spoken German the ellip-
tical formulations (object deletion and verb in first position) "kenn ich nich" or
"weiß ich nich" in contexts where there is a direct display of not knowing are
highly standardized. In the English translation neither the unusual position of
the subject, the object deletion, nor the deletion of 't' from "nicht" are apparent.
For a second-grader like Felix the conspicuous difference in style is helpful to
mark the irony so that it must be noticed. The implicatum is: I know him too well
to regard him as a friend any longer. Felix has a sense of ironic style and uses it
very effectively, without necessarily being aware of this; see Andersen (1996) on
the development of children's register knowledge. Felix frames his words as an
overly formal statement that is contextually unsuitable. The language level is typical of communicating distance, and he indexes distance in regard to Jimmi. The
dictum makes sense as a formal notification of a change in the relationship. With

this change of style Felix helps Ruth to identify and understand his irony. Jimmi seems to have fallen out of favor with Felix.

Ruth expresses surprise. Felix laughs. In lines 6–7 Ruth asks Felix about his relationship with Jimmi, also using a very formal style in line 7 (how may I interpret these words). Now, Felix repeats his question (8) – with a marked intonation. It is only in line 10 that Felix makes it clear that he knows Jimmi very well. Felix demands some processing effort from Ruth. Involved in his irony is a transparent feint. Irony, of course, demands to be recognized. That is what makes it different from lying and deception. Sometimes even two-year-olds produce transparent feints, trying to coax adults to follow a false scent and react with pleasure if they succeed (Kotthoff 2003). Irony can be contextualized via stylistic marking (as is the case in (2)), but can also be communicated dry (without special performance features). Felix borrows his style from a formal adult discourse. The format of a query about an acquaintance and the ironic repudiation according to the formal linguistic pattern, "I do not know this person ("ich kenne diesen Menschen nicht"), make situative transmission possible. As children often temporarily (though harshly) distance themselves from friends, this context is highly relevant for them. In the next section we discuss something as easy to grasp as Felix's stylistically marked comments: the commonplace "great" when things are really not "great" at all.

5.2   Simple positive comments as critique

Irony is communicated in various activity types (e.g., more or less friendly teasing, comments, verbal attacks, playing with others' voices). A form of irony often mentioned in the classical literature is standardized praise used to express critique. Here we witness that type as a reaction to children's boasting, for example, regarding skill in playing soccer. This is also a context that is almost standardized among boys. The ironic speaker communicates a disparity of stances. Martin's "yeah great" reacts to Fabian's endorsement claims that he belongs to the best group. In his opinion it is not at all the best group. Martin mirrors Fabian's boasting in his own stance and at the same time distances himself from it.

(3)   Fabian (F), Martin (M), David (D), Nino (N), Tina (T, 22), Eva (E, 28)

    23   F: bischt du ⟨↑E:⟩ oder ⟨↓EF⟩ jugend.
    24   D: e: drei'
    25   F: e: drei;
    26   D: ja;
    27   F: dann isch ⟨↑ZÄ:Hringe⟩ nit erschter.
    28   (2.0) oder'
    29   D: ne:'

30	F:	ef Eins bin ICH (-) und WIR sind erschter;
31	M:	ja tOLL' (-) wir spielen e: drei'
32	D:	wIr sind doch e: drei. (-) ich bin doch <u>BEsser</u>
33		als du;
34	F:	ach [wa:s(--)e: EIns isch höher;
35	D:	°[↓do:ch°
36	M:	wIr spie:len in der e: eins;
37	D:	ja?
38	M:	ja tOll. wir spielen in der e: zwEI.
39		also ↑bist du nIcht bei uns. (3.0)

23	F:	are you ⟨↑E:⟩ or ⟨↓F⟩ youth. (E and F designate levels of play)
24	D:	e: three
25	F:	e: three;
26	D:	yes;
27	F:	then ⟨↑ZÄ:Hringe:⟩ is NOT the first.
28		(2.0) or'
29	D:	nah:'
30		I am ef: one (-) and WE are the first;
31	M:	yeah great' (-) we play e: three'
32	D:	wE are of course e: three. (-) i am too BEtter
33		than you;
34	F:	ah [nonsense(--)e: One is higher;
35	D:	°[↓oh yes°
36	M:	wE play in e: one;
37	D:	yeah?
38	M:	yeah great. we play in e: twO.
39		so ↑you are nOt with us. (3.0)

All the speakers play soccer. In Example (3) the boys disagree about their soccer skills. Especially in regard to soccer they compete very directly. Fabian claims in line 30 to play in the first rank of the region's youth soccer clubs. In lines 31 and 38 Martin produces a short ironic reaction: ja toll (yeah great). The implicature is that this group is not really so great at all. Then he explicitly rejects Fabian's claim to belong to the best group. In the context a "mental space structure" is opened up (Kihara 2005) in which a positive confirmation can be expected. It is given in a dry tone. Also Clark and Gerrig's "pretense theory" is consistent with the irony of "ja toll." The attitude that Fabian's stance is great is attributed to the addressee; the speaker, however, disputes precisely this.

In Example (4), nine-year-old Klaus and the student Michaela agree that a certain boy (not present) thinks it is a great accomplishment to write ten sentences. Together they distance themselves with the help of irony from the stance attributed to that absent boy.

(4)   Michaela (M) (university student) and Klaus (K) (9-year-old)
    1   M: in musIk heute (--)
    2   dem christian gings SEHR schlecht.
    3   K: warUm?
    4   M: dem christian gings sE::hr schlecht.
    5   der musste zE::hn sätze schreiben.
    5   K: ja tOll. (-) ich musste DREIßig sätze schreiben.

    1   M: today in music (--)
    2   things went very badly for christian.
    3   K: why?
    4   M: things went ve::ry badly for christian.
    5   he had to write tEn sentences.
    5   K: yeah great. (-) i had to write thIrty sentences.

Nine-year-old Klaus understands Michaela's irony. She is mocking Christian for complaining because he had to write a mere ten sentences. She represents his point of view (ten sentences is a lot), and at the same time her own stance, which is diametrically opposite. Michaela exaggerates (by using adverbs, repetitions and lengthening). Klaus's answer (ja toll/yeah great) in line 5 reacts to the dictum. He recognizes and supports her irony and maintains the tension with the implicatum. Then he counters it with his own words. Ten sentences is really not so much. The one who really had to work hard was Klaus, who had to write thirty sentences. Michaela and Klaus communicate a shared stance.

The strategy of "praise as critique" is as old as irony. It is constantly being brought up in the literature, from Quintilian to today, and is easy to perform. The group around Norbert Groeben (1984) has formulated a psychic antecedent condition for this strategy, according to which resistance is offered in the case of really difficult possibilities to influence a scene. The boys cannot prevent others from boasting or from complaining about trivialities but can display their stance.

This type of "great" irony occurs thirteen times in the five to six hours of our data. It seems to be easy for the children, because the context has a format that is easy to identify. The reaction pattern is short and simple. Ninio and Snow (1996) have identified various phases in which children acquire the ability to produce new types of statements. Children first produce utterances in formatted settings before they begin to produce them in unformatted ones. Another type of setting where the processing of irony-like remarks is easy for nine-year-olds is one where someone constructs fantastic scenes; examples of how adults create this genre in informal discourse are discussed in Kotthoff (2007). These contexts sometimes have critical components.

5.3   Contrastive fantasizing

In the group of nine-year-old boys, also David often claims to be an expert soccer player. He insists he likes to train outdoors in stormy March weather. In Example (5) the university student Eva emphasizes the intensity of his commitment to the sport with a pseudo-acknowledging comment that he plays without an umbrella, which causes even David to laugh. Eva then asks whether he perhaps really runs after the ball holding an umbrella. Another university student, Sonja, ironically underlines that it is practical to play football with an umbrella. One of the boys, Fabian, imagines David leaping into the air while still holding onto the umbrella (line 8); he joins in this construction by imagining how David jumps into the air with the ball in his hand and easily scores. The students tease one boy, and another boy plays along. Fabian co-constructs the frame shift and the fantasy construction. Again, some speakers jointly rebuff the boasting of one boy.

(5)   (Corpus homework)
      David (9), Fabian (9), Eva (22), Sonja (28)

      1   D: WIR spielen drAUßen.
      2   E: uaah. aber OHne rEgenschirm.
      3   D: hahaha
      4   E: DU spielst mIt regenschirm?
      5   DU läufst hinter dem ball her mit=m rEgenschirm in
      6   der hand?
      7   S: ist ja zIEmlich praktisch. hahaha
      8   F: schwebsch AB wenn de den ball lupfsch,
      9   nimmsch den ball in die hAnd
      10   und dann TO:::R
      11   m: hahaha
      12   S: genAU. hebst Ab und fliegst mit dem ball zum tOr
      13   und SCHMEIßT den da rein.

      1   D: WE play outdoors.
      2   E: uaah. but withOUT an umbrella.
      3   D: hahaha
      4   E: YOU play with an umbrella?
      5   YOU run after the ball with an umbrella in your hand?
      6   S: that's QUITE practical. hahaha
      7   F: you TAKE off when you pick up the ball,
      8   you take the ball in your hand
      9   and then GOAL
      10   m: hahaha
      11   S: exactly. you take off and fly with the ball to the goal
      12   and CHUCK it in.

Fabian is able to continue the ironic-absurd remarks of the students, so that a coherent fantasy scene is created where David is teased as a braggart and as someone who would go so far as to score using preposterous or unfair means. The children laugh, and David joins in. Another context is that of provocation. The boys also sometimes tease the students.

5.4   Teasing and provocation

(6)   (Corpus homework) "Eva is the oldest"
David (9), Fabian (9), Eva (22), Sonja (28)

1	F:	die EVA ist die älteste.
2	S:	das glaub ich nIcht.
3	E:	meinst dU?
4	F:	(nickt)
5	E:	seh ich so wAhnsinnig ALT aus oder wie?
6	F:	ja.
7	S:	oh guck mal die ganzen schrUmpeln
8		und die ganzen rUnzeln. haha
9	F:	graue haare hAt sie schon.
10	E:	ja. ich muss DRINgend wieder zum frisEUr und
11		nachfärben.
12	F:	haha
13	E:	du machst mich ganz TRAUrig. fAbian.
14	F:	nee. der dAvid ist der ÄLteste. der ist so
15	D:	ach was. der herr kirschner. der ist nOch älter

1	F:	EVA is the oldest.
2	S:	I don't believe that.
3	E:	you think so?
4	F:	(nods)
5	E:	do I look so terribly old or what?
6	F:	yes.
7	S:	oh look at all the crows' feet
8		and all the wrinkles. haha
9	F:	she's already got gray hair.
10	E:	yes. I urgently need to go to my hairdresser and
11		have it touched up.
12	F:	haha
13	E:	you make me quite sad. fabian.
14	F:	no. david is the oldest. he is so
15	D:	come off it. herr kirschner. he is still older.

Nine-year-old Fabian starts to tease university student Eva. In line 5 Eva asks whether she looks so old, whereby Fabian does not qualify his claim, but rather reaffirms it. Then Sonja ostentatiously exaggerates his provocation of Eva as being the oldest to the point of absurdity (7–8), and Fabian, by going a step further (9), expands the frame of the provocation. In the lines 10 and 11 Eva reacts to the dictum, which here means that she goes along with the playful provocation. When Eva explicitly (but not necessarily seriously) states in line 13 that this makes her sad, Fabian heightens the absurdity of his statement by declaring nine-year-old David to be the oldest in the group. Through this invention, the fictitiousness of the provocation becomes clearer. David instead refers to a teacher who is not there as even older.

An important skill for using irony in everyday life is, as shown in Example (6), being able to play along with others in adding to an already-created unrealistic narrative or to top it. Irony and irony-related episodes are often emergent constructions. By pointing to Eva's (non-existent) wrinkles, she enables the boys to add another contra-factual component (to define her blond hair as grey). The boys seem to have sufficient knowledge about societal beauty discourses. With her question in line 5, Eva makes the boys aware for the first time of the provocation potential of the topic.

5.5   Prototypical echo irony

In Examples 7, 8, 9, the boys stage the voices of authoritarian adults that one could refer to as "teacher types." These voices are naturally omnipresent in the everyday lives of the children. It is therefore not surprising that they would perform these voices ironically.

In Example 7 Matthias animates a critical teacher, who orders Laurent, the other pupil present, to write a word thirty times that he couldn't spell correctly. Voicing a teacher or an authority figure is highly relevant (in Attardo's sense – 2007) for the boys.[4] They do it quite often. Laurent tries to write "Donald" on the blackboard but makes a mistake. Matthias notices this and ostentatiously tries to correct him (7 and 9–10). He then repeats this in a more demonstrative manner (13). Eva, a student, ironizes his knowledge by attributing to him "seventy-five years of Walt Disney." He lends his voice to the attribution, with a minor change (Mickey Mouse).

(7)   Matthias (M) (9), Laurent (L) (9), Eva (22), Sonja (28)

    01   M: DO:N (-) DO:N wAs?
    02   L: DOnAld. ((schreibt "Donalt" an die Tafel))
    03   M: so schreibt man das aber GAR
    04   nicht.
    05   L: dOch.
    06   S: pA pA pA pA pA. (-) haha?
    07   M: ich ZEIG dir mal wAs.

---

4.   Normally, voices are stylized in reported speech. Günthner 1996b discusses strategies of speaker stylization in orally reported dialogue. As already said, Andersen 1996 shows how early children start to play with such stylizations.

```
08  S:    [hehehe.
09  M:    [hallo ich ZEIG dir mal wAs.
10        (-) wie man DOnald schreibt.
          ⟨((schreibt das Wort an der Tafel))⟩
11  E:    (?   ?)
12  M:    gibt mal (-) gIb mal KREIde.
          ((korrigiert das Wort))
13        ich- sO schreibt man DOnald.
14  E:    ne? fÜnfundsiebzig jahre walt
15        DISney oder so was.
16  M:    NEIN.
17  E:    war das nicht [ganz (?grad?)
18  M:                  [MIcky maus. (-)
19  L:    °°mIcky maus°°
20  S:    fÜnfundsiebzig jahre [MIcky
21        maus.
22  E:                        [ja
23  M:    sO. SO schreibt man dOnald.
24  S:    ja war FAST rIchtig (?   ?) bis
25        aufs TE am schlUss. genAU.
26  M:    sO.
27  S:    ist doch fast (?fast?)
28  M:    DREIssig mal dOnald schreiben.
          ⟨((Zeigegeste auf Laurent hin))⟩
29  L:    ⟨((haut Matthias))⟩
30  S:    [hehehe
31  E:    [hehehe
32  S:    DU wärst ja ein strEnger lehrer
33        matthias.

01  M:    dO:n (-) dO:n whAt?
02  L:    dOnAld. ((writes "Donalt" on the blackboard)
03  M:    it's not spelled like that
04        at all.
05  L:    yes it is.
06  S:    pA pA pA pA pA. (-) haha?
07  M:    i'll show you something.
08  S:    [hehehe.
09  M:    [hey i'll show you something.
10        (-) how to spell dOnald.
          ⟨((writes the word on the board))⟩
11  E:    (?   ?)
12  M:    just give me (-) just give me some chalk.
          ((corrects the word))
```

```
13        I- that's how you spell dOnald.
14   E:   hm seventy-five years of walt
15        disney or like that.
16   M:   nO.
17   E:   wasn't that [just (?now?)
18   M:              [mIckey mouse. (-)
19   L:   °°mIckey mouse°°
20   S:   seventy-five years of [mickey
21        mouse.
22   E:                        [yes
23   M:   that's. thAt's how you write dOnald.
24   S:   yeah almost right (?   ?) except
25        for the t at the end. exactly.
26   M:   like that.
27   S:   it's really almost (?almost?)
28   M:   write dOnald THIRTY times.
         ⟨((points to Laurent))⟩
29   L:   ⟨((beats Matthias))⟩
30   S:   [hehehe
31   E:   [hehehe
32   S:   you would be a really strIct teacher
33        matthIas.
```

In line 28 Matthias orders Laurent to write Donald thirty times. Animating a classical teacher statement here functions as teasing (not as irony). Matthias is not in
a position to give orders like that. Sonja assesses his behavioral style in lines 32/33.
Between 3 and 9, children develop a range of forms of playing with borrowed
utterances. Echo or pretense irony only functions if one can rely upon the other
to identify the source of the borrowed utterance. To this extent, irony has something to do with social knowledge, above all knowledge of typical attitudes, speech
activities and speech styles.

    An ironic gap between the borrowed and the child's own voice is evident
(and made explicit) in the next scene (Example 8). The students and the boys play
with the attribution of contrastive stances. Pretending to have an attitude oneself
and to attribute contrastive attitudes to others requires knowledge about potential
stances and attitudes. It enables them to unite in sharing unofficial stances. Laurent
echoes a typical voice of a sensible adult (Sperber and Wilson 1981). In line 5 he
harshly forbids the students to bring candy for Christmas.

    (8)   Matthias (M) (9), Laurent (L), Eva (22), Sonja (28)

```
01   L:   kriegen krIEgen wir dann
02        was ANderes?
03   S:   °klAr. vor wEIhnachten GIBTS
```

04   ne kleinigkeit°
05   L: KEIne sÜßigkeiten.
            ⟨((erhobener Zeigefinger))⟩
06   E: [hö?
07   S: [°°sÜßigkeiten?°°
08   S: würden (-) ts (-) wIr sind (-)
09   wir sind doch von der
10   pädaGOgenschule.
11   würden WIR euch sÜßigkeiten geben?
12   SO was Ungesundes.
13   E: ICH bring die chIps mit,
14   du die cOla.
15   S: geNAU.
16   E: hehehe
17   (- -)
18   L: das ist UNgesund.
            ⟨((erhobener Zeigefinger))⟩
19   E: 'h
20   S: °weisst ja GUT bescheid.°
21   S: eva bring [mal eva dann
22   nImm mal kaROTten mit.
23   M: [°°(?   ?) am tag
24   drEI liter COla [[trinkt?°°
25   L: [[Ungesund.
26   E: und minerAlwasser.
27   L: uAh.
28   a: hehehe

01   L: then do we get do we get
02   something different?
03   S: °sure. before christmas
04   there is a little something°
05   L: NO candy.
            ⟨((with raised index finger))⟩
06   E: [ha?
07   S: [°°candy?°°
08   S: would (-) ts (-) we are
09   (-) we are after all from the teacher's
10   college
11   would WE give you candy?
12   something so unhealthy.
13   E: I will bring the potato chIps,
14   you the cOla.
15   S: right.

```
16   E:   hehehe
17        (- -)
18   L:   that is unhealthy.
          ⟨((with raised index finger))⟩
19   E:   'h
20   S:   °you're in the know.°
21   S:   eva you bring [just eva
22        just bring carrots then.
23   M:               [°°(? ?) everyday
24        he drinks three liters [[of cOla°°
25   L:                          [[unhealthy.
26   E:   and minerAl water.
27   L:   uAh.
28   a:   hehehe
```

It is evident from contextualization cues like prosody/mimicry and gesture (he admonishes the student exaggeratedly with his index finger) and body language (he turns to Sonja) that Laurent is mirroring to the students the sensible and authoritative attitude of the prototypical adult. The two students at first play along by pretending that it is self-evident that students from a teacher's college would not give candy to children (9–12).

Eva then suggests bringing other junk food and drinks (chips and coke), which gives Laurent another opportunity to vehemently object (line 18). Then Sonja asks Eva to bring carrots (21–22), and Laurent inserts an interjection of disgust (27) that reveals his actual stance. The boys display their knowledge of contrastive stances. The students and the boys co-construct a play with the official attitude that candy, coke and potato chips are unhealthy, whereas carrots and mineral water are nutritious, but they agree in an unspoken positive stance towards nutritionally deficient, but popular snacks. Matthias in lines 23–24 has already admitted that he drinks a lot of cola.

Likewise in Example (9) below, Laurent displays his knowledge oft official evaluation standards (here in regard to cheating on exams). He again speaks using a quasi-authoritarian adult voice to Sonja. Eva suspects that Sonja has written crib notes on her hand. She begins to tease Sonja by speaking in the third person about Sonja's cheating on a test. Sonja defends herself in lines 9 to 12.

(9)   Matthias (M) (9), Laurent (L), Eva (22), Sonja (28)

```
01   L:   wAs hast du da in der HAND?
          ⟨((zeigt auf Sonja))⟩
02   M:   schErz[frage
03   E:         [spIckzettel
04   L:   [spIckzettel
```

```
05  S:   [('h)
06  E:   merkt euch das NICHT für
07       die zUkunft, aber die sOnja
08       mogelt immmer in klauSUren.
09  S:   nEI:n (-) a kUck mal. ich hab
10       ich hab SIEBzehn sEIten geschrieben
11       und EInen sAtz da aufgeschrieben.
12       das ist ja nIcht °VIEL oder°?
13  L:   dU MOgelst.
         〈((zeigt auf Sonja))〉
14  M:   °hehe. dU MOgelst.°
15  S:   war nur (-) und zwar nur
16       (-) nur eine erInnerungsstütze.
17  E:   [hehe. erInnerungs [[stütze.
18  S:   [hehehe.
19  L:                       [[dU MOgelst.
20       (-)
21  L:   und DU mOgelst auch.
         〈((zeigt auf Eva))〉
22  E:   ich hab noch NIE gemOgelt in klausUren.
23  L:   〈°°ojE du ARme.°°              〉
         〈Abwendung, zur Seite gesprochen〉
24  S:   [hehehe
25  M:   [hehehe
26  L:   °du hast noch NIE gemOgelt?°
27  E:   nein hab ich NIE. ich war immer
28       SEHR gut in der schUle u:nd
29       em hab NIE gemOgelt.
30       (- -)
31  L:   HÖR auf zu lÜgen.
         〈((zeigt auf Eva))〉
32       (-)
33  M:   hehehe
34  L:   in MAthe warst du sEhr sEhr
35       schlecht.
36  E:   hehe. das stImmt. ('h) hm.
37  L:   dann HÖR auf zu lÜgen. (?tanz?)
38       da warst du °schon° gUt.

01  L:   what do you have in your hand there?
         〈((points at Sonja))〉
02  M:   joke[question
03  E:       [crib card
04           [crib card
```

05	S:	[('h)
06	E:	don't remember this for
07		the future but sonja always
08		cheats on exams.
09	S:	nO: (-) ah look. i wrote-
10		i wrote seventeen pages and
11		one sentence there.
12		that's not °much is it°?
13	L:	you are cheating.
		⟨((points at Sonja))⟩
14	M:	°hehe. you are cheating.°
15	S:	was just (-) and that is just
16		(-) just a memory aid.
17	E:	[hehe. memory [[aid.
18	S:	[hehehe.
19	L:	[[you cheat.
20		(-)
21	L:	and you cheat too.
		⟨((points at Eva))⟩
22	E:	i never cheated on an exam.
23	L:	°°oh you poor thing.°°
		⟨turning away, spoken on the side⟩
24	S:	[hehehe
25	M:	[hehehe
26	L:	°you never cheated?°
27	E:	no i nEver did. i have
28		always been vEry gOOd in schOOl
29		and: em nEver cheated.
30		(- -)
31	L:	stOp lying.
		⟨((points at Eva))⟩
32		(-)
33	M:	hehehe
34	L:	in mAth you were vEry vEry.
35		bAd
36	E:	hehe. that's right. ('h) hm.
37	L:	then stop lying (?dance?)
38		you were really good at that

In Example (9) we first see how the students tease each other. Sonja has written some words on her hand, and Eva interprets these words as notes for cheating on an exam. She tells the boys in lines 6–8 not to do this in their future, but Sonja cheats with cribs. Sonja defends herself in lines 9–12 in a playful modality (she has only written one sentence on her hand).

The boys strongly reproach her in lines 13, 14 and 19. In line 21 Laurent addresses Eva and accuses her, too, of cheating. They ironically overdo the accusations, thereby implicating that they don't find cribbing so very bad. Eva defends herself after being accused by Laurent of cribbing (21), and then Laurent again shifts the frame. In an unofficial, whispered aside he pretends to pity Eva for never having cribbed (23).

The students and the boys play with the attribution of contrastive moral perspectives and stances. Pretending to have a stance oneself and to attribute a contrasting one to others requires good knowledge about potential stances and ways of speaking (voices of typical characters). It enables them here to unite in sharing unofficial stances. The boys know that Sonja and Eva are students and not real teachers. In a certain sense they belong to both the world of the children and that of teachers. It seems to be fun for the boys to discover unsatisfactory behavior in future teachers. They can playfully attack these with typical accusatory utterances. The boys are able to manage not only the pragmatics of irony, but also the meta-pragmatics (Verschueren 1995). They create playful alliances and joint irony activities. For irony research it is also interesting that the ironists can sometimes also explicitly express their real positions, as, e.g., Laurent in line 23. The conception that the speaker only produces an isolated ironic act and the hearer decodes this working alone is derived from a monological model of talk.

6.   Concluding remarks: Communicating knowledge about contradictory morals and official and unofficial stances

In this article I linked irony research to an exploration of multi-voicedness. I suggested that:

> Irony only works if the interlocutors can rely on their partners to infer what they really mean. Thus, irony production and comprehension are based on various sorts of knowledge, above all knowledge about typical situational developments, stances, behavioral norms, speech styles and formats. Irony gains relevance in everyday social life as a game of mirroring typical expectations that are actually not the case.

Irony is usually embedded in longer sequences and is in our data seldom found as an isolated act. Other speakers may join in co-constructing ironic activity types. This leads to different social alignments. Those present can demarcate themselves from others present or from absent persons.

For older children, as we see in Examples 7, 8, 9, it is apparently relevant to animate the voices of authority figures and to present official, acknowledged positions in relation to people who are in reality hierarchically above them, but thereby positioned in the role of pupils. Role reversal is an important technique in these data. The students play along and thereby form an egalitarian participation structure with the boys. They are not typical teachers reproducing official voices.

Irony plays a role in the negotiation of shared morals. The children use it to communicate their knowledge about inconsistent behavioral standards. Highly inferential discourse is anchored in the construction of the ongoing relationship, here a more or less symmetrical relationship. The boys mirror to the university students the positions one could expect from them, and at the same time they communicate distance from these positions (and the knowledge that the students do not adopt official stances). The students play along the same lines and thereby support the children's offer to attribute to them the identity of atypical adults. Highly inferential discourse thus helps them to create an in-group with the students. Most 9-year-old boys in our data know how to practice the ironic mode of communication.

I hope to have shown the scope of ironic and other highly inferential contrastive activities that approach irony and how they are anchored in ongoing relationship constructions. Routinization of the contexts in which children can try out new modes of behavior helps them to participate in the dynamic joint negotiation of stances.

Transcription conventions

The conventions are based on GAT (Selting at al. 1998)

(-)	one hyphen indicates a short pause
(- -)	two hyphens indicate a longer pause (less than half a second)
(0.5)	pause of half a second; long pauses are counted in half seconds
(? what ?)	indicates uncertain transcription
(? ?)	indicates an incomprehensible utterance
..[..
..[.... .	indicates overlap or interruption
=	latching of an utterance of one person; no interruption
hahaha	laughter
hehehe	slight laughter
goo(h)d	integrated laughter
(h)	audible exhalation
('h)	audible inhalation
,	slightly rising intonation
?	rising intonation
.	falling intonation

,	continuing intonation
:	indicates elongated sound
°blabla°	lower amplitude and pitch
COME ON	emphatic stress (pitch and volume shift)
cOme ON	primary and secondary accent syllable within a sentence (only in the original language of the transcript)
↑_	high onset of pitch
↓	pitch goes down
⟨↓blabla⟩	low pitch register within the brackets
⟨(smiling)⟩	comments
((sits down))	nonverbal actions or comments

References

Ackermann, Brian P. 1984. "Form and Function in Children's Understanding of Ironic Utterances." *Journal of Experimental Child Psychology* 35: 487–508.

Andersen, Elaine S. 1996. "A cross-cultural study of children's register knowledge." In *Essays in honor of Susan Ervin-Tripp: Social interaction, social context, and language,* Slobin, Dan Isaac et al. (Eds), 125–143. Mahwah, NJ: Erlbaum.

Aronsson, Karin & Thorell, Mia. 2002. "Voice and Collusion in Adult-Child Talk: Toward an Architecture of Intersubjectivity." In *Talking to Adults. The Contribution of Multiparty Discourse to Language Acquisition,* Shoshana Blum-Kulka & Catherine Snow (Eds), 277–295. Mahwah, NJ: Erlbaum.

Attardo, Salvatore. 2007. "Irony as Relevant Inappropriateness." In *Irony in Language and Thought. A Cognitive Science Reader*, R.W. Gibbs & H.L. Colston (Eds), 135–173. New York: Erlbaum.

Bakhtin, Mikhail M. 1981. "The dialogic imagination." In *The dialogic imagination: Four essays by M.M. Bakhtin*, C. Emerson & M. Holquist (Eds), Austin, TX: University of Texas Press.

Bakhtin, Mikhail M. 1984. *Problems of Dostoevsky's poetics.* Manchester: Manchester University Press.

Barbe, Katharina. 1995. *Irony in context.* Amsterdam: Benjamins.

Bearison, David J. & Dorval, Bruce. 2002. *Collaborative Cognition. Children Negotiating Ways of Knowing.* Westport, London: Ablex.

Berger, Peter & Luckmann, Thomas. 1967. *The Social Construction of Reality.* New York: Anchor Books.

Berman, Ruth A. (Ed.). 2004. *Language Development across Childhood and Adolescence.* Amsterdam: Benjamins.

Boxer, Diana & Cortés-Conde, Florencia. 1997. "From Bonding to Biting: Conversational Joking and Identity Display." *Journal of Pragmatics* 27: 275–294.

Brown, Penelope & Levinson, Stephen. 1987. *Politeness. Some Universals in Language Usage.* Cambridge: Cambridge University Press.

Bruner, Jerome. 1990. *Acts of meaning.* Cambridge, MA: Harvard University Press.

Clark, Herbert H. 1996. *Using language.* Cambridge: Cambridge University Press.

Clark, Herbert H. & Gerrig, Richard J. 1984. "On the Pretense Theory of Irony." *Journal of Experimental Psychology: General* 113(1): 121–125.

Clift, Rebecca. 1999. "Irony in Conversation." *Language in Society* 28: 523–553.

Cook-Gumperz, Jenny & Gumperz, John. 1976. "Context in Children's Speech. Papers on Language and Context." *Working Papers No. 46*. Berkeley, CA: Language Behavior Research Laboratory.

Coulson, Seana. 2005. "Sarcasm and the Space Structuring Model." In *The Literal and the Nonliteral in Language and Thought*, Seana Coulson & Barbara Lewandowska-Tomaszyk (Eds), 129–147 Frankfurt: Lang.

Creusere, Marlena. 2007. "A Developmental Test of Theoretical Perspectives on the Understanding of Verbal Irony: Children's Recognition of Allusion and Pragmatic Insincerity." In *Irony in Language and Thought. A Cognitive Science Reader*, Raymond W. Gibbs & Colston, Herbert L. (Eds), 409–424. New York: Erlbaum.

Dews, Shelly & Winner, Ellen. 1995. "Muting and Meaning: A Social Function of Irony." *Metaphor and Symbolic Activity* 10(1): 3–19.

Dews, Shelly & Winner, Ellen. 1997. "Attributing Meaning to Deliberately False Utterances: The Case of Irony." In *The Problem of Meaning. Behavioural and Cognitive Perspectives*, C. Mandell & A. McCabe (Eds), 377–414. Amsterdam: Elsevier.

Eisenberg, Ann R. 1986. "Teasing: Verbal Play in Mexican Homes." In *Language Socialization Across Cultures*, Schieffelin B.B. & E. Ochs (Eds), 182–199. Cambridge: Cambridge University Press.

Garvey, Catherine. 1974. "Some properties of social play." *Merill-Palmer Quarteley* 20: 163–180.

Gibbs, Raymond W. Jr. 1994. *The Poetics of mind: Figurative thought, language, and understanding.* Cambridge: Cambridge University Press.

Gibbs, Raymond W. Jr. 2000. "Irony in Talk among Friends." *Metaphor and Symbol* 15 (1–2): 5–28.

Gibbs, Raymond W. Jr. & O'Brien, Jennifer. 1991. "Psychological Aspects of Irony Understanding." *Journal of Pragmatics* 16: 523–530.

Gibbs, Raymond & Colston, Herbert L. (Eds). 2007. *Irony in Language and Thought. A Cognitive Science Reader.* New York: Erlbaum.

Giora, Rachel. 1995. On irony and negation. *Discourse processes* 19: 239–265.

Giora, Rachel. 2003. *On our Mind: Salience, Context and Figurative Language.* New York: Oxford University Press.

Goffman, Erving. 1974. *Frame Analysis. An Essay on the Organizations of Experience.* New York: Harper & Row.

Goffman, Erving. 1981. *Forms of Talk.* Philadelphia: University of Pennsylvania Press.

Goodwin, Marjorie H. 1996. "Shifting Frame." In *Social Interaction, Social Context, and Language. Essays in Honor of Susan Ervin-Tripp*, Slobin, Dan Isaac et al. (Eds), 71–83. Mahwah, NJ: Erlbaum.

Grice, H. Paul. 1975. "Logic and conversation." In *Syntax and Semantics*, Vol. 3: *Speech acts*, Peter Cole & Henry Morgan (Eds), 41–58. New York: Academic Press.

Grice, H. Paul. 1978. "Further notes on logic and conversation." In *Syntax and Semantics*, Vol. 9, Peter Cole (Ed.), 113–127. New York: Academic Press.

Groeben, Norbert & Scheele, Brigitte. 1984. *Produktion und Rezeption von Ironie. Bd. 1: Pragmalinguistische Beschreibung und psycholinguistische Erklärungshypothesen.* Tübingen: Niemeyer.

Günthner, Susanne. 1996a. "Zwischen Scherz und Schmerz. Frotzelaktivitäten im Alltag." In *Scherzkommunikation. Beiträge aus der empirischen Gesprächsforschung*, H. Kotthoff (Ed.), 81–109. Opladen: Westdeutscher Verlag.

Günthner, Susanne. 1996b. "The Contextualization of Affect in Reported Dialogue." In *The Language of Emotions*, S. Niemeyer & R. Dirven (Eds), 247–277. Amsterdam: Benjamins.

Gumperz, John. 1982. *Discourse strategies*. Cambridge: Cambridge University Press.

Haiman, John. 1990. "Sarcasm as theater." *Cognitive Linguistics* 1: 181–205.

Hancock, Jeffrey, Dunham, Philip J. & Purdy, Kelly. 2007. "Children's Comprehension of Critical and Complimentary Forms of Verbal Irony." In *Irony in Language and Thought. A Cognitive Science Reader*, Raymond W. Gibbs & Herbert L. Colston (Eds), 425–447. New York: Erlbaum.

Hartung, Martin. 1997. *Ironie in der gesprochenen Sprache. Eine gesprächsanalytische Untersuchung*. Opladen: Westdeutscher Verlag.

Kihara, Yoshiko. 2005. "The mental space structure of verbal irony." *Cognitive Linguistics* 16–3: 513–530.

Kotthoff, Helga. 1998. *Spaß Verstehen. Zur Pragmatik von konversationellem Humor*. Tübingen: Niemeyer.

Kotthoff, Helga. 2002. "Irony, Quotation, and Other Forms of Staged Intertextuality." In *Perspective and Perspectivity in Discourse,* Graumann, Carl & Werner Kallmeyer (Eds), 201–233. Amsterdam: Benjamins.

Kotthoff, Helga. 2003. "Responding to Irony in Different Contexts. On Cognition in Conversation." *Journal of Pragmatics* 35: 1387–1411.

Kotthoff, Helga. 2003b. "Witz komm raus! Komik und Humor bei Kindern. Ein Überblick." *TelevIZIon* 16(1): 4–11.

Kotthoff, Helga. 2006. "Pragmatics of performance and the analysis of conversational humor." *Humor. International Journal for the Study of Humor* 19(3): 271–304.

Kotthoff, Helga. 2007. "Oral genres of humor. On the dialectic of genre knowledge and creative authoring." *Pragmatics* 17 (2): 263–297.

Levinson, Stephen. 2000. *Presumptive Meanings. The Theory of Generalized Conversational Implicature*. Cambridge: MIT Press.

Markman, Ellen. 1979. "Realizing that you don't understand: Elementary school children's awareness of inconsistencies." *Child Development* 50: 643–655.

Müller, Marika. 1995. *Die Ironie. Kulturgeschichte und Textgestalt*. Würzburg: Königshausen und Neumann.

Ninio, Anat & Snow, Catherine. 1996. *Developmental Pragmatics*. Boulder, CO: Westview.

Perner, Josef & Wimmer, Heinz. 1985. "'John thinks that Mary thinks that...' Attributions of second-order beliefs by 5–10-year-old children." *Journal of Experimental Child Psychology* 39: 437–471.

Schieffelin, Bambi B. 1986. "Teasing and Shaming in Kaluli Children's Interactions." In *Language Socialization Across Cultures*, Bambi B. Schieffelin & Elinor Ochs (Eds), 165–182. Cambridge: Cambridge University Press.

Schütte, Wilfried. 1991. *Scherzkommunikation unter Orchestermusikern*. Tübingen: Niemeyer.

Selting, Margret et al. 1998. "Gesprächsanalytisches Transkriptionssystem." *Linguistische Berichte* 173: 91–122.

Sperber, Dan & Wilson, Deirdre. 1981. "Irony and the Use/Mention Distinction." In *Radical pragmatics*, P. Cole (Ed.), 295–318. New York: Academic Press.

Straehle, Carolyn A. 1993. "'Samuel?' 'Yes, Dear?': Teasing and Conversational Rapport." In *Framing in Discourse*, Deborah Tannen (Ed.), 210–229. New York: Oxford University Press.

Turner, Victor. 1986. *The Anthropology of Performance*. New York.

Verschueren, Jef. 1995. "Metapragmatics." In *Handbook of pragmatics*, J. Verschueren, J.-O. Östman, & J. Blommaert (Eds), 367–371. Amsterdam: Benjamins.

Wilson, Deirdre & Sperber, Dan. 1992. "On Verbal Irony." *Lingua* 87: 53–76.

Winner, Ellen. 1988. *The Point of Words: Children's Understanding of Metaphor and Irony*. Cambridge: Harvard University Press.

Wu, Ruey-Jiuan Regina. 2003. *Stance in Talk. A conversation analysis of Mandarin final particles*. Amsterdam: Benjamins.

Multimodal and intertextual humor
in the media reception situation

The case of watching football on TV

Cornelia Gerhardt

Based on natural data from media reception, the talk of television viewers watching football matches is analysed with regards to humor. Remarks on television are often greeted by (shared) laugher of the fans. However, laughter as such does not necessarily indicate humor. Instead, the celebrating fans also often laugh after goals. Principally, the fans appropriate the media text humorously either by multimodally referring to the pictures on the screen or by intertextually hinging their talk on the televised language. Formally, second person pronouns or sequences co-constructed with the sports announcers are used. Functionally, humor marks the activity as leisure. It helps the viewers negotiate world-views serving as contextualisation cue in the interpretation of the media text.

1. Introduction[1]

This paper aims to describe the use of humor in the media reception situation. The larger context of this work thus lies at the hinge between mass media and everyday face-to-face interaction. It is concerned with "the social practices by which the discourses of the media are appropriated in common face-to-face interactions" (Scollon 1998: vii). Although mass media have acquired an enormous importance in Western societies and the television, being one important kind, takes a central place in the households of most people, linguistics has only recently discovered this particular setting (Scollon 1998; Baldauf 1998; Hepp 1998; Klemm 2000; Holly et al. 2001). The current chapter will focus on the role of humor in the reception situation. It is data-driven and based on a corpus of naturally occurring interaction in this setting, i.e., talk by television viewers in their homes. We will see that humor as a social practice plays an important part in the appropriation of media texts in the reception situation. Laughter is a recurrent phenomenon in the corpus, since watching football is a form of recreation for the viewers. Their

---

1. The author would like to thank Neal Norrick heartily for commenting on her paper.

shared laughter mirrors their enjoyment of the situation and contributes to a feeling of belonging and warmth. They laugh joyfully in response to positive actions of their team. Furthermore, they laugh about humorous remarks on television. More importantly though, the television viewers create their own humor against the backdrop of the media text. By linking their talk to the pictures, they create humor multimodally, and by tying their words to the sportscasting, intertextual humor is constructed.

The study is based on the ATTAC (Analysing The Television Audience's Conversations) corpus, which consists of transcriptions from video tapes of naturally occurring talk. Five different groups of predominantly British English native speakers were recorded while they were watching football games on television. The recorded consist of families or groups of friends. The age range is wide with the youngest participant being a toddler and the oldest over 70 years of age. The recorded are mainly middle class and from a non-immigrant background. One group lives in Sheffield and the others in the Greater Thames estuary. They were all found through personal contacts by the author. Generally, the video camera was either given to them so that they could record themselves and get acquainted to the camera being present, or the researcher set up the camera herself and left the premises prior to recording. The ATTAC-corpus encompasses transcriptions of fourteen half-times from seven different games consisting, all in all, of more than 45,000 words.[2] Generally, the viewers are absorbed in the games so that they seem oblivious to the camera after a few minutes. Since the football fans are watching the World Cup, the televised program appears fully to grasp the attention of the football fans, as one of them puts it: *I have been waiting for four years.* The corpus exemplifies situated talk in the *reception situation* (Charlton et al. 1997), the verbal *appropriation* (Holly et al. 1993; Faber 2001; de Certeau 1980) of media texts. On the same ground, it instantiates talk-in-interaction in the presence of another text, i.e., the media text. Since the media text, i.e., the televised program, consists of talk and pictures, both multimodality and intertextuality become an issue.[3] Both concepts have found a lot of recent attention (Tannen 2007; Norris 2004; Schmitt 2007). Here the terms will be used restrictedly: multimodality will pertain to the relation of the viewers' talk to the pictures, and intertextuality will only be used to focus on the ties between the participants' language use and the language in the medium, i.e., *SAT sports announcer talk* (Ferguson 1982).

2. The ATTAC-corpus is currently not available for use by the interested public because it is not in a format that would allow publication.

3. The term 'media text' will be used in the following to denote both the pictures on television as well as the accompanying football commentary.

I will first give a short account of the principal features of talk in front of the television (Gerhardt 2008a) to furnish a basis for the ensuing discussion. This will be followed by a description of a very specific kind of laughter found in the ATTAC-corpus which cannot be taken as an indication of humor. How the viewers treat humor in the football commentary will be the following topic. Finally, in the two main parts, I will focus on multimodal and intertextual connections between the talk at home and the media text with respect to humor.

2.   Talk in the football reception situation

Generally, the conversations by television viewers represent an *open state of talk* (Goffman 1981). Interactions in front of the television often consist of *free units* (Baldauf-Quiliatre 2004) or short *Gesprächsinseln* (Baldauf 2002 'islands of talk', my translation C.G.) only, i.e., there is no obligation to talk for the viewers. Also, the obligation to respond can be superseded. Different *footings* (Goffman 1979) account for the differing status of cohesion (Halliday et al. 1976) and coherence in the viewers' talk. For instance during story-telling sequences, the participants' talk-in-interaction is fully cohesive. No links to the media text may be found on the verbal level. However, even then, *view signs* (Scollon 1998) such as gaze or posture signal that the television is part of the viewers' *contextual configuration* (Goodwin 2000). These view signs are *embodiments* (Goodwin 2000) of the constant likelihood of a shifting footing to the 'watching football' frame. *Contextualization cues* (Gumperz 1982) such as interjections or rise in volume mark these shifts to the 'watching football' frame. In other words, depending on the *notability* (Gerhardt 2008a) of a given scene on television, the talk may at any moment be interrupted or abandoned without any prior interactional work. Contrariwise, the watch (Scollon 1998) may also at any moment be reframed as a *with* (Goffman 1981), for instance during 'story-telling' or 'catching up'.

Within the 'watching football' frame, the viewers' talk is only coherent with reference to the media text. A number of cohesive ties (Halliday et al. 1976) such as personal pronouns link the interpersonal interactions of the viewers intertextually to the media text. Furthermore, the interlocutors at these moments also construct coherence interactionally (Schegloff 1990) e.g., by backchanneling to utterances on television or by using discourse markers. At times, the football fans intertwine their conversation and the commentary by producing discontinued talk which accommodates SAT into the gaps left in their interactions by granting turn-rights to the sportscasters. In this way a prohibition to talk may also be negotiated amongst the viewers. Besides the use of personal address (e.g., terms of address (cf. Chapter 2), imperative verb forms or second person pronouns), another intriguing finding is the co-production of adjacency pairs: then the viewers construct coherent passages with the telecasters by furnishing second pair parts to the sports announcer talk. The (other) viewers may then only be 'present' (*anwesend* in Norris' terminology (2004)), that is, there is no interaction between the viewers.

Structurally in the viewers' talk-in-interaction, these passages of intense interaction with the sports casters or other TV personae often consist of *side-sequences* (Jefferson 1972), i.e., the viewers interrupt themselves to comment on the game. This is mainly the case for the groups of friends, who talk continuously, despite being part of a watch. Towards the end of the games and also for the families watching football, the interaction with the television represent the free units and islands of talk mentioned above, since mostly the viewers are silent and follow the game intently. This behavior by the viewers mirrors the *para-social interaction* (Horton et al. 1956) on television. This common feature of media texts consists of the direct address of the viewers at home, for instance when a show host greets the audience at home: *Good evening, ladies and gentlemen.* So both the viewers and the persons on TV attempt to bridge the *co-presence gap* (O'Keeffe 2006) between presenter and audience in this mediated discourse.

Regarding multimodality (Norris 2004), the media text takes on high modal density in the interaction of the viewers, when the viewers do 'watching football'. 'Watching television' is foregrounded, which may go so far as to a prohibition of inter-viewer communication when the television is granted turn-rights. By contrast, when the participants move into a 'story telling' frame, the television in the viewers' talk takes on much less modal density. Instead, states of gaze take on more importance as a communicative mode (Gerhardt 2007) to negotiate turn-taking among the viewers. To sum up, the role of the pictures and talk on television in the viewers' interactions can be represented on a continuum ranging from a full orientation to the medium to being *nearly* utterly disregarded e.g., when the viewers sort out the mail, or talk on the phone (Baldauf 2001).

3.   Laughter as jubilation in the football reception situation

I will first present an instance of laughter by the participants which cannot be taken as an indication of humor. In the first example, one of the participants laughs out loud over a prolonged stretch of time. The kind of laughter we find in this scene is typical for the football reception situation. It does not however signal the presence of humor.

This transcript represents the first half of England versus Brazil, one of the quarter finals of the World Cup. From an English perspective this represents their most important game in this series. The video has been recorded at the home of a young family with Andrew, Ursula, and their 18-month-old toddler Laurie. The following scene represents the English goal which results in a lot of physical and verbal excitement by Andrew.

Transcript 1 EB1A 25:44–26:06[4]

1	TV	Owen's sprinting away,=
2		=for the left here,=
3		=to get to [Lucio.]
4	Andrew	[OH] [{jumps up}]
5	TV	MICHAEL OWEN,
6		GREAT HEA[DER,...]
7	Ursula	I can't-
8		I can't SEE.=
9		{jumps from left to right on the sofa to see past husband}
10	Andrew	=YEEEEEEEAAAAAAHHHHHH.
11		{screams at the top of his voice finishing in laughter}
12	Ursula	I didn't see,
13		you were [blocking it from] me, {laughingly}
14	Andrew	[I'm sorry,]
15		{laughs hysterically, jumps up and down}
16		{laughs}
17		{jumps with his head on his wife's lap}
18	Ursula	stop that. {smiles}
19	Andrew	{laughs hysterically}
20	Ursula	what's (?)ing you.= {smiles}
21	Andrew	=well I can't help that? {in a high pitched coarse voice}
22	Ursula	[but you should HAVE]
23	Andrew	[{laughs}] {sits down again}

The first three lines of the transcript deliver the media context for the ensuing reaction: Owen, one of England's principal strikers, attacks. Andrew can anticipate the outcome: he jumps up in excitement (line 4) when Owen chips the ball over Marcos, the Brazilian goalie. Andrew then screams at the top of his voice finishing in laughter of pure joy (line 10). While his wife laughingly complains *I didn't see, you were blocking it from me,* (lines 12 – 13) he jumps around in the living room

---

4.   The letters and numbers indicate the game (here England vs. Brazil), the half-time (here the first half), the recorded group (here Andrew's family), and the time in the recording, which is roughly also the game time. It can be used to retrieve the passages under discussion in the ATTAC-corpus. TV refers to the commentator and pundit to the color commentator.

saying *I'm sorry* (line 14). His answer is more a reflection of the normative nature of a complaint in making an answer relevant (Sacks et al. 1974) than an actual apology. Andrew continues in his jubilations by laughing again (line 15) while jumping up and down. Then he laughs again (line 16), before putting his head on his wife's lap and, concurrently, jumping with both feet high into the air. After Ursula makes him stop, he again laughs hysterically (line 19). Finally in line 23, the whole passage ends with his laughter while he sits down again. Hence, the whole scene is interspersed by laughter (lines 11, 13, 15, 16, 19, and 23) and by smiles (lines 18 and 20). However, these cannot be taken as markers of a reflex to humor. Laughter here is part of the celebration of an important English goal (in a quarter final, in the World Cup, against Brazil, the best ranked national football team in the world). It can be taken as a sign of psychological relief. (cf. *catharsis* Aristotle's "Poetics") since the England team is battling vicariously for the fans and the fans at home live through these battles (cf. Sloan 1979 for this function of sports in society). Also, laughter represents a contextualization cue here which displays the viewers' orientation to the media text. This kind of high involvement by the viewers tends to appear in clusters. The football fans use an array of vocal and bodily means to signal their stance at the media text to their co-viewers: singing, laughter, moaning, sighing as well as clapping, getting up, and jumping up and down can be found in the corpus. To sum up, this kind of jubilating laughter will not be taken as a marker of humor.

4.   Humor in the media text

Sportscasting as a genre for discourse studies has a long tradition by now (Ferguson 1982; Gerhardt 2008b; cf. Lavric et al. 2008 for a recent bibliography). However, humor in sportscasting has not been described so far. As we will see with the help of the following examples, the telecasters construct watching the matches amongst other things as a pleasurable and entertaining enterprise by using hyperbole, funny expressions or other means of making humorous remarks. The ATTAC-corpus shows that these jokes are indeed taken up by the viewers. The fans at home accept the invitation to be entertained. This may take the form of a simple laugh as in the following example:

Transcript 2 ES1R 05:56–06:02

1	TV	here we go,
2		for another white-knuckle ride,
3		with the England football team.
4	Gerard	uchu {short snorty laugh}

In line 4, Gerard, who is watching England versus Sweden together with his wife and their teenage son, signals his appreciation of the humorous hyperbole in the SAT *white-knuckle ride* (line 2). This establishes his general willingness to be positively distracted by the game and the accompanying SAT. Some jokes also make him laugh out loud:

Transcript 3 BB1R 12:13–12:36

1	TV	the uh-
2		England headquarters is,
3		only about twenty-five miles,
4		from Kobe,
5		but the press corps,=
6		=that have been travelling around,=
7		=with uh- England,
8		have been-
9		stationed in this city,
10		much to the delight,
11		of the local bar tenders.
12	Gerard	[{laughs}]
13	TV	[only kidding boys,]
14	Gerard	{continues laughing}

In this example, *much to the delight of the local bar tenders* (lines 10 – 11) triggers Gerard's mirth. It plays on the image of the football fan and, in extension, also the football commentators as 'one of the boys': regular fellows who like to drink (a lot) in pubs (cf. Wanta et al. 1988 on the use of clichés in SAT). In response, Gerard laughs out loud for a longer amount of time. This appreciative laughter by the viewers is often accompanied by head-turns to fellow viewers (Gerhardt 2007) so that a feeling of belonging and sharing can be built in this way. This can be seen in the following example:

Transcript 4 EB2R 41:30–41:45

1	TV	and uhm,
2		FOUR minutes,
3		plus stoppage time,=
4		for England,=
5		=to rescue their World Cup chances,
6		that's where we're at now,
7		(3.4tv)
8		having breakfast in the LAST-chance saloon.
9		(0.8TV)
10		Rivaldo,
11	Gerard	{laughs and turns to wife}

Here, the creative expression *having breakfast in the LAST-chance saloon* (line 8) makes Gerard laugh, albeit a little belatedly. In line 11, his shift of posture and change of gaze direction invites his wife to join him in his laughter. In this way, he tries to negotiate a mutual stance and, again, his laughter serves as a contextualization cue in the interpretation of the media text (Gerhardt 2007).

The ATTAC-corpus in general does not contain any talk-in-interaction which does not involve laughter and humorous remarks: each and every transcript contains passages where the viewers laugh, giggle, snigger or smirk, be it triggered by humorous passages on television or be it about a remark they themselves make (see below). By enjoying jokes from the television, they directly react to SAT taking up the commentators' invitation to enter into a quasi-communicative situation.

5.   Multimodal humor in the reception situation

After having considered cases where the humorous remarks are to be found in the media text, we will now turn to instances where the viewers themselves create humor against the backdrop of the media text. We will first consider connections to the televised pictures, before turning to the field of intertextuality, i.e., connections to SAT, in the next section.

Let us recall at this point that the term *multimodality* is used here to describe ties between the pictures shown on television and the talk by the viewers at home. The term *multimodal* is used because it denotes a connection from one mode (pictures) to another (spoken language) or physically from changing colored dots on a screen to streams of sounds. For the production format this implies that the viewers are automatically *authors* (Goffman 1981), i.e., they have to verbalize physical events. Linguistically, multimodality is often achieved in the ATTAC-corpus through the use of pronouns (Gerhardt 2008a). For instance, a player visible on the screen (and *not* concurrently mentioned on SAT to exclude intertextual ties methodologically) can be addressed directly with the help of a second person pronoun *you* or he can be referred to with the help of a 3rd person pronoun *he*. Especially the demonstrative pronoun *that* is used to connect the viewers' talk to current or salient events on the screen. Also comparative reference is often used by the viewers for instance when comparing a current state of affairs to a prior one as in *that's better* meaning *that is better than what we witnessed earlier*. Also *conjunctions* (Halliday et al. 1976) or *discourse markers* (Schiffrin 1987) can be used to link the interactions to the pictures (e.g., *well, that should liven it up*). In the following we will see how humor is employed multimodally.

In this first example of multimodal humor, Maria, a middle aged Londoner who is watching with her lodger and an acquaintance, addresses a person on TV directly. The scene happens towards the end of the second half of Germany against

Saudi-Arabia, a game which the Saudis lost 8:0. Germany is already 7:0 in the lead at this moment in the match.

Transcript 5 GS2L 51:17–51:24

1	Maria	come on.=
2		STOP funning about,
3		{laughs}
4		o::h nasty man.
5		just because you've won.

It is not quite clear who exactly Maria is referring to, since nobody takes up her remark, the other viewers treating her utterance as a free unit. Evidently, though, Maria criticizes the behavior of someone associated with the German team. She uses the fixed expression *come on* (line 1) and an imperative verb form, *STOP funning about* (line 2), and a term of address *nasty man* (line 4). The referent of her talk can only be located in the pictures on television, hence multimodally. In this first example, it is only one viewer who amuses herself by linking her talk to the media text.

In the following piece of data, one of the viewers refers directly to a scene in the match. Frank and Tom, two friends in their 30s to 40s who live in East London, are watching the second half of Japan versus Russia here. Both use the reception situation for jokes and shared amusement (cf. Klemm's function for talk in the reception situation 'creating an atmosphere of sociability and enjoyment', my translation, CG, *Schaffung einer geselligen und vergnüglichen Stimmung* 2000).

Transcript 6 JR2T 16:54–17:02

1	Frank	it's just like schoolboy football.
2	Tom	yeah, {laughingly}
3	both	{laughter}
4	Frank	it's-
5		I'll get that in, {in boyish voice}
6	both	{laughter}

Frank's simile *it's just like schoolboy football* opens up a humorous frame (Norrick 1993, 2004). The referent of *it* (line 1) can only be found in the pictures: it is the current way of playing that can be witnessed live on the screen. Frank's 'constructed dialogue' (Tannen 2007) (line 5), the high-pitched voice with a pouting quality, the use of glottal stops for plosives indexing the prototypically less well educated football player, and the foolish grin on his face continue the humorous frame. The manner of execution of line 5 relates back to the assessment as *schoolboy football* (line 1). The media text is used a backdrop here to create conviviality and also, subsequently, by the fact that they laugh together, a feeling a belonging and sharing (cf. Klemm's function for talk in the reception situation 'creating a feeling of belonging to the same group', my translation CG, *Vergemeinschaftung der Zuschauer* 2000). Also, the viewers position themselves within the setting with respect to their co-viewers and to the media text building identities such as being an entertaining fellow (Bamberg 1997, 2000; Davies et al. 1990)

The reception situation also allows for crude forms of *impoliteness* such as insults (Bousfield 2008), because of the *unidirectionality* (Klemm 2000) of the setting. The following example represents a form of face-threatening humor that would generally not be possible if the 3rd person was actually within hearing distance.

Transcript 7 JR1T 03:43–03:50

1	Frank	he's got that Putin look=
2	Tom	=yeah yeah,
3		[it's-
4		yeah,]
5	Frank	[{laughs}] {laughs}
6	Tom	a real hatchet [face,]
7	Frank	[{laughs}]
8		(0.9)
9	Tom	Slav, {jocular}

This scene happens roughly at the beginning of the game when close-ups of the players are shown. Frank comments on the physical appearance of one of the Russian players *he's got that Putin look* (line 1). The 3rd person singular pronoun is used multimodally here to refer to the pictures on television. This remark is ratified by Tom (lines 2 – 4), while Frank's laughter (line 5) contextualizes his own words as a joke rather than a neutral comment about the likeness between the Russian president and the player. Tom then continues in this wake: *a real hatchet face* (line 6). These words are again tied to the pictures, i.e., multimodal, since they describe what the viewers see or, in other words, they verbalize the pictures. This derogatory remark also reaffirms the uncomplimentary nature of Frank's first utterance. In other words, for the two participants, it is not a good thing to look like the Russian president. Frank's laughter (line 7) at the end of Tom's remark ratifies Tom's comment and, again, underlines the humorous framing of the exchange. Finally, after a short pause (0.9 seconds), Tom smilingly says *Slav* (line 9) in a jocular tone to account for the likeness between the two Russians and their specific physiognomy, hence also for his and his friend's remarks. Although this moves the whole exchange from being specifically about two men to being a racial remark based on stereotypes and prejudice, Tom does sound very sympathetic for the player in question. So Tom's accounting here also justifies the player's look or apologizes for it, in the sense that he, the player, cannot help looking the ways he looks (being a Slav). With this short multimodal humorous exchange, the two have confirmed and aligned their world-view or prejudice about male Slavic physiognomy generally not being particularly pleasing in the eyes of English men. So here the reception situation also allows the viewers to position themselves against larger Discourses (with a capital D) (Hepp 1998) negotiating their meaning in their talk.

As the last example of multimodal humor, we will move into the living room of an older English couple who watch Argentina versus England together with an old friend. The men share a background of refereeing, but they have by now retired from this pastime. This pairing is marked by the long history of rivalry between these two great football nations (cf. Maradona's 'hand of God') and, outside of the pitch, also by the Falkland war. So emotions can easily run high. This moment in the game is preceded by a number of Argentinean fouls.

Transcript 8 AE1C 32:45–32:57

1	Henry	from a technical point of view,
2		the Argentineans are so HAIry.
3		[aren't they {laughingly}]
4	Darrell	[{laughing}] [{continues laughing}]
5	Henry	[long hair,]
6		(0.7)
7		like David Seaman,=
8		ALL of them.=
9	Darrell	=yeah,

In lines 1 – 2, Henry evaluates the playing of the Argentineans *from a technical point of view, the Argentineans are so HAIry.* Based on the current state of the game, i.e., multimodally on the pictures, the term here seems to be used in the sense 'excited, angry, out of temper'. (OED) However, the expression used triggers the speakers and Darrell's mirth, so Henry continues in a joking manner based on the literal meaning of the term *long hair* (line 5). He then foregrounds his English perspective by comparing the Argentineans to David Seaman who also has long hair. (line 7) His turn finishes with *ALL of them.* (line 8) to refer back to *the Argentineans* (line 2) hence recasting his whole earlier utterance in the light of the second frame: *long hair, ... ALL of them.* Both readings of the term are based on the pictures, i.e., the media text is used multimodally as a resource for entertainment by the viewers.

To conclude, we were able to see that the viewers often base their humorous remarks directly on the pictures on television for multifarious functions such as the creation of an atmosphere of conviviality and pleasure and the building of a feeling of belonging and solidarity. Because of unidirectionality, politeness with TV personae is not called for. This allows for a much more open airing of emotions or prejudice than other settings. This in turn helps align world-views and positioning against topics triggered by the television text so that the viewers can negotiate their more local, discursive identities (e.g., being entertaining) as well as their transportable identities (e.g., Englishman).

6.   Intertextual humor in the reception situation

Besides the pictures, the talk on television, i.e., the football commentary or SAT, can also be used as a springboard for humorous activities by the viewers. Intertextual connections between the media text and the talk by the viewers abound in the ATTAC-corpus (Gerhardt 2008). Besides reference and the use of conjunctions (in the sense of Halliday et al. 1976), which can both also be used multimodally, intertextually the viewers have a number of linguistic means at their disposal. Since, intertextually, text is linked to text, *a priori*, any cohesive device can also be employed across texts (just as it can be employed within a text). For this reason, the viewers can also use substitution and ellipsis to connect their talk to SAT. Also, lexical repetition can serve to connect the two strands of talk in the ATTAC-corpus. All three means are not available for multimodal connections since they can only link language to language. Furthermore, the viewers use backchannelling, discourse markers and direct address to tie their conversations to the talk on television. Interactionally, they sometimes grant turn-rights to the television and co-construct talk by furnishing second pair parts to adjacency pairs started on television. As we will see, again the joint creation of humor plays an important part in this setting.

Sometimes the connection between the viewers' talk and SAT consists of simple repetition. Repetition has been described as a source of intertextuality and identity construction (cf. Tannen 2007; Tovares 2006; Gordon 2004, for a more general account cf. Johnstone 1994). This is again the opening match between Germany and Saudi-Arabia which Germany won 8:0. At this point in the game, Klose, a German player, has already scored two goals.

> Transcript 9 GS1L 24:42–24:46

1	TV	maybe it's a little early, {jocular}
2		to start thinking about-
3		golden boot.
4	Maria	golden boot. {laughingly}
5	all viewers	{general mirth}

The sports reporter jokes about Klose already being the top scorer of the tournament: *to start thinking about golden boot* (lines 2 – 3). The joke is based on the discrepancy between the time elapsed at that point and the 63 other matches still to come. Maria repeats the joke verbatim and laughs *golden boot* (line 4). Verbatim reiteration is frequent in the corpus when participants mark parts of the commentary as entertaining. It allows them to draw attention to the humorous parts inviting in a reaction by their co-viewers. Concurrently, they construct themselves as humorous persons and the situation as leisurely and entertaining.

The following transcript is again a part featuring the two friends in East-London who are watching Japan versus Russia.

Transcript 10 JR2T 02:11–02:42

1	TV	Izmailov, [zmaɪlɔv]
2		corner.
3		(2.6)
4	Frank	is his name REAlly Smirnoff.
5	Tom	{laughter} [{continued laughter}]
6	Frank	[{laughter}]=
7	Tom	=well he's not supposed to-
8		what if he was,
9		be called Smirnoff.
10		who would do that.=
11	Frank	={short laugh}
12		(0.9)
13		{laughs}
14		that's like there was people in Italy called Bacardi,
15		{laughter} [{continued laughter}]
16	Tom	[I mean there ARE are there,]
17		[Martini,]
18	Frank	[{continued laughter}]
19	both	{laughter}
20	Frank	RON Bacardi.
21	Tom	and yeah- {laughter} Ron Bacardi {laughingly},

In the first two lines, the sports announcer does *play-by-play announcing* (Ferguson 1982), i.e., he describes the ongoing action on the pitch. A Russian player, Izmailov, is conceded a corner. The way the commentator pronounces the name [zmaɪlɔv] (line 1) reminds the viewers of the Russian vodka brand Smirnoff pronounced [zmɜ:nɔf] by Frank (line 4). The connection between the viewers' talk and SAT is established with the help of anaphora *his name* (line 4). Clearly, the referent of *his* must be located in the prior talk on television (and not in the pictures or the prior talk at home.) First, in the World Cup the players wear jerseys with numbers only and no names. Primarily though, there is only a phonetic resemblance in unstressed fast English speech. Hence, the televised text here is used by the viewer as a resource for joke-telling reinforcing their friendship by shared laughter. They manage to execute this practice by Frank (line 4) intertextually referring to a player just mentioned on television with the help of the 3rd person pronoun his.

The following example is similar: again it is Gerard, the father, who is watching England versus Brazil together with his son. It is the end of the second half; Brazil are leading 2:1 which means England will most probably be out of the World Cup.

Transcript 11 EB2R 45:32–45:44

1	TV	but there's a bonus here for England,
2		FOUR minutes of stoppage time.
3		(0.7TV)
4		a lot of that's down,=
5		=to the time it took,=
6		=to send off Ronaldinho.
7		(5.4)
8	Gerard	{laughs}
9		(2.9)
10		nice of him,

With *nice of him* (line 10), Gerard connects his talk to the media text (lines 1 – 6). The 3rd person referred to with *him* can only be located with the help of SAT. It is nice of Ronaldinho that he caused extra stoppage time in which England might be able to score and, as a consequence, might still be able to win the game. Ronaldinho had earlier been the source of some critical remarks both by the sportscasters and the viewers at home. The referee's decision now seems to punish Ronaldinho's earlier behavior. Gerard in hitching up to the media text can display an ironic stance towards Ronaldinho's doings. Furthermore, since his remark evaluates earlier doings by one of the protagonists, Gerard weaves a meaningful narrative out of the, in principle, unconnected events on the pitch (cf. Martinez 1999; Morris et al. 1985 for the same function for SAT).

Often demonstratives are also used for this purpose. Their nature as verbal 'pointers' make them useful instruments in this setting. The following example is again taken from the beginning of the game Japan versus Russia being watched by the two friends Tom and Frank. Again, the viewers use SAT for humorous purposes to their shared amusement.

Transcript 12 JR1T 02:59–03:17

1	TV	includes a lawyer,
2		also from Germany,
3		(0.5)
4		a scientist,
5		(0.6)

6		from,
7		the Czech republic,=
8		=from Prague,
9		and yet another dentist,
10		from Paraguay.
11		(1.4)
12		[(?)…]
13	Frank	what?
14		{laughs}
15		is that the [Russians.]
16	Tom	[on the team?]=
17	Frank	[{laughs}]
18	Tom	=[I was gonna say,
19		is that-]
20	Frank	{laughs}
21		[a dentist,
22		from Paraguay.] {laughingly}
23	Tom	[a new relaxed Russian immigration][policy.]
24	Frank	[{laughs}]

In lines 1 – 10, the telecaster is presenting the match officials: the referee and his linesmen. After a pause of 1.4 seconds, Frank signals his confusion with the help of the wh-pronoun *what?* (line 13). Seemingly, the two had not been paying attention so they do not understand the significance of this list of non-Russian (and clearly non-Japanese) names. As their talk generally has a humorous keying, Frank starts laughing about his or their bewilderment (line 14). He then uses the demonstrative *that* to refer to the commentators talk *is that the Russians* (line 15). In overlap, Frank (line 16) states the same non-sense suggestions *on the team?* While Frank laughs again, Tom aligns himself with Frank's failure to contextualize the information in SAT correctly. First he signals that his words will represent another version of Frank's aberrant suggestion. The *marker of standpoint continuity* in line 18, *I was gonna say* (cf. *I'm just saying* Craig et al. 2000), indicates that the speaker could renounce from voicing his intended utterance because the prior speaker has already stated the same. Still, in line 19, Tom continues *is that-*. Again *that* refers intertextually back to SAT. The break-off and pause may be a result of his endeavor to find a more entertaining formulation for the thought already expressed by Frank. While Frank repeats the dubious denomination more or less verbatim, *a dentist from Paraguay*, Tom comes up with a more entertaining reformulation *a new relaxed Russian immigration policy* (line 23). The laughter which accompanies this exchange underlines the humorous keying i.e., they both know that the people mentioned on television are not part of the Russian team. Instead, SAT is exploited for comic purposes here. This again emphasizes that the viewing is seen as a past-time in which the viewers want to 'enjoy themselves' (cf. *sich vergnügen*, my translation CG, Klemm 2000). The demonstrative pronouns link the viewers' talk and the commentary.

This final example is taken from the game England versus Denmark which is watched by the father Gerard and his son Benjamin again. Here, Jodie, the mother, has joined them for the viewing. As we will see, this interchange raises a number of methodological questions in this specific setting.

Transcript 13 ED1R 31:12–31:31

1	TV	it was Töfting,
2		who uh-
3		(0.6)
4		bounced the ball in frustration,
5		and got a yellow card.
6		(1.4tv)
7	Gerard	he looks like a BOUncer.
8	Jodie	yeah,=
9	Pundit	=wouldn't meet-
10		like to meet him in a dark alley.=
11		=would you.
12		(?)= (1.1tv)
13	Jodie+Gerard	={loud laughter}
14		[{continued laughter}]
15	TV	[no.] (0.8tv)
16	Jodie+Gerard	{continued laughter}
17	TV	see his tattoos.=
18		[=anyway.]
19	Jodie+Gerard	[renewed laughter]
20		{rest incomprehensible}

On television, the commentators assign a yellow card to a specific player, a common act on SAT, since the pictures do not always make it clear which player exactly was penalized *it was Töfting who uh- (0.6) bounced the ball in frustration, and got a yellow card* (lines 1 – 5). Gerard then seems to utter a rather clever pun *he looks like a BOUncer* (line 7). On the one hand, this is based on Töfting bouncing the ball earlier, hence, on his activity: he seems to be the kind of person who would do what was just mentioned on SAT (intertextual connection between *BOUncer* and *bounced* and between *he* and *Töfting*). On the other hand, it is based on Töfting's physical appearance which apparently is similar to that of a chucker-out (multimodal connection between *he* and the person visible on the screen). Hence, the more immediate meaning of the verb *to bounce* is replaced by its extended meaning in the derivative noun *bouncer*. However, in taking the intonation pattern into account it becomes apparent that *BOUncer* is the new information in this utterance marked by the tonic pitch movement (Halliday 1967) and not *looks*. In other words, if Gerard had based his remark on the earlier mention of the lexical stem *bounce*, he would have had to say: *he LOOks like a bouncer*, since *bouncer* would be the given information and *looking like* one the new information. Hence, the information structure signaled through the intonation pattern clearly rules out this intertextual connection in an interactional sense, albeit semiotically in describing these texts as texts, this connection exists. For our current endeavor, namely a description of the humorous practices of television viewers or an analysis of the verbal appropriation of the media text by the viewers with respect to humorous uses, this instance does not represent an intertextual humorous connection (cf. a similar point in Norrick 2003 about jokes as performance in contrast to jokes as texts). The ensuing utterances raise a similar point. After Jodie's ratification, the pundit's states a similar opinion which, in terms of timing, latches on to Jodie's short acquiescence (line 8) *wouldn't meet- like to meet him in a dark alley. would you. (?)* (line 9 – 12). Since the pundit cannot hear the viewers, the 3rd person pronoun *him* must either point back textually to the commentator mentioning *Töfting* on television (line 1) or multimodally to the pictures on television.[5] It cannot, for a start, be said to point intertextually to Gerard's earlier utterance in his living room (line 7). However, taken the next turn into account, i.e., the sequential place where we find the participant's treatment of the prior turn, we can discern that the couple evidently orients to this intertextual connection. Their loud laughter is only explicable on the basis that the pundit's remark is *heard* as a response to the husband's remark. So part of the loud merriment of the couple is grounded in the coincidence that the pundit voices similar ideas as the husband with sequentially appropriate timing. Hence, to come to a conclusion as far as the nature of this connection is concerned: in line with the *next-turn-proof-procedure* of CA (Sacks et al. 1974) I will assume an intertextual relation here since the participants themselves orient to this moment of intertextuality.

As we have seen, the viewers exploit the talk on television for humorous purposes and for their shared amusement. They use the language on television as a resource for humor. In repeating verbatim what has been said on television they can draw attention to humorous bits. Furthermore, they can pick out individual words or utterances to subvert them for their own comic purposes, irrespective of their

---

5.   The television commentators have monitors in the stadium which allow them to follow the televised pictures in order to synchronize their commentary with them.

meaning or function in SAT. Also, talking back to the television is done for the pleasure and entertainment of the speaker him/herself and the co-viewers.

7. Conclusion

The reception situation offers fruitful ground for humor. Since television viewing is a form of entertainment for the families and groups of friends, an atmosphere of sociability and enjoyment is built by the viewers. The media text serves as a backdrop for jokes, humor and clever ironic commentary. Both the language on television and the transmitted pictures can be built on. These humorous practices often result in common laughter signaling and fuelling the shared mirth. The shared laughter about the media text reinforces a feeling of sharing and belonging to the same group. Furthermore, common laughter helps negotiate mutual stance on world-views and, hence, serves as a contextualization cue in the interpretation of the media text. In this light, the prototypical image of the *couch potato* seems questionable, at least, when groups of viewers watch together.

Finally, the data also point to this basic differentiation that has to be maintained between jokes as texts and humor in interaction. Depending on the perspective of the researcher, one and the same piece of data will lead to different analyses. However, it must be recognized that spoken language is the cradle of humor and jokes. Especially the reception situation, the setting under discussion, calls for a treatment of humor as an element of spoken talk-in-interaction.

References

Baldauf, Heike. 1998. "Aufschreien und Stöhnen: Äußerungsformen emotionaler Beteiligung beim Fernsehen." In *Neuere Entwicklungen in der Gesprächsforschung*, Alexander Brock & Martin Hartung (Eds), 37–54. Tübingen: Narr.

Baldauf, Heike. 2001. "Reden gegen die Wand? Einige Überlegungen zu Äußerungen ohne erkennbaren Adressaten." *Gesprächsforschung* 2. www.gespraechsforschung-ozs.de. (23 January, 2003)

Baldauf, Heike. 2002. *Knappes Sprechen*. Tübingen: Niemeyer.

Baldauf-Quiliatre, Heike. 2004. "Some problems of addressivity from a conversational point of view." In *Aspects of the Dialogical Self*, Marie-Cécile Berteau (Ed.), 129–156. Berlin: Lehmanns.

Bamberg, Michael. 1997. "Positioning between structure and performance." *Journal of Narrative and Life History* 7(1–4): 335–342.

Bamberg, Michael. 2005. "Positioning". In *The Routledge Encyclopedia of Narrative Theory*, David Herman, Manfred Jahn & Marie-Laure Ryan (Eds), 445–446. New York: Routledge.

Bousfield, Derek. 2008. *Impoliteness in Interaction*. Amsterdam: Benjamins.

Charlton, Michael & Schneider, Silvia. 1997. *Rezeptionsforschung: Theorien und Untersuchungen zum Umgang mit Massenmedien*. Opladen: Westdeutscher.

Craig, Robert T. & Sanusi, Alena L. 2000. "'I'm just saying': Discourse markers of standpoint continuity." *Argumentation* 14(4): 425–445.

Davies, Bronwyn & Harré, Ron. 1990. "Positioning: The discursive production of selves." *Journal for the Theory of Social Behaviour* 20(1): 43–63.

de Certeau, Michel. 1980. *L'invention du Quotidien, vol. 1, Arts de faire*. Paris: Gallimard.

Faber, Marlene. 2001. "Medienrezeption als Aneignung." In *Der sprechende Zuschauer: Wie wir uns Fernsehen sprechend aneignen*, Werner Holly, Ulrich Püschel & Jörg Bergmann (Eds), 25–40. Opladen: Westdeutscher.

Ferguson, Charles A. 1982. "Sports announcer talk: Syntactic aspects of register variation." *Language in Society* 12: 153–172.

Gerhardt, Cornelia. 2007. "Watching television: The dilemma of gaze." *Toegepaste Taalwetenschap in Artikelen* 78: 91–101, 140.

Gerhardt, Cornelia. 2008a. *Talk by television viewers watching live football matches: Coherence through interactionality, intertextuality, and multimodality*. (unpubl. dissertation)

Gerhardt, Cornelia. 2008b. "Turn-by-turn and move-by-move: A multimodal analysis of English live television football commentary." In *The Linguistics of Football*, Eva Lavric, Gerhard Pisek, Andrew Skinner & Wolfgang Stadler (Eds), 270–283. Tübingen: Narr.

Goffman, Erving. 1979. "Footing." *Semiotica* 25: 1–29.

Goffman, Erving 1981. *Forms of Talk*. Philadelphia: University of Pennsylvania Press.

Goodwin, Charles. 2000. "Action and embodiment within situated human interaction." *Journal of Pragmatics* 32: 1489–1522.

Gordon, Cynthia. 2004. "'Al Gore's our guy': Linguistically constructing a family political identity." *Discourse & Society* 15(4): 607–631.

Gumperz, John J. 1982. *Discourse strategies*. Cambridge: Cambridge University Press.

Halliday, M.A.K. 1967. "Notes on transitivity and theme in English Part 2." *Journal of Linguistics* 3: 199–244.

Halliday, M.A.K. & Hasan, Ruqaiya. 1976. *Cohesion in English*. Harlow: Longman.

Hepp, Andreas. 1998. *Fernsehaneignung und Alltagsgespräche: Mediennutzung aus der Perspektive der Cultural Studies*. Wiesbaden: Westdeutscher Verlag.

Holly, Werner, Püschel, Ulrich & Bergmann, Jörg (Eds). 2001. *Der sprechende Zuschauer: Wie wir uns Fernsehen kommunikativ aneignen*. Wiesbaden: Westdeutscher.

Holly, Werner & Püschel, Ulrich. (Ed.). 1993. *Medienrezeption als Aneignung: Methoden und Perspektiven qualitativer Medienforschung*. Opladen: Westdeutscher.

Horton, Donald & Wohl, Richard. 1956. "Mass communication and parasocial interaction: Observations on intimacy at a distance." *Psychiatry* 19: 215–229.

Jefferson, Gail. 1972. "Side sequences." In *Studies in Social Interaction*, David N. Sudnow (Ed.), 294–338. New York: Free Press.

Johnstone, Barbara (Ed.). 1994. *Repetition in discourse: Interdisciplinary perspectives*. Norwood, NJ: Ablex.

Klemm, Michael. 2000. *Zuschauerkommunikation: Formen und Funktionen der alltäglichen kommunikativen Fernsehaneignung*. Frankfurt: Lang.

Lavric, Eva, Pisek, Gerhard, Skinner, Andrew & Stadler, Wolfgang (Eds). 2008. *The Linguistics of Football*. Tübingen: Narr.

Martinez, Matias. 1999. "Nach dem Spiel ist vor dem Spiel: Erzähltheoretische Bemerkungen zur Fußballberichterstattung." *Jahrbuch für Finnisch-Deutsche Literaturbeziehungen* 31: 20–29.

Morris, Barbara S. & Nydahl, Joel. 1985. Sport spectacle as drama. *Journal of Popular Culture* 18. 101–110.

Norrick, Neal R. 1993. *Conversational Joking*. Bloomington, IN: Indiana University Press.

Norrick, Neal R. 2003. "Issues in conversational joking." *Journal of Pragmatics* 35: 1333–1359.

Norrick, Neal R. 2004. "Humor, tellability, and conarration in conversational storytelling." *Text* 24(1): 79–111.

Norris, Sigrid. 2004. *Analysing multimodal interaction: A methodological framework*. London: Routledge.

O'Keeffe, Anne. 2006. *Investigating media discourse*. London: Routledge.

Sacks, Harvey, Schegloff, Emanuel & Jefferson, Gail. 1974. "A simplest systematics for the organisation of turn-taking for conversation." *Language* 50: 696–735.

Schegloff, Emanuel A. 1990. "On the organization of sequences as a source of 'coherence' in talk-in-interaction." In *Conversational Organization and its Development*, Bruce Dorval (Ed.), 51–77. Norwood: Ablex.

Schiffrin, Deborah. 1987. *Discourse Markers*. Cambridge: Cambridge University Press.

Schmitt, Reinhold (Ed.). 2007. *Koordination: Analysen zur multimodalen Interaktion*. Tübingen: Narr.

Scollon, Ron. 1998. *Mediated Discourse as Social Interaction: A Study of News Discourse*. London: Longman.

Sloan, Lloyd R. 1979. "The function and impact of sports for fans: A review of theory and contemporary research." In *Sports, Games, and Play*, Jeffrey H. Goldstein (Ed.), 219–262. Hillsdale: Erlbaum.

Tannen, Deborah. 2007. *Talking Voices: Repetition, Dialogue, and Imagery in conversational discourse*. Cambridge: Cambridge University Press.

Tovares, Alla. 2006. "Public medium, private talk: Gossip about a TV show as 'quotidian hermeneutics'." *Text & Talk* 26(4/5): 463–491.

Wanta, Wayne & Leggett, Dawn. 1988. "'Hitting paydirt': Capacity theory and sports announcers' use of clichés." *Journal of Communication* 38: 82–89.

PART II

Doing gender with humor in talk at work

Using humor to do masculinity at work

Stephanie Schnurr & Janet Holmes

Workplaces constitute sites where individuals "do gender" while at the same time constructing their professional identities and meeting their organisation's expectations. In most workplaces, a rather narrow range of masculine styles of interaction are considered normative. Discursive strategies associated with stereotypically masculine speech styles, as well as behaviours associated with the enactment of hegemonic masculinity are generally viewed as paradigmatic ways of interacting at work. Drawing on data recorded in a range of New Zealand professional organizations, this chapter investigates a range of ways in which normative masculinity is manifested in participants' discourse, and how notions of masculinity are explored and exploited in workplace interactions. The investigation focuses on one particularly versatile discursive strategy frequently employed in talk at work, namely humor.

1. Introduction[1]

Until recently, most workplaces have been dominated by men (Holmes 2000b: 3). Consequently, discursive strategies associated with stereotypically masculine speech styles, as well as behaviors often perceived as 'masculine' in their approach are generally viewed as paradigmatic ways of doing things at work (Kendall and Tannen 1997; Pauwels 2000). While researchers in the area of language and gender have recently begun to examine the "multiplicity of experiences of gender" (Eckert and McConnell-Ginet 2003: 47) in different communities of practice, and some have focused on the range of 'masculinities' which may be discursively enacted in different contexts (e.g., Cameron 1997a; Kiesling 2001, 2004; Meân 2001;

1. The authors would like to thank Adam Jaworski and two anonymous reviewers for their valuable comments on earlier versions of the paper. We would also like to express appreciation to the participants who allowed us to record their interactions, and to other members of the Language in the Workplace team, especially Bernadette Vine (Corpus Manager) who ensured the transcriptions were accurate, and Meredith Marra who provided comments on a draft of this paper. The research described here was made possible by grants from Victoria University of Wellington's Research Fund.

Coates 2003), we focus here on the range of ways in which hegemonic or normative masculinity may be dynamically accomplished in the workplace.

Normative or hegemonic masculinity is associated with styles of discourse which have been described as direct, often confrontational and relatively aggressive, and as outcome-oriented rather than relationally-oriented (Coates 1994; Holmes and Stubbe 2003a; Tannen 1995). Features of communication stereotypically ascribed to masculinity include assertiveness, competitiveness, task-orientation, and the display of power – all of which are highly valued in many workplace contexts (Hearn and Parkin 1988; Still 1996). Research in the area of language and gender has indicated that these features are expressed linguistically in a variety of ways, including, for instance, one-at-a-time construction of the floor (Coates 1997), the "use of competitive and confrontational devices" (Case 1988: 56; Coates 2003), the frequent occurrence of interruptions (Case 1988; Zimmerman and West 1975), as well as unmitigated face-threats and directness (Coates 2003).

Though, as will become evident, our own humor analyses take a more nuanced approach, it is important to note that these findings on features of gendered speech styles have been supported and reinforced by humor research. In particular, the observation that women tend to be supportive, encouraging, and other-oriented conversationalists, while men are more typically competitive in their conversational style (e.g., Coates 1993; Crawford 1995; Holmes 1995; Romaine 1999) seems to be supported by evidence on women's and men's styles of humor. In a number of studies, women were found to prefer self-denigrating humor, for instance, oriented to making the addressee feel good, whereas men tended to make use of more challenging types of humor (Hay 1995a; Jenkins 1985; Ervin-Tripp and Lampert 1992).

This pattern is also supported by findings from studies investigating gender differences in the use of humor in the workplace. Most researchers argue that in a workplace context women not only use fewer instances of humor, but they also appreciate it less than men (Cox et al. 1990; Ehrenberg 1995). These stereotypical perceptions have, however, been challenged by some researchers. Smith et al's (2000) investigation of flight attendants' use of humor, for instance, did not indicate that men used more humor than their female colleagues. In another study, Decker and Rotondo (2001: 457) found that, although the use of humor by workplace leaders was generally perceived as positive by their subordinates, female leaders were rated higher than their male counterparts on "relationship and effectiveness when using positive humor". Moreover, Holmes and associates, who investigated gender differences in the use of humor by recording and analyzing authentic spoken interactions (rather than by relying on participants' self-perceptions and judgments as in most humor research), found that humor is a significant linguistic tool in the socio-pragmatic repertoire of professional women. Their studies show, for example, that in larger meetings women produced more humor than men, and that female chairs made effective use of humor in managing meetings (Holmes 2006; Holmes et al. 2001). Nevertheless, because men are typically perceived as having a better sense of humor, especially at work (Duncan et al. 1990), researchers have claimed that "humour seems to be less a part of the female's communicative patterns" (Cox et al. 1990: 287).

Interestingly, most of the discussion in the research literature of the use of humor at work seems to refer predominantly to the competitive and aggressive style of humor associated with stereotypical masculinity, which is perceived as indexing and reinforcing masculine norms in this context (e.g., Collinson 1988; Linstead 1985; Vinton 1989). In fact, our earlier research suggests that a more feminine style of humor is equally identifiable in many workplaces (Holmes and Stubbe 2003a; Holmes 2000a; Holmes 2006), although few researchers have previously paid attention to it. Clearly, then, humor can be characterized as a gendered discourse resource on which both men and women regularly draw when negotiating their professional and their gender identities in the workplace (see also Holmes 2006; Schnurr 2009b). In a previous paper (Holmes and Schnurr 2006), we explored the diverse ways in which femininity is constructed through workplace humor. In this paper we focus on how hegemonic masculinity is instantiated in humorous interactions at work.

Our approach emphasizes that any individual's use of humor needs to be understood in the particular context in which it occurs. Workplaces, and, in particular, specific work teams, develop their own linguistic repertoire of normative communication patterns. Thus, norms of what counts as appropriate and normatively gendered behavior in a workplace are typically negotiated and enacted on a day-to-day basis in so-called communities of practice (this point is explored in detail elsewhere, e.g., Holmes and Stubbe 2003a; Holmes and Schnurr 2005). The notion of a community of practice (henceforth CofP) evolved from a social constructionist theoretical framework, i.e., a CofP approach focuses on the ways in which people dynamically construct and negotiate their membership of certain groups through their language use, as they acquire the verbal practices that membership involves. Eckert and McConnell-Ginet (1992: 464) define a community of practice as:

> an aggregate of people who come together around mutual engagement in an endeavor. Ways of doing things, ways of talking, beliefs, values, power relations – in short, practices – emerge in the course of this mutual endeavor.

Wenger (1998) identifies three crucial criteria for distinguishing different CofPs, namely, mutual engagement (including regular interaction), a joint, negotiated enterprise (e.g., the shared organizational objectives of the team or group), and a shared repertoire developed over a period of time (which may include specialized jargon, routines, running jokes etc). Humor not only constitutes one aspect of a group's shared linguistic repertoire, but the type of humor which members typically use to convey different meanings as well as the style in which they deliver their humorous utterances are both influenced by norms developed among members of communities practice (e.g., Holmes 2006; Holmes and Schnurr 2005; Holmes and Stubbe 2003a; Mullany 2004; Schnurr 2009a).

Using a CofP framework highlights the importance of membership in a particular group in relation to distinct ways of behaving appropriately in the workplace, and in particular of adhering to and sometimes even challenging prevailing norms of gendered speech behavior. Ways of doing gender by drawing on elements of masculine and feminine speech styles are influenced by the group or CofP within which organisational members are communicating; and conversely their ways of doing gender actively contribute to the construction of different kinds of CofP (e.g., Bergvall 1996; Eckert and McConnell-Ginet 1992). By adhering to the norms of acceptable and appropriate behaviors negotiated among members of a CofP, interlocutors not only reinforce those norms but at the same time accept prevailing gendered expectations and stereotypes. Conversely, by exploiting and challenging these norms, they question and attempt to subvert the existing norms and assumptions about what constitutes appropriate ways of doing gender in their CofP.

2. Data

In order to explore the various ways in which people make use of humor in the workplace to enact and respond to gender stereotypes while simultaneously meeting professional expectations, we draw on natural data recorded for the Language in the Workplace Project (LWP) housed at Victoria University of Wellington (see www.vuw.ac.nz/lals/lwp; Holmes and Stubbe 2003b; Stubbe 1998). The Project includes material from a wide variety of New Zealand workplaces, and uses a methodology which allows workplace interactions to be recorded as unobtrusively as possible. Ethnographic information and follow-up interviews provide a rich basis for interpreting the data, as well as categorization in terms of different types of community of practice. The LWP corpus currently comprises over 2000 workplace interactions, involving around 500 participants.

In this paper we draw on video and audio-recorded interactions together with interview and ethnographic data collected in a range of white-collar organizations in order to explore the range of ways in which stereotypically masculine styles of humor are exploited in different communities of practice.

3. Analysis

Our data provides abundant evidence that people are very aware of the relevance of gender stereotypes in the workplace, and furthermore, this awareness is often indicated through humorous exchanges. In this section, we illustrate, some of the ways in which humor contributes to the construction of workplace relationships and social identities, and also provides a means of challenging and contesting workplace norms and stereotypes.

Elsewhere we have illustrated how humor may sometimes act as a channel for more explicitly gendered discourse at work which may be used to reinforce particular gendered stereotypes (e.g., Holmes 2006; Holmes and Schnurr 2006; Schnurr 2009b). In some of these instances, participants' gender identities are explicitly invoked or become the focus of the humorous exchange, and gender may emerge as an overt topic.

In Examples 1 and 2, expectations of feminine and masculine behaviors and gender stereotypes are exploited as a basis for workplace humor. These examples are also discussed in Holmes and Marra (2002).

(1) Context: Meeting of 7 women and 7 men, members of a project team in a multinational white-collar commercial organization. Clara, the section manager, and Peg, a senior team member, comment on a male colleague.

1	Clara:	he wants to get through month end first
2		he's [smiling voice] : he can't multitask :
3		[females laugh]
4	Peg:	it's a bloke thing
5		[general laughter]
6	Clara:	it's in the genes
7	Peg:	[laughs]

Clara makes a disparaging, teasing comment on the limitations of a specific colleague in relation to managing complex work demands: *he can't multi-task* (line 2). The humorous effect is achieved not only by her tone, which is arch and teasing, but also by the group's knowledge that women have been promoted as 'multi-taskers' in the media recently. Peg's supportive humor, *it's a bloke thing* (line 4), makes the gender orientation of Clara's point explicit, broadening the scope of her remark to men in general. The humor constructs and emphasizes female solidarity, while simultaneously subverting wider societal values which, especially in this large commercial organization, tend to value male skills more highly than female.

This example nicely illustrates how women employ humor to make fun of the masculine stereotype of being 'a bloke' and thus not being able to work on more than one task at the same time. In Example 2, by contrast, which was recorded in a different organization, it is the men who make fun of the stereotypical female preference of engaging in small talk before moving on to more task-focused discussions.

> (2)   Context: This exchange occurs at the beginning of a meeting between Jason and Rob to discuss their relative responsibilities in relation to a project. Jason is the general manager of the company and Rob is the business development manager.
>
> | 1 | Rob: | I I broke it down [clears throat] |
> |---|------|-----------------------------------|
> | 2 | | what I what I figured was what I thought was the most logical |
> | 3 | Jason: | what happened to the small talk |
> | 4 | Rob: | [laughs] [laughs]: just I love the col- |
> | 5 | | I love what you're doing with your hair |
> | 6 | | //these days: [laughs]\ |
> | 7 | Jason: | /[laughs]\\ |
> | 8 | | oh you're just I mean |
> | 9 | | you're so //straight into it you know [laughs]\ |
> | 10 | Rob: | /[laughs]\\ um when we talked about [sighs] the style of |
> | 11 | | operation of of the type of buyer … |

Jason and Rob here make fun of the idea that small talk is a necessary preliminary to transactional or business talk. With his humorous comment *what happened to the small talk* (line 3), Jason disrupts Rob's attempt to start straight into the meeting with a report of his analysis *what I thought was the most logical.*[2] Rob replies by continuing the humor: using a sarcastic tone of voice, he makes fun of feminine stereotypes by imitating the supposed content of women's small talk: *I love what you're doing with your hair these days* (line 5). They then both laugh uproariously for some seconds. The humorous comments and reactions of both men make it clear that they view 'doing small talk' as stereotypical feminine activity, and as something 'real men' do not do. As in Example 1, Jason and Rob's humor focuses explicitly on gender stereotypes and indicates an awareness of the relevance of gender stereotypes and norms in workplace interaction.

Gender has been described as a "pervasive social category" (Weatherall 2000: 287), an ever-present influence on how we behave, even if our level of awareness of this influence varies from one interaction to another, and from moment to moment within an interaction (see Holmes 2006 for a discussion of this issue). Our workplace data supports the view that gender is always potentially relevant to understanding what is going on in face-to-face interaction. It is constantly there – a

---

2. Although there is no speech overlap, it is clear that Jason interrupts Rob's utterance by jumping in and disrupting his topic.

latent, omni-present, background factor in every communicative encounter, with the potential to move into the foreground at any moment. Humor is clearly one means by which workplace participants indicate their awareness of the omni-relevance of gender and gender stereotypes at work.

In what follows we first distinguish unmarked from marked uses of normatively masculine styles of humor in New Zealand workplaces. We then examine some examples of marked humor in more detail, describing ways in which this type of humor may provide a means of conveying critical comments in an acceptable way in workplaces where a contestive interactional style is not the norm. Employing normatively masculine styles of humor in a marked and contestive way enables these professionals to challenge workplace norms and stereotypes, and thus potentially contribute to change.

3.1 *Unmarked* normatively masculine humor

In some of the workplaces in which we recorded our data, stereotypically masculine styles of humor are considered unmarked and normative. In these workplaces, and in particular in a range of working groups (which form CofPs), contestive and challenging humor are interpreted by members as normal, appropriate, and acceptable strategies for performing a range of interpersonal functions, such as reinforcing solidarity and 'creating team' (Fletcher 1999). In these groups (which can often be characterized as relatively 'masculine' CofPs) employing speech styles that are indexed for masculinity is considered normative behavior by members, as evidenced by their reactions and comments.

In many workplace meetings, these normatively masculine styles of humor are used by men to 'do gender', and in particular to enact hegemonic masculinity in a conventional way. The same discursive behavior may be perceived as gender atypical if used by a woman in the same workplace in the same context. This is particularly true for humor that is contestive and competitive in style, as well as for swearing and jocular abuse (Coates 2003; Hay 1994; de Klerk 1997). The limits of tolerance for men seem in general to be wider. While women can and do use abusive and contestive humor, for them there are more contexts in which such behavior is perceived as marked.

We discuss five examples of this kind of stereotypically masculine humor. The first two instances occurred in meetings of the senior managers at a large IT company, Company S. Based on its overall composition and its style of interaction, this group can be characterized as a decidedly 'masculine' CofP. Interactions among members of this working group contain a high amount of challenging humor: members frequently engage in teasing and jocularly insulting each other, and their overall style of using humor is highly contestive and competitive (see also Schnurr 2009a). Hence, stereotypically masculine ways of using humor have become part of the negotiated repertoire on which members regularly draw in order to reinforce solidarity and assert their group membership.

These aspects are illustrated in Example 3, which is taken from the end of a meeting of the senior managers at Company S with Neil, the HR consultant, and Jacqueline, the marketing expert, who have joined the team recently. Neil is gradually learning the ways of talking appropriately in this very masculine CofP. After having decided to invite the entire staff (almost 300 employees) to a presentation about the new HR strategies, the meeting participants discuss the details of informing staff about this event. This example illustrates the 'biting' teasing style (see Schnurr 2009a) on which members of this team regularly draw when reinforcing solidarity with each other. This example is also discussed in Schnurr (2009b).

(3) Context: Towards the end of a meeting which is attended by 4 men and 1 woman. Neil, is an HR consultant and Jacqueline is a marketing expert; both have recently joined the senior management team of company S. Shaun and Chester are well-established members of the senior management team.

1	Shaun:	(yeah so) you've got four weeks of build up
2		(so Jacq) can start doing some clever things
3		to start building them up to that date
4		making sure they're booking it in their diaries
5		and //( ) yeah\
6	Jacqueline:	/do you know where we're going [laughs]\\
7		//[laughs]: come\ along and find out:
8	Neil:	/yeah\\
9	Chester:	the search for the holy grail
10	Jacqueline:	[laughs]
11	Chester:	Harrison Ford Vic's Harrison Ford
12		[general laughter]

In lines 9 and 11 Chester makes use of a range of different types of humor which have been associated with masculinity. In particular, his mocking tone in line 9 *the search for the holy grail,* followed by jocular abuse directed at his boss Victor *Vic's Harrison Ford* (line 11) are not gender neutral but are clearly indexed for masculinity. Chester's suggestion that his boss is facing an impossible task (finding *the holy grail*), with the implication that he needs to be a real man (like Harrison Ford) to meet the challenge could potentially be perceived as insulting. However, interlocutors' reactions (in particular the joint laughter in line 12) indicate that Chester's comments are interpreted as 'playful/nonserious', which is typical for teasing humor (Alberts 1992: 155).

Like the boys in Eder's (1993) study, Chester's teasing of Victor is characterized by a competitive style of delivery, which is manifested in the witty one-liners, for instance, and the one-at-a-time construction of the floor. These challenging types of humor were also found to characterize the discourse of male workers in a factory manufacturing lorries in the UK. A study conducted by Collinson (1988) shows that these men also frequently made use of banter and teasing when interacting with each other – a behavior which has been associated with normative masculinity, and in particular working class masculinity. This very masculine, and even rather macho type of masculinity (Coates 2003: 144) is further emphasized by Chester who portrays Victor as Indiana Jones (played by the actor Harrison Ford), referred to here in his role of searching for *the holy grail*.

This example thus illustrates that Chester's use of teasing and jocular abuse, as well as the overall style in which he delivers these types of humor constitute normative and unmarked behaviors in this particular CofP, although they are clearly indexed for masculinity. This interpretation is further supported by the fact that there are many more examples of this kind in the data recorded in this senior management team. In fact, the majority of the instances of humor collected in this CofP contain teasing or other challenging types of humor, and most are delivered in a contestive and competitive style. (See Schnurr 2009b for a more detailed analysis of the humor used in this CofP.) Behaving in ways typically associated with masculinity, and displaying discursive behaviors and speech styles that are indexed for masculinity are clearly considered normative and unmarked behavior in this CofP.

The masculine normativity of the styles of interaction in this CofP is reinforced in this instance by the overall very male composition of the workforce and the explicitly masculine values to which they subscribe: not only are the majority of staff members men, but when asked to describe a typical company S person, one interviewee commented: *It's a boy. It's a boys club and by boys as a + general gender (generic) term.* Hence stereotypical masculinity is evident at a variety of levels: in members' behavior and dress, in comments which express hegemonic masculine values and which single out women as marked exceptions to the norm in the workplace context, and above all, in members' discourse (and in particular, their style of humor). Displaying ways of 'doing humor' which construct masculinity constitutes normative, unmarked behavior in this overall 'masculine' CofP.

The next example provides further support for the claim that masculine ways of using humor are the norm in this professional white-collar workplace, and particularly in this CofP. Example 4 indicates that the norms in this group permit strong expletives and abusive language. This example is also discussed in Schnurr (2009b).

(4)   Context: A meeting of the senior management team at Company S. The meeting is attended by 5 men. Victor is the Managing Director. Neil is new, but the others are well-established team members. Joel, another team member, is on a phone link.

    1   Shaun: I get you two
    2   no nah I get you and Dean mixed up quite often mm

3	Chester:	fuck off Shaun
4		[laughter] //[laughter]\
5	Chester:	/[laughs]: for the record:\\
6		[laughter]
7	Neil:	… Joel we're taping the session
8		so we were trying to keep all four letter words out
9		but that //hasn't really worked\
10	Victor:	/[laughs]\\
		[laughter throughout next turns]
11	Shaun:	Chester was toning down his normal er
12	Victor:	no they insist on us having // + the normal meetings\
13	Neil:	/yeah yeah\\ (yeah) yeah
14	Chester:	oh right
15	Neil:	it's two minutes thirty seconds into the
16		discussion + they'll be thinking oh that's a record

This exchange makes it clear that swearing at each other is considered part of 'normal' interaction in this CofP. When Neil remonstrates, albeit with tongue-in-cheek, about the swearing *we were trying to keep all four letter words out* (line 8), Shaun comments that Chester's remark was actually toned down from his normal style (line 11), while Victor humorously challenges his suggestion that they should behave in a way that is not normal *they insist on us having the normal meetings* (line 12). Victor is here referring to our practice of reassuring people that they don't have to change their interactional style because they are being recorded. Neil reinforces this interpretation when he jokes that they had managed to get *two minutes thirty seconds into the discussion* (line 15) before a swear word had occurred.

Chester's use of the expletive *fuck off Shaun* in line 3 can thus be interpreted as normal behavior, functioning to reinforce solidarity (see also Coates 2003; Daly et al. 2004), using a strategy which is considered normative and unmarked behavior in this CofP. The humor in this sequence is generated by the obvious mismatch between Neil's perception that swearing on a tape which will be heard by outsiders is unacceptable, and Victor and Shaun's view that since swearing is normal in their CofP, they should not be concerned about it. As Coates (2003: 46) notes, swearing performs hegemonic masculinity: "Swearing and taboo language have historically been used by men in the company of other men as a sign of their toughness and of their manhood". (See also de Klerk 1997).

In addition to swearing, the very competitive ways in which the other men try to outwit each other in coming up with humorous responses to Chester's remark (lines 7–9, 11–12, 15–16) are speech behaviors that have been described as typical of 'men's talk' (Coates 2003; Hay 1994). Coupland (2000: 10 referring to Johnson and Finlay 1997, and Schwebel 1997) notes that verbal duelling "has been seen as a particularly male activity".

What is also interesting about this humorous instance is the fact that the men pretend to be concerned about the effect that Chester's swearing will have on us (an all-female research team) (lines 7–9, 15–16). Similar observations were also made by Collinson (1988) who was told by the male workers that they did not mind swearing frequently at work with their male colleagues, but found it inappropriate to swear in the company of women. Examples 3 and 4 illustrate that in this particular CofP masculine styles of using humor are considered the norm, and that even relatively challenging and aggressive ways of employing this discursive strategy are regarded as appropriate.

However, Chester's *fuck off Shaun* remark in Example 4 could also be interpreted as a borderline case of unmarked behavior – an attempt to test and perhaps expand masculine norms of what is considered appropriate in this particular CofP. This interpretation is supported by participants' reaction: the joint laughter and the subsequent attempts by Neil and Shaun to downplay the impact of the potentially offensive speech act suggest that perhaps the strength of Chester's swearing and jocular abuse is somewhat marked (i.e., *fuck off* is at the more offensive end of a scale of swear words, in a white collar professional group). This aspect is discussed in more detail below. However, in other workplace contexts where we have recorded data, such as in a factory, the use of the expletive *fuck* constitutes unmarked behavior on which members regularly draw when reinforcing solidarity (see Daly et al. 2004; Schnurr et al. 2008).

A similarly masculine, albeit less challenging and potentially insulting, way of employing humor is illustrated in Example 5. This extract was recorded in a regular meeting of an IT project team in a large commercial organization. In this group too, challenging contributions to the meeting discourse occurred frequently.

(5)   Context: Weekly meeting of 6 men, expert members of an IT project team in a large commercial organization. Barry is the meeting chair; Callum is the minute taker. Callum has failed to update a header leading Barry to think he's got the wrong document.

1	Callum:	I definitely sent you the right one
2	Barry:	[laughs]
3	Eric:	yep Callum did fail his office management
4		[laughs] word processing lesson
5	Callum:	I find it really hard being perfect at everything

In lines 3–4, Eric makes Callum the target of a jocular insult, *Callum did fail his office management word processing lesson*. Callum responds by challenging Eric's claim with his own mock-modest claim *I find it really hard being perfect at everything* (line 5). By asserting his overall superiority, Callum contests Eric's contribution by challenging the put-down intent of his jocular abuse. (See Holmes 2006 for further discussion).

As noted above, this kind of talk, contesting the content of the previous speaker's utterances, tends to be associated with more masculine styles of inter-action (Coates 1997, 2003; Cameron 1997b, Edley and Wetherall 1997). Coates (2003: 56ff.), for instance, describes how many of the men she studied, and espe-cially the younger men, engaged in extremely competitive talk, arguing about issues such as who had drunk most, who had got the better of authority most effectively, and so on. She illustrates this with examples which demonstrate the use of unmitigated face-threatening acts, abusive swearing, and deflating com-ments in response to narratives intended to construct a heroic identity (see Daly et al. 2004 for similar examples from our workplace data set). As men-tioned above, these findings are supported by de Klerk (1997) who argues that swear words are typically ascribed to a masculine register, and Boxer (2002) also observes that verbal challenges and put-downs are a male propensity. Not surprisingly, then, contestive humor is perceived as typical of normatively masculine styles of interaction in the workplace.

The humor in Examples 3–5 thus constitutes instances of paradigmatic masculine humor. The ways in which interlocutors in these examples make use of humor is contestive or challenging in focus and style, the floor is constructed with minimal collaboration and with a focus on one-at-a-time contributions. Moreover, the content of the humorous instances assumes, and implicitly reinforces, masculine conceptions of what counts as acceptable communicative strategies for men at work. In these cases, the humor is predicated on underlying assumptions about gendered norms of interaction and shared understandings about what constitutes appropriately gendered discourse in these 'masculine' CofPs (see also Holmes 2006).

However, this masculine style of humor is not only used by men in white-collar workplaces but may also constitute part of the discursive register of women. Doing gender, whether masculinity or femininity, is an option for both women and men. The next two examples illustrate how women can use humor to do masculinity at work when appropriate. Examples 6 and 7 are from a workplace that could be characterized as predominantly 'masculine' in its overall make-up as well as in the discursive norms typically employed by members. In this work-place contestive and challenging humor are regularly used by men and women. The humor in the first example is aimed at Hine, a team member who is about to undertake work with a group she belongs to in a rural area.

(6)   Context: Executive team of 4 men and 2 women in a regular weekly meeting of
       a relatively large semi-public organization. Hine is a senior manager. Maureen is
       the Personal Assistant to the CEO.

       1   Hine: I'll go and give Steve my contact details
       2   which I didn't even think about / ( )\\

3	Maureen:	//that's right\ cellphones don't work out there eh
4	Hine:	that's right
5	Maureen:	tom tom drums
6		[laughter]

With her sarcastic comments *cellphones don't work out there eh* (line 3) and *tom tom drums* (line 5) Maureen implies the people in the rural area, who are Hine's people, are primitive. She is using a sarcastic quip which can be classified as jocular abuse in this context. However, Hine is perfectly capable of managing this kind of challenging and stereotypically masculine humor. Rather than being upset by the jocular abuse, she agrees with Maureen's comment (line 4) and joins in with the laughter.

Example 7 occurred in the same workplace. Daniel is the team manager and he is the focus of Maureen's comment, since the team is aware that we, as researchers, are interested in styles of leadership.

(7)   Context: Team of 8 men and 8 women in a regular weekly meeting.

1	Maureen:	he's being assessed
2	MX:	[laughs]
3	Maureen:	so we should all get up and walk out

Maureen suggests that, instead of supporting Daniel, they should all walk out of the meeting to suggest that he is a poor leader. This jocular abuse is quite typical of the repartee which occurs in the meetings of this team; members regularly challenge each other, contest each other's statements, and make sarcastic and teasing remarks. By engaging in contestive humor in ways that are indexed for normative masculinity, members draw on and reinforce the masculine norms of interaction that prevail in their workplace. In these contexts displaying behaviors typically ascribed to hegemonic masculinity constitutes unmarked and normative behavior.

Elsewhere we have described in great detail the ways in which Ginette, a team leader in a factory, makes use of a range of elements (including contestive humour and swearing) typically indexed for normative masculinity (Holmes and Schnurr 2005; Daly et al. 2004; Holmes and Stubbe 2003a, 2003b). As in the context of the white-collar workplace in which Examples 6 and 7 were recorded, in Ginette's blue-collar workplace, these stereotypically masculine behaviors also constitute normative, unmarked ways of interacting with each other.

In Ginette's factory, as well as in the white-collar workplaces in which Examples 3–7 were recorded, contestive and stereotypically masculine humor occurs frequently and is normative behavior. However, as the analysis of Example 4 has suggested, this contestive and potentially face-threatening humor may also sometimes be used to test the boundaries of acceptable behavior and workplace norms. This idea is explored further in the next section, which focuses on workplaces in which the use of challenging and competitive humor does not form part of the normative repertoire, but constitutes *marked* behavior.

3.2   *Marked* contestive, stereotypically masculine humor

In workplace contexts where challenging and competitive humor is not unmarked but is considered to be marked, unusual and even inappropriate behavior, this stereotypically masculine style of humor may nonetheless be exploited as a means of conveying a critical message in a relatively acceptable way.[3] Such humor may in the process expand and challenge workplace norms.

Conveying a negative message
In CofPs where direct criticism is generally avoided, stereotypically masculine, contestive or teasing humor can serve as a valuable socio-pragmatic strategy for conveying negative or challenging content in a more acceptable way. Its marked status in these contexts provides a signal that this style of interaction is unusual, and allows the speaker to revert to a more typical unthreatening interactional style after the negative message has been conveyed.

Although a component of a challenging utterance, the humor is nonetheless a useful means of attenuating the criticism. In particular, it serves as a useful resource in contexts where work is being regularly evaluated and assessed. In Example 8, Andy implies that Vince has been too wordy, using humor to convey the critical message. (See Holmes 2000b for further discussion).

> (8)   Context: Two advisors in a government organization comparing their evaluations of an organization. Andy is more experienced and is providing feedback to Vince.
>
>   1   And: apart from that I've just got what you've got
>   2   just in a lot less words //[laughs]\
>   3   Vin: /[laughs] \\

The humor in this example derives from the contrast between the directness of the criticism and the usual more cooperative style typical of interaction in this collaborative and relatively feminine CofP (Holmes and Stubbe 2003a), where attention to face would be predicted.

Humorous insults and jocular abuse are more extreme examples of the same phenomenon. As illustrated above, insulting and aggressive humor may be frequent and unmarked in very masculine CofPs, contributing to creating team. However, more

---

3.   For a more detailed discussion of the ways in which marked behaviour is often associated with impoliteness see Locher and Watts (2005), and for an application to a workplace context see Mullany (2008) and Schnurr et al. (2008).

feminine workplaces, such as the government department from which Example 9 is taken, are characterized by a more cooperative and supportive approach to interaction. In such feminine CofPs, it is regarded as uncollegial to compete very overtly in completing tasks ahead of others. In this context, contestive humor may serve as a marked resource for managing suggestions that could be interpreted as critical, or which were undoubtedly intended to be critical, as in Example 9.

(9)   Context: Three women of equal status in a government department discussing proposals they are working on.

1   Val: and Celia's finished her proposals I'm sure [laughs]
2   Cel: on the last one
3   Val: ah you sod
4   All: [laugh]

Celia's statement that she is *on the last one* (line 2) is clearly perceived as boastful and provocative, and it elicits an insulting response from Val for showing up her colleagues. The insult, which might be considered mild in absolute terms, is strong for this usually very supportive and friendly work context. It conveys aggression based on envy, while the laughter reflects the incongruity or marked status of such a strong term of abuse in this particular work context between colleagues. By treating the remark as humorous, the colleagues manage the challenge and threat to their social relationship conveyed by the insult. Or to use Spencer-Oatey's (2000: 14) terms, they manage their 'sociality rights' – the social expectancies and concerns over fairness, consideration and inclusion in the group. Using marked masculine humor in this context clearly challenges the normally harmonious and non-threatening, non-competitive work-relationship the women share. Their joint laughter as a response to Val's marked use of humor can thus be interpreted as an attempt to prevent tension from building up and to revert to the group's normative and less challenging way of interacting with each other.

When colleagues in more 'feminine' CofPs use insulting terms such as *rotter, sod,* and *bastard,* these terms are clearly marked. They occur in a range of unwelcome situations such as when a colleague passes on an undesirable job, or volunteers them for a task, or lands them with a difficult client. The insult provides a jocular means of protesting, but it is clearly marked in these contexts. So although humor provides a covert strategy for face attack – a means of registering a veiled protest – it is notable that this kind of challenging and contestive humor is unusual in some workplace contexts.

However, in addition to providing one means through which negative messages can be communicated, stereotypically masculine humor when it occurs in 'feminine' CofPs may also serve to challenge workplace norms and stereotypes, and thus potentially contribute to changes in these norms.

Challenging workplace norms

The examples that we discuss in this section go beyond unmarked uses of masculine humor in 'masculine' workplaces (as illustrated in Examples 1–7), and the use of masculine styles of humor in 'feminine' workplaces (as in Examples 8 and 9), to marked instances of humor which actively transgress and challenge norms of acceptable workplace behavior. By employing contestive, masculine humor in workplaces where this kind of behavior is clearly not part of the appropriate and acceptable ways of using humor, members challenge the interactional norms of their workplace, and thereby contribute to the ongoing construction of workplace identities.

Not surprisingly perhaps, there are only relatively few instances of this kind of marked behavior in our workplace data. The first example we discuss here is taken from a one-to-one interaction between Noel, a group leader in an IT organization, and Barbara, his subordinate. Barbara is telling Noel, her boss, how she dealt with a particular problem that arose the week before. She reports that she has received numerous electronic requests which she was supposed to process. This example is discussed in more detail in Schnurr (2009b).

> (10)　Context: Noel is the group leader in an IT organization, and Barbara is his subordinate in his section of the organization.
>
> | 1 | B.: | so I diverted diverted it into a folder |
> |---|-----|--|
> | 2 | | forgot all about it and then like a week later thought |
> | 3 | | oh haven't heard a thing |
> | 4 | | there was four hundred and //seventy emails\ in there you know |
> | 5 | N: | /yeah yeah\\ |
> | 6 | | [*sarcastic tone*] so you didn't bother of course + |
> | 7 | | //yes no\ I wish + it was all as easy but er + anyhow [tut] + |
> | 8 | B.: | /(um)\\ |

Instead of providing support and showing empathy to the no-doubt exaggerated account of Barbara's email disaster, Noel, does the exact opposite. His sarcastic remark (the sarcasm is very clear from his tone of voice) *so you didn't bother* (line 6) challenges her, and the ascertaining pragmatic particle *of course* at the end of his comment renders his remark face-threatening, overtly displaying his disapproval.

Using sarcasm to communicate his disapproval and criticism of his subordinate in this way, Noel displays a range of behaviors typically ascribed to a normatively masculine style of interaction. In particular, his overt display of power, his relative directness and unmitigated face-threat are behaviors which are clearly indexed for hegemonic masculinity (Holmes and Stubbe 2003a). It is notable that his behavior silences his subordinate. This stereotypically masculine style is in stark contrast to the harmonious ways in which members of this workplace normally interact with each other. The vast majority of instances of humor employed by members is characterized by a relatively high degree of supportiveness and collaboration (as reflected, for instance, in the ways in which humor is constructed conjointly, see Schnurr 2009b). Hence, by using a stereotypically masculine humor strategy, namely sarcasm, in a challenging and marked way, Noel accomplishes some very negative interactional work (i.e., criticizing and distancing himself from his subordinate), while at the same time challenging interactional norms of appropriate and acceptable behavior that prevail in this workplace.

When judged against the interactional norms of this workplace (Schnurr 2009b; Marra et al. 2006), Noel's use of sarcasm in Example 10 is marked as particularly negative. However, from another perspective Noel's sarcastic comment could be seen as a face-saving way of conveying disapproval of his subordinate's behavior. Like Examples 8 and 9, the contestive and marked humor provides a somewhat more acceptable means for Noel to convey a negative message: instead of explicitly telling Barbara that he considers her behavior to be inappropriate and disappointing, he wraps this sensitive message in humor. As a consequence, he increases the social distance between them (Seckman & Couch 1989: 328). In this instance, then, by using marked masculine humor in order to communicate a negatively affective speech act, Noel finds an acceptable channel through which to display his disapproval, whilst also maintaining distance between interlocutors.

A similar albeit less face-threatening use of humor is evident in the next example which is taken from a board meeting at a small IT company. Participants returned to the meeting room after a break. During the meeting Tessa has been typing the minutes on the computer, but when she returns, she finds that Donald (her husband) has worked on the computer in the meantime. At this point in the interaction, there are three people in the room, Jill (the company director), Donald, the CEO, and Tessa (a member of the board).

(11)   Context: After the break during a Board meeting at a small IT company. Donald is a company founder and Managing Director. Tessa is also a company founder and Donald's wife. Jill is Chair of the Board.

1	Tessa:	um + oh what have you done
3	Donald:	I've (exited) out the minutes so they don't get lost
4		//cos\ you (weave) them off the server
5	Tessa:	/( )\\
6	Donald:	and the guys have to reboot the server to fix the
7		database ( ) with all the stuff on the projects
8		database so (ju-) don't //oh\ shit
9	Tessa:	/what\\
10	Donald:	//just\

```
11   Tessa:     /what\\
12   Donald:    //don't touch it (just leave it)\
13   Jill:      /don't do anything (don't move it a\\round)
14   Tessa:     (what)
15   Donald:    sit back and eat your biscuit [laughs] […]
16   Jill:      [laughs] [laughs]: he means that in
17              the nicest possible way: [laughs]
```

It is clear from Tessa's remarks and questions that she does not understand what her hsuband Donald is doing with the computer (lines 1 and 5). After he has tried to explain the problem to her (lines 6–8) without any success, he gets irritated and uses humor as a way to express his annoyance. His sarcastic remark *sit back and eat your biscuit* (line 15) is contestive in content. Although it is considerably mitigated by his relatively soft tone of voice and his subsequent laughter, it is nevertheless face-threatening and challenging. The directness of this interchange no doubt reflects in part at least the intimate personal relationship between Donald and Tessa. (This example is discussed from a different angle in Schnurr 2009b).

This challenging and normatively masculine way of using humor is not typical of the interactional style of this workplace. Most of the interactions among members of this CofP are characterized by supportive humor, sometimes with a little edge to it (see Schnurr 2009b). While Tessa and Donald sometimes spat with each other in a friendly way, Donald's use of contestive sarcasm in example 11 clearly oversteps the boundaries of acceptable interactional behavior, as indicated by Jill's attempt to mitigate his behavior by asserting to Tessa that *he means that in the nicest possible way* (lines 16–17).

Donald's sarcastic, and even insultingly patronizing remark in line 15, could be interpreted as 'doing power', using a typically hegemonic interactional strategy. He uses the humor to reinforce gendered stereotypes and thus (ironically) challenges the non-sexist workplace norms which Jill reasserts with some of her comments (see Holmes and Schnurr 2005 for a more detailed discussion of this point). Jill's mitigating response can be interpreted as an attempt to mediate between Donald and Tessa and thereby to reinstall the status quo of harmonious interactions between colleagues. As noted above, workplace interactions in this company are typically characterized by collaborative and supportive contributions rather than by contestive comments.

In the context of this workplace, then, using challenging and sarcastic humor is a marked exception to the interactional norms developed among members of this CofP. And by drawing on this masculine and marked way of doing humor, Donald also challenges these norms of acceptable and appropriate behavior. In particular, due to his special status and authority in the company (as one of the founder members and key personnel), his marked behavior could be regarded as potentially having a considerable effect on perceptions and norms of acceptable behavior.[4]

4. Conclusion

The analysis undertaken in this paper complements our earlier exploration of multiple femininities and ways of constructing femininity at work. Drawing on the concept of the community of practice and using social identity theory, we have here analyzed some of the ways in which hegemonic masculinity is manifested in workplace discourse, and exploited in workplace interactions. Our examples have demonstrated that humor is one means by which professionals indicate their awareness of the omni-relevance of gender and gender stereotypes at work.

Male and female professionals use humor as a means to express and respond to gender expectations and stereotypes. But they also employ gendered humor styles in ways that are considered as marked and/or unmarked in their respective CofP in order to achieve their workplace objectives. In particular, our analyses have demonstrated how stereotypically masculine ways of using humor contribute in particular to the construction of power and distance relationships and particular social identities in the workplace, while they also assist people in challenging and contesting the gendered interactional norms prevailing in their workplaces.

The men and women in our workplace data employ humor as a means to construct, at times, a stereotypical gender identity, while challenging and undermining those norms on other occasions (see also Holmes 2006: 137). They explore and exploit masculine styles of humor in their CofPs in marked and unmarked ways to reinforce as well as to challenge and contest interactional workplace norms. For these individuals humor, and in particular masculine humor, constitutes a valuable means for shifting the boundaries of accepted behavior. They also exploit masculine humour in order to license relatively unconventional behavior, and to express face-threatening messages in a relatively direct way.

Overall, then, humor in the workplace can be viewed as a gendered discourse strategy which serves a range of diverse and interesting functions. Furthermore, our analysis has indicated the overwhelming importance of the specific CofP and the particular workplace context in interpreting the significance of humor in any particular interaction. Our analyses support the claim that the theoretical framework of

---

4. Donald's influence on what is considered acceptable behavior in this workplace is further illustrated in some of the comments that employees made in the interviews, such as Donald "defines a lot of our culture" and the company is driven by "Donald's thinking".

the community of practice provides a rich starting point for examining the ways in which humor is differently exploited in different social contexts, including different workplaces. Complementing this approach, social identity theory has supplied a sound basis for exploring the diverse ways in which humor contributes to the on-going construction of facets of identity, such as gender, ethnicity, and authority in dynamic on-going workplace interaction. Further research building on these sound theoretical foundations will further illuminate our understanding of the important contribution that humor makes in workplace communication.

Transcription conventions

[laughs]	Paralinguistic features in square brackets
+	Pause up to one second
-	Incomplete or cut-off utterance
... // ..... \ ...	
... / ..... \\ ...	Simultaneous speech
(hello)	Transcriber's best guess at an unclear utterance
?	Rising or question intonation
VERY	Capitals indicate emphatic stress
[...]	Section of transcript omitted
ke-	Incomplete word
[laughs]: yeah:	Laughter throughout the utterance of the word in between the colons

All names are pseudonyms.

References

Bergvall, Victoria. 1996. "Constructing and enacting gender through discourse: Negotiating multiple roles as female engineering students." In *Rethinking Language and Gender Research: Theory and Practice,* Victoria Bergvall, Janet Bing & Alice Greenwood (Eds), 173–201. London: Longman.

Boxer, Diane. 2002. *Applying Sociolinguistics. Domains and Face-to-Face Interaction.* Amsterdam: Benjamins.

Cameron, Deborah. 1997a. "Performing gender identity: young men's talk and the construction of heterosexual masculinity." In *Language and Masculinity*, Sally Johnson & Ulrike Hanna Meinhof (Eds), 47–64. Oxford: Blackwell.

Cameron, Deborah. 1997b. "Theoretical debates in feminist linguistics: Questions of sex and gender." In *Gender and Discourse*, Ruth Wodak (Ed.), 21–36. London: Sage.

Case, Susan Schick. 1988. "Cultural differences, not deficiencies: An analysis of managerial women's language." In *Women's Careers. Pathways and Pitfalls*, Suzanna Rose & Laurie Larwood (Eds), 41–63. New York: Praeger.

Coates, Jennifer. 1993. *Women, Men and Language. A Sociolinguistic Account of Gender Differences in Language* (2nd Edn). London: Longman.

Coates, Jennifer. 1994. "The language of the professions: Discourse and career." In *Women and Career. Themes and Issues in Advanced Industrial Societies,* Julia Evetts (Ed.), 72–86. London: Longman.

Coates, Jennifer. 1997. "One-at-a-time: The organization of men's talk." In *Language and Masculinity,* Sally Johnson & Ulrike Hanna Meinhof (Eds), 107–130. Oxford: Blackwell.

Coates, Jennifer. 2003. *Men Talk. Stories in the Making of Masculinities.* Oxford: Blackwell.

Collinson, David. 1988. "'Engineering humour': Masculinity, joking and conflict in shop-floor relations." *Organization Studies* 9(2): 181–199.

Coupland, Justine. 2000. "Introduction." In *Small Talk,* Justine Coupland (Ed.), 1–25. London: Longman.

Cox, Joe, Read, Raymond & van Auken, Philip. 1990. "Male-female differences in communicating job-related humor: An exploratory study." *Humor* 3(3): 287–295.

Crawford, Mary. 1995. *Talking Difference. On Gender and Language.* London: Sage.

Daly, Nicola, Holmes, Janet, Newton, Jonathan & Stubbe, Maria. 2004. "Expletives as solidarity signals in FTAs on the faculty floor." *Journal of Pragmatics* 26: 945–964.

Decker, Wayne & Rotondo, Denise. 2001. "Relationships among gender, type of humor, and perceived leader effectiveness." *Journal of Managerial Issues* 13(4): 451–465.

DeKlerk, Vivian. 1997. "The role of expletives in the construction of masculinity." In *Language and Masculinity,* Sally Johnson & Ulrike Hanna Meinhof (Eds), 144–158. Oxford: Blackwell.

Duncan, W. Jack, Smeltzer, Larry L. & Leap, Terry L. 1990. "Humor and work: Applications of joking behavior to management." *Journal of Management* 16(2): 255–278.

Eckert, Penelope & McConnell-Ginet, Sally. 1992. "Think practically and look locally: Language and gender as community-based practice." *Annual Review of Anthropology* 21: 461–490.

Edley, Nigel & Wetherall, Margaret. 1997. "Jockeying for position: The construction of masculine identities." *Discourse & Society* 8(2): 203–217.

Ehrenberg, Tamar. 1995. "Female differences in creation of humour relating to work." *Humor* 8(4): 349–362.

Ervin-Tripp, Susan & Lampert, Martin. 1992. "Gender differences in the construction of humorous talk." In *Locating Power. Proceedings of the Second Berkeley Women and Language Conference* (Vol. 1), Kira Hall, Mary Bucholtz & Birch Moonwomon (Eds), 108–117. Berkeley, CA: Berkeley Women and Language Group University of California.

Fletcher, Joyce. 1999. *Disappearing Acts. Gender, Power, and Relational Practice at Work.* Cambridge, MASS: MIT Press.

Hay, Jennifer. 1995. *Gender and Humour: Beyond a Joke.* Unpublished MA, Victoria University of Wellington.

Hearn, Jeff & Parkin, P. Wendy. 1988. "Women, men, and leadership: A critical review of assumptions, practices, and change in the industrialized nations." In *Women in Management Worldwide,* Nancy Adler & Dafna Izraeli (Eds), 17–40. London: M.E. Sharpe.

Holmes, Janet. 1995. *Women, Men and Politeness.* London: Longman.

Holmes, Janet. 2000a. "Women at work: Analysing women's talk in New Zealand workplaces." *Australian Review of Applied Linguistics* 7: 89–98.

Holmes, Janet. 2000b. "Politeness, power and provocation: How humour functions in the workplace." *Discourse Studies* 2(2): 159–185.

Holmes, Janet. 2006. *Gendered Talk at Work Constructing Gender Identity through Workplace Discourse.* Oxford: Blackwell.

Holmes, Janet & Marra, Meredith. 2002. "Over the edge? Subversive humour between colleagues and friends." *Humor* 15(1): 65–87.

Holmes, Janet & Schnurr, Stephanie. 2005. "Politeness, humour and gender in the workplace: Negotiating norms and identifying contestation." *Journal of Politeness Research: Language, Behaviour, Culture* 1: 121–149.

Holmes, Janet & Schnurr, Stephanie. 2006. "Doing femininity at work: more than just relational practice." *Journal of Sociolinguistics* 10(1): 31–51.

Holmes, Janet & Stubbe, Maria. 2003a. "'Feminine' workplaces: Stereotypes and reality." In *Handbook of Language and Gender,* Janet Holmes & Miriam Meyerhoff (Eds), 573–599. Oxford: Blackwell.

Holmes, Janet & Stubbe, Maria. 2003b. *Power and Politeness in the Workplace. A Sociolinguistic Analysis of Talk at Work.* London: Longman.

Holmes, Janet, Marra, Meredith & Burns, Louise. 2001. "Women's humour in the workplace: A quantitative analysis." *Australian Journal of Communication* 28(1): 83–108.

Jenkins, Mercilee. 1985. "What's so funny? Joking among women." In *Proceedings of the First Berkeley Women and Language Conference,* Noelle Caskey, Sue Bremner & Birch Moonwomon (Eds), 135–155. Berkeley, CA: Berkeley Women and Language Group.

Kendall, Shari & Tannen, Deborah. 1997. "Gender and language in the workplace." In *Gender and Discourse,* Ruth Wodak (Ed.), 81–105. London: Sage.

Kiesling, Scott Fabius. 2001. "'Now I gotta watch what I say': shifting constructions of gender and dominance in discourse." *Journal of Linguistic Anthropology* 11(2): 250–273.

Kiesling, Scott Fabius. 2004. "Dude." *American Speech* 79(3): 281–305.

Linstead, Steve. 1985. "Jokers wild: The importance of humour in the maintenance of organizational culture." *The Sociological Review* 33(4): 741–767.

Locher, Miriam & Watts, Richard. 2005. "Politeness theory and relational work." *Journal of Politeness Research: Language, Behaviour, Culture* 1: 9–33.

Marra, Meredith, Schnurr, Stepahnie & Holmes, Janet. 2006. "Effective leadership in New Zealand workplaces: Balancing gender and role." In *Speaking Out: The Female Voice in Public Contexts,* Judith Baxter (Ed.), 240–260. Houndmills, Basingstoke: Palgrave.

Meân, Lindsey. 2001. "Identity and discursive practice: Doing gender on the football pitch." *Discourse & Society* 12(6): 789–815.

Mullany, Louise. 2004. "Gender, politeness and institutional power roles: Humour as a tactic to gain compliance in workplace business meetings." *Multilingua,* 23: 13–37.

Mullany, Louise. 2008. "'Stop hassling me!' Impoliteness, power and gender identity in the professional workplace." In *Impoliteness in Language,* Derek Bousfield & Miriam Locher (Eds), 231–251. Berlin: Mouton.

Pauwels, Anne. 2000. "Inclusive language is good business: Gender, language and equality in the workplace." In *Gendered Speech in Social Context. Perspectives from Gown and Town,* Janet Holmes (Ed.), 134–151. Wellington: Victoria University Press.

Romaine, Suzanne. 1999. *Communicating Gender.* London: Erlbaum.

Schnurr, Stephanie. 2009a. "Constructing leader identities through teasing at work." *Journal of Pragmatics,* 41: 1125–1138.

Schnurr, Stephanie. 2009b. *Leadership Discourse at Work. Interactions of Humour, Gender and Workplace Culture.* Basingstoke: Palgrave Macmillan.

Schnurr, Stephanie, Marra, Meredith & Holmes, Janet. 2008. "Impoliteness as a means of contesting power relations in the workplace." In *Impoliteness in Language,* Derek Bousfield & Miriam Locher (Eds), 211–229. Berlin: Mouton.

Seckman, Mark & Couch, Carl. 1989. "Jocularity, sarcasm, and relationships." *Journal of Contemporary Ethnography* 18(3): 327–344.

Smith, Wanda, Harrington, Vernard & Neck, Christopher. 2000. "Resolving conflict with humor in a diversity context." *Journal of Managerial Psychology* 15(6): 606–617.

Spencer-Oatey, Helen. 2000. "Rapport management: A framework for analysis." In *Culturally Speaking: Managing Rapport through Talk across Cultures,* Helen Spencer-Oatey (Ed.), 11–46. London: Continuum.

Still, Leonie. 1996. "Women as leaders: The cultural dilemma." In *Women and Leadership: Power and Practice,* Su Olsson & Nicole Stirton (Eds), 63–76. Palmerston North: Massey University.

Stubbe, Maria. 1998. *Researching language in the workplace: A participatory model.* Paper presented at the Australian Linguistics Society Conference, Brisbane University of Queensland.

Tannen, Deborah. 1995. *Talking from 9 to 5.* London: Virago.

Vinton, Karen. 1989. "Humor in the workplace. It is more than telling jokes." *Small Group Behavior* 20(2): 151–166.

Weatherall, Ann. 2000. "Gender relevance in talk-in-interaction and discourse." *Discourse & Society* 11: 286–288.

Wenger, Etienne. 1998. *Communities of Practice. Learning, Meaning, and Identity.* Cambridge: Cambridge University Press.

Zimmerman, Don & West, Candace. 1975. "Sex roles, interruptions and silences in conversation." In *Language and Sex: Difference and Dominance,* Barry. Thorne & Nancy Henley (Eds), 105–129. Rowley, MA: Newbury House.

Boundary-marking humor

Institutional, gender and ethnic demarcation in the workplace

Bernadette Vine, Susan Kell, Meredith Marra & Janet Holmes

Drawing on recorded workplace meetings of Māori and Pākehā women in one New Zealand government department, this paper illustrates some of the complexities of boundary-marking humor. In particular, we analyze examples where the humor illuminates some of the tensions experienced by less powerful groups working within the institutional parameters or frameworks of more dominant groups or sources of influence. The relevant in-group shifts and the humor may correspondingly orient to boundaries dividing different institutional groups, different sexes, and different ethnic groups at different times. In each case, no members of the out-group are present and the humor functions to build solidarity and rapport between in-group members.

1. Introduction[1]

The role of humor in supporting or enforcing social norms and expressing identity has been noted by a number of humor researchers (e.g., Limon 1977; O'Quin and Aronoff 1981; Duncan 1985; Norrick 1993; Boxer and Cortés-Conde 1997; Pratt 1998; Archakis and Tsakona 2005). From a socio-pragmatic perspective, humor is one of a wide variety of linguistic and pragmatic strategies available to those 'out of power' to construct a positive identity, and also to subvert the pervasive influence of the dominant group by testing, stretching and contesting normative boundaries (Holmes, Stubbe and Marra 2003). In this paper we explore how humor may contribute to the dynamic construction and reinforcement of institutional demarcations, gender divisions, and ethnic group boundaries in the workplace.

Within the New Zealand context, boundary-marking humor, in particular, has been identified in the informal conversations of Māori speakers of New Zealand English, where the humor often derives from their less dominant

---

1. The authors would like express appreciation to the participants who allowed us to record their interactions.

position as Māori people in New Zealand society (Holmes and Hay 1997; Stubbe and Holmes 2000; Benton 1991).[2] Boundary-marking humor in this context constructs and reinforces cultural identity, and often takes the form of self-deprecating jokes that refer to a socially negative stereotype, or may involve giving excessive praise to qualities that are regarded as characteristic only, or mainly, of the in-group. This kind of humor was extensively exploited by the late, much-loved, Māori comedian, Billy T. James. Drawing on a recognizable stereotype of a hick, 'dumb', rural Māori male, he created a wonderfully successful comic character which he used (among other complex functions) to send up the attitudes of Pākehā, the dominant group, and their beliefs about the way Māori behaved. The use of an exaggerated stereotype as a source of entertainment is a well-attested feature of minority group humor (Ziv 1988; Davies 1982, 1990).

Turning to the workplace context, the construction of different aspects of social identity and the delineation of social boundaries between different groups and communities of practice are important ways in which humor contributes to creating and maintaining workplace relationships (Grainger 2004; Fine and De Soucey 2005; Rogerson-Revell 2007). Holmes and Marra (2002a), for instance, described the ways in which humor may signal ethnic and gender boundaries in a workplace context, as well as professional in-group versus out-group boundaries.

In this article we focus on the use of boundary-marking humor by women in two distinct workgroups in the same workplace, examining, in particular, examples where the humor illuminates some of the tensions experienced by less powerful groups working within the institutional parameters or frameworks of more dominant groups or sources of influence. The relevant in-group shifts and the humor may correspondingly orient to boundaries dividing different institutional groups, different sexes, or different ethnic groups at different times. The dynamic flux of talk thus allows different aspects of social identity to come to the fore at different moments. In each case there are no members of the out-group present and the humor functions to build solidarity and rapport; it is bonding humor (Boxer and Cortés-Conde 1997) and can be seen as a device which contributes to the managing of rapport within the workgroup (Spencer-Oatey 2008).

2.   The data

The data analyzed in this paper is drawn from the corpus of the Wellington Language in the Workplace Project; for a detailed description of this project, see

---

2.   Māori are the indigenous people of New Zealand and comprise about 15% of the population (Statistics New Zealand 2001). 'Pākehā' is a Māori word used widely in New Zealand to refer to people of European (mainly British) descent.

Holmes and Stubbe (2003). Reviewing our dataset, we found that we had audio and video recordings of meetings of two remarkably parallel work groups within one government department, often discussing the same business agenda. In both groups, only women were present. In one group, all the women were Māori, and their conversations are referred to below as those of the Māori group. The other group included one Māori woman and one Cook Island woman, while the rest were Pākehā. We refer to this group as the Pākehā group, since it was predominantly Pākehā in composition and unquestionably Pākehā in meeting style (Kell et al. 2007). The examples discussed are selected from the recordings of more than one meeting of each group. In each meeting, there were generally between seven and eleven women present. One example is also drawn from an informal conversation involving four women from the Pākehā group.

The analysis focuses on successful humor: humorous utterances are those for which we as analysts can point to paralinguistic, prosodic and discoursal evidence to support the interpretation that they were intended by the speaker(s) to be funny, and perceived to be amusing by at least some of the participants (Hay 2001). Humor is considered to have failed if no-one indicates that they have found it funny, even if the person making the joke intended to be amusing. More problematic aspects of what constitutes humor are discussed by various researchers including Hay (1996), Holmes (2000) and Holmes and Marra (2002b). See also Mullany (2007: 88).

3. Intergroup theory and boundary-marking humor

Individuals are typically concurrently members of a number of different identity groups. One way of theorizing this complexity is provided by Tajfel's Intergroup Theory and the related concept of social identity. At the heart of intergroup theory lies 'positive ingroup distinctiveness' whereby individuals categorize themselves in their interactions as 'belonging' to a particular group (Tajfel 1974, 1978, 1982; Tajfel and Turner 1979). Tajfel's model highlights the psychological importance of social categories, and emphasizes the individual's orientation to their in-group rather than outsiders, whether the relevant boundaries involve institutions, gender, or ethnicity. Boundary-marking humor may construct and reinforce in-group cohesion, while also providing a strategy for managing the tensions which inevitably arise in intergroup interaction.

Building on Tajfel's concepts, Meyerhoff and Niedzielski (1994) proposed that individual identity might be conceived as a complex of interacting aspects of different group or social identities (see also Meyerhoff 1998). In any interaction, they suggest, while all facets of an individual's social identity are potentially relevant resources, individuals tend to present or focus on particular aspects, sometimes emphasizing gender, sometimes ethnicity, sometimes power, authority or professional status, and sometimes organisational or institutional identity. Moreover, these different identities are constantly in flux:

> The personal and group identities which make up an individual's persona are not static, but rather can be activated or called on to different degrees depending on the situation. (Meyerhoff and Niedzielski 1994: 319).

They propose that individuals draw on different aspects of their social identity in different interactions; different in-groups and out-groups may be brought into focus in different contexts, or even at different points in the same interaction. Hence, individuals and groups can be regarded as constantly engaged in the process of constructing aspects of interpersonal and intergroup identity.

This provides a useful framework for our discussion of boundary-marking humor. Individuals shape and re-shape identity through their workplace talk (Dyer and Keller-Cohen 2000; Mullany 2007), and humor is a flexible discourse strategy which can be manipulated in a wide variety of ways. As we demonstrate in the next section, in response to specific aspects of the on-going interaction, individuals may use humor to highlight their organizational responsibilities at one moment, to focus on their femininity at another, and to draw attention to ethnicity at yet another point. The point of reference is constantly shifting.

4. Analysis

In this section, we examine the ways in which humor is used to mark group boundaries in the workplace talk of the two selected groups, namely the Māori group and the Pākehā group, within the same government department. The analysis indicates how humor contributes to the construction of different facets of social identity (professional, gender, ethnic) whilst also reinforcing group norms and values. Boundary-marking humor makes it clear where salient group boundaries are drawn. At the same time, such humor may subvert and challenge the status quo, making fun of out-group norms and values or conventional stereotypes (Holmes and Hay 1997). The examples which follow illustrate these points.

4.1 Institutional boundary-marking

We begin by examining two examples where the intergroup boundary is drawn between the department as a whole and the wider public service of which it is a part. Hence in these examples, the two groups orient similarly to the out-group, positioning themselves as a beleaguered in-group being persecuted by the demands of an officious out-group. This orientation is particularly clear in these examples, since although the excerpts occur in different meetings, both groups are responding to precisely the same issue. And they both make use of boundary-marking humor to do so.

In Example 1, the group of Māori women is discussing the impact that a government-wide change in procedure will have on their day-to-day work. Genevieve has been reporting back to the group on what was said at an information seminar, during which it became clear to her that a newly implemented change in procedures will bring forward a daily work deadline, creating a serious time-squeeze. Transcription conventions can be found in the appendix.

(1) (Māori Group)
    1   Genevieve: … as Fred Jeffries was saying by the time it gets to
    2   actually on my desk it'll probably be quarter to twelve
    3   Hera: [laughs]
    4   Genevieve: and he was like [rolls her eyes and raises her face] +
    5   Tracey: yeah (and it'll) probably need to be reviewed //(   )\
    6   Hera: /I might\\ miss it when I'm in the toilet [laughs]
    7   [laughter]

As Genevieve unfolds the likely scenario that they will be required to turn the work around within minutes instead of the hours that were previously available, Hera, the manager, laughs cynically (line 3). Encouraged by Hera's laughter, Genevieve then mimics the exasperated gesture made by the speaker at the seminar, another public servant. Tracey does not respond with a supporting laugh, but with the anxious observation that getting the work done involves review (line 5), implying that this will add to the timing problem. The finished task (a draft reply to a Question in Parliament) also needs approval by the manager before it can be sent, which underpins Hera's joke *I might miss it when I'm in the toilet* (line 6), as if only a few seconds would be left for her to fulfill this responsibility at the end of the process. Tracey then joins in with the general laughter that follows Hera's witty line (line 7). Hera's use of humor could be interpreted as effectively reassuring her staff that even though they have no power to alter this rule change, they are together in this, and will manage somehow. Hera identifies with her team and not those making the demands; her use of humor builds solidarity.

Although this is a meeting of Māori women, there is nothing here to indicate a general sense of difference from the dominant Pākehā culture. The example contains no explicit linguistic indication that the participants are Māori. The focus of the humor is entirely on the boundary between the in-group they form as members of a government department and the out-group who is imposing change on them.

Example 2 shows that the women in the Pākehā meeting respond to this very same issue in a very similar way – by using boundary-marking humor. Grace has attended the same information seminar on behalf of the Pākehā group, and at this point has told the others about the new deadlines. Ruth, the manager, also knows the details and she is helping to explain.

(2)   (Pākehā Group)
1	Ruth:	and then they get but they get edited those questions
2		get edited they're probably not at a minister's office
3		till about eleven fifteen
4	Grace:	mm
5	Ruth:	which means you've probably er in reality
6		only got about an hour to turn it around
7	XF:	mm
8	Grace:	yes there was some comment that at our seminar
9		that there seems to be an awful lot of attention paid
10		to revising the standing orders that the MPs were
11		going to use to give them plenty of time but not
12		//[laughs]: the ones that the public servants: were\
13		going to have to use
13	XF:	/[laughs]\\
14		[laughter]

The group gradually realizes that the time for this task is going to be much shorter than formerly available, and this obviously causes some anxiety. In this meeting it is Grace who provides the humor which triggers the laughter, and relieves the tension. She reports for the amusement of her colleagues a cynical observation which pointed to the difference in the impact of the revision of the new procedures for the MPs (Members of Parliament), which *give them plenty of time* (line 11), as opposed to their impact on the people who will be doing the work. Her laughter as she makes this contribution indicates that she considers it amusing.

In the meetings of both groups, then, the same joke is made about the less powerful position of this small government department, in relation to the greater dominance of the wider public service. In these examples, both groups position themselves similarly, as members of the same in-group in relation to external institutional forces.

4.2   Gender boundary-marking

The second type of boundary-marking humor which occurs in these meetings is oriented to gender. Examples 3 and 4 illustrate boundary-marking humor which uses parody of one's own group for humorous effect, exemplifying one way of joking about gender differences. The comments on appearance in both examples can be instantly decoded by all of the women present as referring to the conventional stereotype of women as constantly preoccupied by their appearance.

In Example 3, people are arriving at the start of the meeting. Hera comments that Ella isn't there. Because the meeting is being videoed Ripeka suggests that Ella is putting lipstick on (for the camera). She then develops this further by referring to false eyelashes (line 3).

> (3) (Māori group)
> 1   Hera: Ella isn't here
> 2   Ripeka: Ella Ella she's putting her lipstick on ++
> 3   [dramatically]: I'll get my eyelash: [laughs]
> 4   [laughter]

In Example 4, the group's talk is anticipating their next meeting being videoed. Until now the meetings have only been audio-taped.

> (4) (Pākehā group)
> 1   Ruth: … whether we'd like to have that meeting videotaped
> 2   Barbara: well that's good that's //given us lots\ of warning
> 3   Leigh: /doesn't worry me\\
> 4   Kelly: that's //right we can get our hair [laughs] done\
> 5   Stacey: /[laughs]\\
> 6   Kelly: [drawls]: and: you //know er you know\
> 7   Barbara: /get our hair cut\\
> 8   Stacey: //[laughs]\
> 9   Barbara: /buy a new wardrobe\\ [laughs]

It is not clear whether Barbara's observation that *lots of warning* (line 2) has been given before the meeting will be videoed is intended to be funny, but Kelly exploits the possibility by suggesting *we can get our hair done* (line 4). Her drawly delivery suggests she is looking for other things to add (line 6). Barbara obliges, picking up the idea *get our hair cut* (line 7) and adding *buy a new wardrobe* (line 9). Barbara has supported Kelly's humor by contributing more humor (Hay 2001: 60–62).

It is worth noting the normatively feminine interactional style used by the women in Example 4 on a stereotypically feminine topic. Whereas elsewhere in their meetings (see Kell et al. 2007), these women often adhere to the one-at-a-time (OAAT) rules of formal interaction normatively associated with men's talk (Coates 2003), here they exploit the all-together-now (ATN) conventions associated with women's talk (Coates 1996).

Example 5 exemplifies another way of joking about gender differences, this time male symbols and values are parodied. Example 5 comes from an informal interaction between four of the women from the Pākehā group (including the Cook Island woman). Ellen and Nell had seen some overseas male ambassadors the day before standing by a BMW car with some golf clubs. Ellen has recounted this story to Carole and Katie earlier in the interaction. Example 5 comes later in the meeting after they have been discussing a visit Katie had from an occupational health and safety nurse who had been assessing her workstation. They are referring to Nell's office chair.

(5)	(Pākehā group)	
1	Ellen:	I like your chair
2	Nell:	yes I do too …
3	Carole:	… aspirations for //c[hief] e[xecutive] got the chair
4		next\ step the job
5	Nell:	/aspirations for c[hief] e[xecutive]\\
6	Nell:	[laughs]: ne- //next step: the\ the ( ) [laughs]
7	Katie:	/[laughs]\\
8	Katie:	what you need is golf clubs though
9	Ellen:	yeah you gotta have a BMW and some golf clubs
10	Nell:	oh no we're working on the BMW
11		even if it is rented for a week [laughs]

Carole sets the humorous tone by joking that Nell has "aspirations for chief executive" because she has been given a fancy office chair (line 3–4). Nell supports Carole's humor here by echoing her words (line 5) (Hay 2001) and then extends the humor (line 6). The women collaboratively build on this, and the excerpt is normatively feminine in discursive style; this is classic cooperative humor expressed in a collaborative style (Holmes 2006). The women build on and support each other's comments, lexically and prosodically repeating and echoing the previous suggestions. They bring in status symbols strongly associated with male power and wealth, such as golf clubs and driving a BMW car. Katie introduces this aspect of the humor by suggesting *what you need is golf clubs* (line 8). Ellen expands on the suggestion *you gotta have a BMW and some golf clubs* (line 9). Nell then reinforces the humor with her suggestion that the only way they could afford this would be to rent the BMW *for a week* (line 10–11). This is gendered talk i.e., feminine in style, making a point about women's ways of behaving compared to men's. The male symbols become objects of derision and satire and so the women distance themselves from rich and powerful men.

4.3   Ethnic boundary-marking

An added facet of their identity which the Māori group mark with humor is their ethnicity. On a number of occasions, the Māori women use humor oriented to ethnicity, in a way characteristic of Māori speakers of New Zealand English described in earlier research, reflecting Māori participants' sensitivity to potentially discriminatory behaviors, and their awareness of the pervasiveness of unequal treatment

(Holmes and Hay 1997). Example 6 illustrates this well. The issue being discussed at the start is not one which relates specifically to Māori. The group is discussing the lack of progress on an issue that they acknowledge is beset with political tensions.

(6) (Māori group)
    1 Tracey: it's always been like that though eh ( )
    2   //I don't know\ how many reviews there's been
    3 Hera: /it's a political issue\\
    4 Ripeka: just like the Māoris
    5   [*people smile and look amused*]
    6 Hera: it's a political issue not a not an issue
    7   it's not it's not it's got nothing to do with logic
    8 Tracey: no

In lines 1–2 Tracey refers to a situation they have been discussing which keeps surfacing and attracting criticism. The standard political response in such a situation is to set up a review. Hence her comment *I don't know how many reviews there's been* (line 2). Hera makes the point quite explicit *it's a political issue* (line 3), implying that the lack of progress has nothing to do with logic, a point she spells out explicitly in lines 6–7. In between these comments Ripeka inserts an ironic remark *just like the Māoris* (line 4), drawing on a familiar negative stereotype of Māori interactional style in which, in the New Zealand popular imagination, political tension and fractious argument are considered to be major features. Another feature of the stereotype, which may also be relevant, is the (from a prejudiced Pākehā perspective) repeated iterations of politically-motivated argument which characterize Māori political speeches. All these negative allusions can be derived without any effort by the women at the meeting for whom such a remark serves as a compressed shorthand for the dominant group's predictable prejudices about Māori behavior.

Although there is no explicit laughter, looks of amusement are clearly visible on the video. Ripeka's humor clearly emphasizes the boundary between Māori and Pākehā. This is a good example of a remark which is perfectly acceptable when made by a Māori among other Māori, where it clearly signals in-group solidarity and shared knowledge of damaging racist stereotypes. Uttered by a non-Māori person in the same context, it would almost certainly be interpreted as insulting and racist, no matter how sympathetic the speaker was known to be to Māoridom.

A second example of ethnically-oriented boundary-marking humor occurs when Ripeka refers to a South African person she had spoken to. In this example the boundaries constructed are more complex, and the humor draws on a positive view of Māori rather than a negative stereotype. Ripeka is telling the group how she discovered that the person she was speaking to on the phone was a South African man.

(7)   (Māori group)

1	Ripeka:	Hera gave me contacts over in in [department]
2		and I finally got a South African guy
3	Hera:	[laughs] //[laughs]\
4	Ripeka:	/[clears throat] I don't know whether he's the same colour but
5		he's South African\\ a South African chap in [department]
6	Ella:	for what?
7	Ripeka:	to to to talk with about [topic] ...
8		Brad Bayford I said oh [Māori]: kia ora: I know some Bayfords
9		he says //( )\ I'm from South Africa
10	Ella:	/[laughs]\\
11	Ripeka:	I said oh
12		[laughter]
13	Ripeka:	I'll just say are you the right colour
14		but the wrong tribe but I didn't say that
15	Ella:	[laughs]

Ripeka reports how she contacted the guy and greeted him in Māori *kia ora* (line 8) and then said that she knew some people with the same name as his. This is standard Māori greeting style, namely a greeting formula followed by an attempt to establish links by identifying a person's family connections, tribal affiliations, tribal area and so on. She is clearly somewhat taken aback when he tells her he is South African as evidenced by her response *I said oh* (line 11), uttered in a surprised and somewhat disappointed tone which elicits laughter from others (lines 12). She then goes on to develop the humor by reporting what she thought in response to this information, *are you the right colour but the wrong tribe* (lines 13–14). Though introduced with *I'll just say*, this is subsequently qualified with the information that she didn't actually say it (line 14).

The humor here rests on Ripeka paying the South African man the compliment of including him in her in-group. Since Ripeka thinks he may be non-white *the same colour* (line 4) and subsequently *the right colour* (line 13), he is, Ripeka implies, like all Māori, part of a much wider in-group of people who are not white. This is the first layer of meaning; Ripeka's joke draws a boundary between white and non-white and includes the South African man in it.

Clearly, however, the man is not part of all possible in-groups for Ripeka. While the obvious distinction is gender, Ripeka's humor is all the more effective because it focuses on the less expected boundary of tribal affiliation. Here *the wrong tribe* (line 14) clearly means 'not Māori'. Ripeka's humor here draws a boundary between non-white Māori and non-white non-Māori.

Interestingly here, both categories, *right colour* and *wrong tribe*, refer to non-dominant groups. The South African shares with the Māori women in the workplace the status of being less dominant and less powerful than members of the white, dominant, Pākehā culture in New Zealand. And even though he is not Māori, the fact that Ripeka refers to his *tribe* indicates another level of affiliation; the word *tribe* underlines the fact that he is different from the dominant Pākehā group.

5.   Discussion

The examples discussed in the previous section provide interesting evidence that individuals simultaneously enact different aspects of their social identity, and that even with the same group of people in the same context, such as a formal meeting, people orient to a diverse range of dimensions of identity. More specifically, the examples illustrate how simultaneous membership of more than one subordinate group provides a range of opportunities for individuals to contribute rapport-enhancing, boundary-marking humorous utterances to workplace discourse.

In Examples 1 and 2, the women in both the Māori and Pākehā groups orient to the same boundary. Both groups respond wryly, with a humorous tone, to their lack of power as employees in a relatively small government department, in relation to the authority of the wider public service. The rules have changed without consultation and as a relatively powerless pawn in the game, their department will simply have to comply. The focus of the boundary marking humor here is not gender or ethnicity, but rather the institutional demarcations which lie at the heart of the power difference.

Examples 3, 4 and 5 illustrate moments in their meetings when the focus of the women's humor shifts to gender, and they joke about the predicament of being a woman in a man's world. These examples exploit masculine and feminine stereotypes both in content and style. Through their parodic humor in Examples 3 and 4, they indicate their awareness of how women are stereotypically perceived in this world – as consumed by their appearance rather than by serious workplace issues. They also parody men in Example 5, with their derision of male symbols of power and status. Thus they use humor to handle the complexities of daily workplace interaction and especially the challenge of constructing an acceptable gender identity in the male-dominated world of work.

Examples 6 and 7 illustrate moments in the meetings when the focus of the Māori women's humor shifts to ethnicity. The humor in these examples is about their membership of the group of all-Māori, both within and beyond this workplace. For this group, in these particular examples, all Māori count as insiders while all non-Māori are outsiders. The examples exploit both negative and positive stereotypes of Māori, with Example 6 looking from the outside in and drawing on majority group negative stereotypes of Māori, while Example 7 looks from the inside out, representing Māori tribal membership as a desirable affiliation. The Māori women exploit the potential of their distinctive minority identity within a wider Pākehā system, using humor to affirm their cultural identity as Māori, and to draw a firm boundary between themselves and the powerful non-Māori 'others'.

By contrast, there are no such examples, nor even a hint of humor in the Pākehā meetings referring to their position as members of the dominant culture. As noted in Holmes and Hay:

> Minority groups are much more sensitive to areas of difference between their norms and those of other groups than are those in power. Powerful groups take their norms for granted; they are given, assumed, unquestioned and even unconscious. Members of minority groups are generally much more attuned to areas of cultural difference between their own patterns of interaction and those of the majority group. (Holmes and Hay 1997: 135).

Consequently, minority or marginalized groups tend to use boundary-marking humor oriented to their point of difference more often than do dominant or powerful groups. Our analysis of the humor in these meetings certainly supports these observations, since the Pākehā meetings included not a single example of boundary-marking humor along ethnic lines.

6.   Conclusion

Drawing on recorded workplace meetings of Māori and Pākehā women in one New Zealand government department, this paper has illustrated some of the complexities of boundary-marking humor. The analysis has demonstrated that boundary-marking humor is a versatile tool in the construction of different dimensions of social identity, in constructing collegial workplace relations, and in maintaining close-knit work teams.

This analysis has illustrated some of the diverse ways in which boundary-marking humor is used at different moments in meetings, to create rapport with different in-groups, and position a group in relation to a range of out-groups. The dynamic flux of talk allows different positions to be taken at different times; different aspects of social identity come to the fore at different moments. The definition of the relevant in-group and out-group differs not only from situation to situation, but even within one situation at different moments. This constantly changing positioning is evident in all talk, though we are not always aware of it, especially when the boundaries involved are ones we take for granted.

Finally, the analysis has suggested that multiple aspects of individual identity, in particular simultaneous membership of more than one subordinate group, expands the range of opportunities for individuals to contribute rapport-enhancing, boundary-marking humorous utterances to mundane, primarily transactionally-oriented workplace discourse. Boundary-marking humor is a means of creating, maintaining and reinforcing facets of an individual's social identity, and it is also a means of constructing and sustaining membership of particular workplace teams, and communities of practice, and reinforcing particular cultural values.

Appendix – Transcription conventions

[laughs]	Paralinguistic features in square brackets
+	Pause up to one second
-	Incomplete or cut-off utterance
... // ..... \ ...	
... / ..... \\ ...	Simultaneous speech
( )	Unclear utterance
(hello)	Transcriber's best guess at an unclear utterance
?	Rising or question intonation
...	Section of transcript omitted

All names are pseudonyms.

References

Archakis, Argiris & Tsakona, Villy. 2005. "Analyzing conversational data in GTVH terms: A new approach to the issue of identity construction via humor." *Humor* 18(1): 41–68.

Benton, Richard A. 1991. *The Māori Language: Dying or Reviving*. Wellington: NZCER.

Boxer, Diana & Cortés-Conde, Florencia. 1997. "From bonding to biting: Conversational joking and identity display." *Journal of Pragmatics* 27(3): 275–294.

Coates, Jennifer. 1996. *Women Talk*. Oxford: Blackwell.

Coates, Jennifer. 2003. *Women, Men and Language* (2nd Edn). London: Longman.

Davies, Christie. 1982. "Ethnic jokes, moral values and social boundaries." *British Journal of Sociology* 33(3): 383–403.

Davies, Christie. 1990. *Ethnic Humor Around the World*. Bloomington/Indianapolis: Indiana University Press.

Duncan, W.J. 1985. "The superiority theory of humour at work: Joking relationships as indicators of formal and informal status patterns in small task-oriented groups." *Small Group Behaviour* 16(4): 556–64.

Dyer, Judy & Keller-Cohen, Deborah. 2000. "The discursive construction of professional self through narratives of personal experience." *Discourse Studies* 2(3): 283–304.

Fine, Gary Alan & De Soucey, Michaela. 2005. "Joking cultures: Humor themes as social regulation in group life." *Humor* 18(1): 1–22.

Grainger, Karen. 2004. "Verbal play on the hospital ward: Solidarity or power?" *Multilingua* 23(1): 39–59.

Hay, Jennifer. 1996. "No laughing matter: gender and humour support strategies." *Wellington Working Papers in Linguistics* 8: 1–24.

Hay, Jennifer. 2001. "The pragmatics of humor support." *Humor* 14(1): 55–82.

Holmes, Janet. 2000. "Politeness, power and provocation: How humour functions in the workplace." *Discourse Studies* 2(2): 159–185.

Holmes, Janet. 2006. "Sharing a laugh: Pragmatic aspects of humor and gender in the workplace." *Journal of Pragmatics* 38(1): 26–50.

Holmes, Janet & Hay, Jennifer. 1997. "Humour as an ethnic boundary marker in New Zealand interaction." *Journal of Intercultural Studies* 18(2): 127–151.

Holmes, Janet & Marra, Meredith. 2002a. "Humour as a discursive boundary marker in social interaction." In *Us and Others: Social Identities Across Languages, Discourses and Cultures*, Anna Duszak (Ed.), 377–400. Amsterdam: Benjamins.

Holmes, Janet & Marra, Meredith. 2002b. "Over the edge? Subversive humor between colleagues and friends." *Humor* 15(1): 65–87.

Holmes, Janet & Stubbe, Maria. 2003. *Power and Politeness in the Workplace. A Sociolinguistic Analysis of Talk at Work*. London: Longman.

Holmes, Janet, Stubbe, Maria & Marra, Meredith. 2003. "Language, humour and ethnic identity marking in New Zealand English." In *The Politics of English as a World Language*, Christian Mair (Ed.), 431–455. Amsterdam: Rodopi.

Kell, Susan, Marra, Meredith, Holmes, Janet & Vine, Bernadette. 2007. "Ethnic differences in the dynamics of women's work meetings." *Multilingua* 26(4): 309–331.

Limon, J. 1977. "Agringado joking in Texas Mexican society." *New Scholar* 6: 33–50.

Meyerhoff, Miriam. 1998. "Accommodating your data: The use and misuse of accommodation theory in sociolinguistics." *Language and Communication* 18: 205–225.

Meyerhoff, Miriam & Niedzielski, Nancy. 1994. "Resistance to creolization: An interpersonal and intergroup account." *Language and Communication* 14(4): 313–330.

Mullany, Louise. 2007. *Gendered Discourse in the Professional Workplace*. London: Palgrave Macmillan.

Norrick, Neal R. 1993. *Conversational Joking. Humor in Everyday Talk*. Bloomington: Indiana University Press.

O'Quin, K. & Aronoff, J. 1981. "Humor as a technique of social influence." *Social Psychology Quarterly* 44: 349–57.

Pratt, Steven B. 1998. "Razzing: Ritualised uses of humor." In *Communication and Identity Across Cultures*, Dolores V. Tanno & Alberto Gonzalez (Eds), 56–79. Thousand Oaks, London: Sage.

Rogerson-Revell, Pamela. 2007. "Humour in business: A double-edged sword. A study of humour and style shifting in intercultural business meetings." *Journal of Pragmatics* 39(1): 4–28.

Spencer-Oatey, Helen (Ed.). 2008. *Culturally Speaking: Managing Talk through Rapport Across Cultures* (2nd Edn). London: Continuum.

Statistics New Zealand. 2001. *2001 Census of Population and Dwellings: Results*. Wellington, Statistics New Zealand.

Stubbe, Maria & Holmes, Janet. 2000. "Talking Māori or Pākehā in English: Signalling identity in discourse." In *New Zealand English*, Allan Bell & Koenraad Kuiper (Eds), 249–278. Wellington: Victoria University Press.

Tajfel, Henri. 1974. "Social identity and intergroup behaviour." *Social Science Information* 13: 65–93.

Tajfel, Henri. (Ed.). 1978. *Differentiation between Social Groups: Studies in the Social Psychology of Intergroup Relations*. London: Academic Press.

Tajfel, Henri. 1982. "Social psychology of intergroup relations." *Annual Review of Psychology* 33: 1–39.

Tajfel, Henri & Turner, John C. 1979. "An integrative theory of intergroup conflict." In *The Social Psychology of Intergroup Relations*, William G. Austin & Stephen Worchel (Eds), 33–47. Monterey, CA: Brooks-Cole.

Ziv, Avner. 1988. *National Styles of Humor*. Westport, CN: Greenwood Press.

PART III

Failed humor and its interactional effects

Impolite responses to failed humor

Nancy D. Bell

The data discussed in this paper come from a larger project designed to address the neglected area of failed humor. A corpus of 207 elicited responses to failed humor was collected. The focus here is on the 44% that were coded as impolite. Findings show that most responses attacked the speaker using offensive, positive impoliteness strategies. Given that failing at humor is already humiliating, why might these interlocutors have opted to further punish the tellers with aggravated face attacks? Four somewhat overlapping reasons are suggested: the disruptive nature of humor, the expectations hearers held of the teller's behavior, the characteristics of the study participants, and the identity concerns or face claims of the hearer.

1. Introduction

Until relatively recently, psychologists and philosophers could claim humor studies almost exclusively; however, the past 15 years or so have seen growing interest in this topic from linguists. In particular, sociolinguistic investigations of humor have revealed a great deal about how humor functions in everyday interaction. Current research has tended to focus on the forms, functions, and negotiation of humor in local contexts. Generally implicit in these studies is the idea that the humor has succeeded; that is, it has been found funny by at least some participants. Attardo (2005; see also Palmer 1994: Part IV) notes the examination of failed humor as an important gap in current research, observing that "most analysts merely ignore the issue or when they are aware of it, dismiss it for simplicity's sake (cf. Holmes 2000: 163)." Some studies, such as Hay (1994) and Norrick (1993), deal with specific instances of failed humor as they arise; however, broad, systematic investigations of failed humor are lacking (see, however, Bell in press, Eisterhold 2007). Yet, a complete theory of humor must also take into account its failure. Thus, the present study begins to address this neglected area through an examination of responses to failed humor.

In American society, having a good sense of humor is generally seen as a positive trait. In surveys asking about important qualities in a friend or spouse, Americans consistently place a good sense of humor as the first or second most desirable quality (Maritz Ameripoll 1999, Roper's Public Pulse 1998, The Roper Center for Public Opinion Research 1993). Humor is so highly valued that even politi-cians, whom we might expect to avoid humor while operating in their professional capacity, often joke in both formal and informal contexts, with some even employ-ing joke-writers. Given this positive valuation, failing at humor can be seen as a serious face threat. In fact, I recently witnessed how a woman changed seats on the bus after her attempt to amuse her seatmate, a stranger, failed miserably. As most people have experienced the embarrassment and humiliation that follow such an occurrence, we might expect to see interlocutors responding to unamusing jokes with positive politeness strategies (Brown and Levinson 1987) in an effort to mini-mize the teller's humiliation. Yet, as the data I present here will demonstrate, this is frequently not the case. Instead, individuals were subjected to firm rebukes after having shared a joke that did not amuse their interlocutors. In order to examine these responses I draw on recent research on (im)politeness theories, with a focus on the work of Helen Spencer-Oatey.

2.   Background

2.1   (Im)politeness theory

Despite the strength of Brown and Levinson's (1987) work on face and politeness, it has been subject to a great deal of criticism (e.g., Eelen 2001; Watts 2003: Chapter 4). Current promising approaches that build on this work see (im)politeness as an interactional phenomenon, grounded in the dynamic, situated, and *value-laden* interpretations and negotiations that occur between interlocutors within a given context. Thus, utterances are no longer seen as inherently polite or impolite, rather these assessments are judgments made based on community norms (e.g., Fraser and Nolen 1981; Holmes 1995; Spencer-Oatey 2000, 2005; Watts 2003; Locher 2004; Locher and Watts 2005, Mills 2005). Current definitions reflect this emic shift. Spencer-Oatey (2005: 97), for example, defines (im)politeness as "the subjective judgments people make about the social appropriateness of verbal and non-verbal behavior." Similarly, Locher and Watts (2005: 10) see politeness as "a discursive concept arising out of interactants' perceptions and judgments of their own and others' verbal behavior." Such definitions situate analysis in interaction, and, by focusing on judgments, open analysis to include those often neglected occasions on which interlocutors do not treat each other nicely.

Spencer-Oatey's (2000, 2002) discussion of rapport management is one exam-ple of these reconceptions, and has led to a more culturally sensitive and theo-retically sophisticated approach to (im)politeness phenomena. She sees rapport management as "the use of language to promote, maintain, or threaten harmonious social relations" (2000: 3). As described above, this is not a one-sided endeavor, as any such linguistic behavior is judged by all interlocutors, which highlights the co-constructed nature of (im)politeness. Building on this earlier work, Spencer-Oatey (2005: 98) identifies behavioral expectations as the primary source of our judgments regarding appropriacy. These expectations, in turn, are based on contractual/legal requirements, role specifications, behavioral conventions, and interactional principles. The latter three are of particular interest here in understanding how people perceive attempts at humor as unamusing and how they frame their subsequent response. With regard to role specifications, the types of humor that are appropriate vary according to the teller. For example, riddles are not normally shared between adults in the U.S., and such humor will likely be judged quite differently than if it were told by a child. Behavioral norms can influence, for example, whether humor is even acceptable within a certain context, or what type of humor is appropriate. In some communities, canned jokes are a common genre, whereas in others this type of behavior will be seen as juvenile and spontaneous humor will be valued. Finally, Spencer-Oatey likens interactional norms to conversational maxims, but stresses their link to personal and community values. She proposes the association principle as one guide to interactional norms: "people have a fundamental belief that they are entitled to an association with others that is in keeping with the type of relationship that they have with them" (2005: 100). This principle is made up of components of involvement, empathy, and respect.

Face, too, in these discussions moves from being conceived of as a primarily individual trait to a social one (Arundale 2006). Spencer-Oatey (2007) ties the concept of face closely to identity. In contrast to Brown and Levinson's (1987) fairly static conception of positive and negative face, both face and identity are related to self-image; however, face is restricted to those aspects of a person's personality that she or he values positively and wishes others to do so as well. A relevant example here would be the quality 'good sense of humor'. The speaker who wishes to be seen as someone with such a trait will perceive a face threat or loss when his or her joke is not appreciated. Similarly, Spencer-Oatey (2007) points out that the ascription of a quality with which an individual does not want to be associated, such as a 'bad sense of humor', will also impinge on his or her face. Because people will value different qualities differently across different contexts, face must be seen as a dynamic notion and can only be assessed interactively.

Spencer-Oatey's use of the term rapport management encompasses all types of behavior, including those which are perceived as rude or inappropriate. Some scholars, however, have focused specifically on impoliteness. Beebe (1995), for example, showed how rude behavior is no accident, but rather, as part of our pragmatic competence, face attacks can be carefully constructed to achieve certain goals. Kienpointner (1997: 251), too, questions the emphasis researchers have placed on polite behavior and suggests that, far from being viewed as "the marked, abnormal, and irrational counterpart of politeness," both politeness and impoliteness exist together on a continuum of more or less cooperative behavior. Similarly, Locher and Watts (2005) emphasize the equal importance of impolite talk in the construction of relationships, and note that assessments of verbal behavior go well beyond the binary polite/impolite. Instead, like Kienpointner (1997), they see a continuum, on which 'rudeness' is one type of negatively marked behavior that can be perceived as impolite, non-politic, or inappropriate.

The theoretical perspectives discussed thus far emphasize that politeness is a value-laden perception and that the interpretation of an utterance as polite or rude is co-constructed by interlocutors. Such views imply that the phenomenon would best be investigated in its context, suggesting that audio or video taped interaction should be used to gain a rich understanding of the ways that failed humor is negotiated by interlocutors. Such a close examination is indeed advisable; however humor does not fail so regularly as to make the creation of a good-sized corpus from tapes feasible. In such cases, elicitation and field notes are often used in order to obtain a data set more quickly, as for the present study. This method results in the loss of the kind of nuanced information obtained from recordings (e.g., paralinguistic cues, extended turns at talk) and must also be analyzed accordingly. For this reason, although Spencer-Oatey's views on (im)politeness reflect my own theoretical preference, for this paper I have largely adopted Culpeper's (1996) work on impoliteness strategies in this analysis.

By inverting the four super-strategies in Brown and Levinson's (1987) politeness paradigm, Culpeper (1996) develops a framework specifically addressing impolite behavior. Briefly, for Brown and Levinson, a bald on record formulation is the strategy used when the face threat is smallest, followed by positive politeness, negative politeness, and finally off-record strategies for those FTAs that are the most threatening. In contrast, Culpeper proposes bald on record *im*politeness for speakers wishing to attack their hearer's face with the most force. This super-strategy is followed by positive impoliteness and negative impoliteness, which, in keeping with Brown and Levinson, can each be used for slightly less aggressive face attacks. Positive impoliteness strategies are those that attack or impinge upon the other's desire to be liked and accepted, whereas negative impoliteness strategies affect the other's ability to act independently. Specific examples of the former cited by Culpeper include the use of taboo words and name-calling, attempts to disassociate from the other, snubbing or ignoring the other, or excluding the other through the use of in-group jargon or secretive language. As negative politeness strategies he suggests that speakers can frighten the other, condescend to the other, or invade the other's space. Finally, Culpeper proposes sarcasm or mock politeness as off-record super-strategies. Culpeper, Bousfield, and Wichmann (2003: 1562–1563) further develop this framework, noting that the strategies speakers use to counter a face attack fall broadly into the categories of offensive or defensive strategies. While these are not to be considered as mutually exclusive, offensive strategies counter a face attack with a face attack, whereas defensive strategies work to protect one's own face.

In responding to critiques to Culpeper's (1996) original formulation of the theory, Culpeper, Bousfield and Wichmann (2003) defend the need for such a theory, particularly from supporters of the Brown and Levinson framework, who would argue that impoliteness is already accounted for by the bald-on-record strategy. They emphasize and provide examples to illustrate that the strategies selected and the judgments that ensue from their use are highly dependent on the context. Despite this acknowledgement, a direct inversion of Brown and Levinson's politeness super-strategies runs the danger of suffering its same shortcomings, in particular that of viewing (im)politeness as encoded in language, rather than as negotiated by language users (see also, Mills 2005 for a discussion of problems with presenting impoliteness as the opposite of politeness). In keeping with the contextually sensitive approach to (im)politeness outlined above, Culpeper's proposed strategies should and in this paper will be used solely as a heuristic device for analysis.

2.2 Humor and rapport management

The role of humor in rapport management has historically been simplified. One line of thought with a long history (see Morreall 1983 for an overview), sees humor as largely aggressive. In this view, humor is thought to function as a socially acceptable means of expressing hostility and criticism. When some forms of humor, such as teasing, are directed at group members, they can often mask criticisms and thus function to regulate the behavior of members, or would-be members, as has been illustrated in numerous studies (e.g., Eder 1993; Jorgensen 1996; Yedes 1996; Goldberg 1997; Holmes and Marra 2002). Further empirical support has come from Sacks' (1974) analysis of the telling of a sexual joke by adolescents, which has given rise to the notion that humor is aggressive because it tests the hearer's knowledge. In addition, some types of humor, such as puns (Sherzer 1978) and canned jokes (Norrick 1993) can be viewed as aggressive in that they disrupt the flow of conversation. Norrick (1993) compares these forms to humorous narratives, noting that the latter fit in to the ongoing talk, rather than interrupt it.

On the other hand, humor has been seen as largely affiliative. Brown and Levinson (1987: 124), for example, describe joking solely as a positive politeness strategy, noting that humor builds on and exploits shared understandings, and can be used to mitigate face threats by making participants feel comfortable. This position, too, has received a great deal of support from empirical studies of humor (e.g.,

Basso 1979; Straehle 1993; Holmes and Marra 2006; Holmes 2007). With regard to the aggressive 'testing' function of humor, Norrick (1993: 109) argues that if any sort of testing is taking place it may be a check of "the audience's willingness to laugh about the subject matter in question." In this way, humor seems instead to be used more often as an opportunity to establish and maintain intimacy, which is revealed in the ways the people provide background information that may be necessary to interpret and appreciate the humor (Norrick 2003: 1342).

Thus, humor is, in fact, neither exclusively positive/mitigating nor aggressive. Its functions, to borrow the words Boxer and Cortés-Conde (1997) used to describe different types of teases, range from bonding, to slightly aggressive 'nipping', to harsh 'biting'. As with other utterances, the exact nature of any humorous utterance arises through the interplay of a variety of factors, including the genre of humor used, the context, and interlocutor factors, such as gender, ethnicity, and social relationship. Humor is constructed and understood interactively, and as sociolinguistic analyses of humor have multiplied, it has become increasingly apparent that its functions are locally negotiated (see, e.g., Norrick 1993; Kotthoff 1996; Holmes 2000). Thus, a full account of the pragmatics of humor must take into account both the speaker and the hearer.

While the joint *production* of humor has been attested to, responses have received less attention. Intuition suggests that laughter would be the expected, unmarked response to humor; however studies such as Hay's (2001) use of examples of naturally-occurring speech to illustrate the ways in which interlocutors support humor in conversation show that the range of options is actually quite broad. Interlocutors can, for example, show their appreciation by adding more humor, or by echoing the speaker's words. She also demonstrates that reactions to even failed humor are more varied than previously thought. Given the positive value placed on having a 'good' sense of humor, unappreciative hearers must acknowledge the attempt at humor, in order to present themselves as competent interlocutors, but can simultaneously show that they did not appreciate the humor. Fake laughter and groaning, as suggested by Sacks (1974), are commonly cited as possible ways of doing this (e.g., Chiaro 1992: 111; Norrick 1993: 123). Hay's (2001) research also showed that explicit statements of understanding and/or non-appreciation and ironic statements of enjoyment are common and, when the attempt at humor is very obvious, silence can be used to indicate lack of amusement.

In terms of politeness, failed humor is often discussed as face-threatening for the speaker, who risks embarrassment if the joke is not well-received; however, Zajdman (1995) points out the risk to the hearer, as well, given the dilemma described above in which he or she must demonstrate understanding while withholding appreciation. In light of Spencer-Oatey's (2007) discussion of face and identity we can expect face and identity consequences of being on the receiving end of a bad joke to go beyond the issue of getting the joke. Being selected as an appropriate audience for a stupid joke suggests that there is something amiss with the hearer's sense of humor. Described in terms of face/identity and rapport management, hearers of a bad joke make claims about their own competence in signaling their understanding of the joke. Their response to the would-be joker can orient toward that person's positive face needs, for example, by using laughter that is clearly polite rather than genuine or, at the other end of the continuum, as with the responses to be presented here, can attack the speaker, damaging his or her positive face, a response that simultaneously defends the hearer's face claims regarding his or her 'good' sense of humor.

Having made a case for the need to examine both (im)politeness and humor in their interactional contexts, I will now discuss the make-up and origins of my relatively decontextualized corpus of responses to failed humor.

3. Methods

Humor does not frequently fail in interaction, therefore it can be difficult to build a substantial corpus of instances for analysis. Because of this, I instead opted to expose individuals to humor that I hoped would not be funny, thus eliciting responses to failed humor.[1] The following joke was chosen because, for the largely middle-class communities in the U.S. where data was gathered, its form would be easily recognizable as an attempt at humor (a riddle), it would be unlikely to cause offense in any way (i.e., it is not racist or sexist), and it would be likely to fail (i.e., not be found amusing by the hearer):

> What did the big chimney say to the little chimney?
> Nothing. Chimneys can't talk.

This example had the additional advantage of being easily tailored to specific situations, making it possible to fit it naturally into the flow of conversation: What did the big [inanimate object X] say to the little [inanimate object X]? For example, if someone pointed out a new pair of shoes, this person could be presented with the riddle in this form: What did the big shoe say to the little shoe? Thus, natural responses to failed humor could be collected quickly and unobtrusively.

Data collection took place between March and October of 2007. In addition to my own efforts, both graduate and undergraduate students enrolled in sociolinguistics courses participated in the data collection. These students were provided

---

1. Many thanks to Salvatore Attardo whose idea it was to debase myself in this way.

with a handout, describing data collection procedures in detail. In addition, they participated in role-plays to practice judging whether or not to record the responses (since in some cases the joke met with an enthusiastic response) and how to record it when it indicated failure. Investigators told the joke, and upon receiving the response, recorded the exact words in writing as soon as was practicable. In addition, the participant's sex, relationship to the investigator, and approximate age were noted, in order to allow for a more detailed analysis of responses.

In total, 207 tokens were collected. Of these, 44% (n = 91) were classified as impolite following Culpeper (1996), who describes impoliteness as the use of strategies that "are oriented towards attacking face" and thus achieving "social disruption" (p. 350). What counts as a face attack depends on the particular community, and I did not have access to every community in which data was collected. Investigators usually noted when they interpreted an apparently appreciative response as merely 'polite', because otherwise the data might have been discarded as the humor would not appear to have failed. However, when responses openly evaluated the joke or the teller negatively, failure was clear, so there was no need to note whether the response was perceived as rude and aggressive, or simply as a normal mode of abuse between close friends. In order to account for this, I removed all responses that combined aggressive comments (e.g., "that's so stupid!" or "you asshole") with mitigating strategies, such as smiling or the use of terms that have largely negative denotations, but that tend to have neutral or even affectionate connotations (e.g., replace *stupid* with *silly*, or *asshole* with *dork*, above), thus placing them in the realm of "mock politeness" (Culpeper 1996: 352). I was left with a corpus of apparently impolite responses. Coding the data in this way is not ideal, given the emic perspective on impoliteness that I have already advocated, and leaves open the possibility that I have included examples that the participants would not have identified as impolite. At the same time, it seems necessary given the preliminary nature of the research, as well as the type of data. In addition, what is relevant in analyzing these responses is the previous turn, that is, the punch line of the joke. Following an important principle of conversation analysis, next turn validation, the joke-recipient's response is important in understanding her or his interpretation of the joke. In addition, as the data were elicited, the turn following the hearer's reaction to the joke would not be likely be useful for this study, as, in order to redress face loss, it was most probably an explanation that the joke was a homework assignment.

Data collectors ranged in age from 18 to mid-30s. In relation to their respondents, in the majority of instances (63), both participants were between 18 and 34 years old. In 18 examples ages ranged from 20 to late 80s, with more than 10 years disparity between the interlocutors. In just eight examples the participants were between ages 35 and 69, with no more than 10 years between them. Most examples were collected between friends (42) or family members (31), with 15 instances of data collection between acquaintances and one with a stranger. Thus, the majority of the data came from interaction with intimates, which was true for the larger corpus from which this subset was taken as well.

In general, the responses took the following forms:

> 13 = silence, non-verbal response only
> 21 = minimal responses (oh, okay, thanks)
> 55 = comments/questions denigrating the joke, the teller, or both

I relied on Culpeper (1996) as a heuristic for classifying the impoliteness strategies used in the responses, making modifications as required by the data. Thus, although I used Culpeper as starting point, much of the analysis was inductive and data-driven.

4.   Impoliteness strategies

Respondents made overwhelming use of offensive, positive impoliteness strategies. That is, their responses oriented almost exclusively toward attacking the speaker, rather than defending themselves, and these attacks aimed at social exclusion or humiliation of the speaker, rather than toward the use of tactics that might impinge on the speaker's ability to act freely. Below I describe the impoliteness strategies found in the data, using Culpeper's (1996) classification as a basis for organization. Of course, as discussed in the first section of this paper, impoliteness is a judgment, rather than a result of any particular utterance and thus its meaning can only be construed by examining it in its context. Because of this, some of Culpeper's strategies appear under different classifications here, many are not used, others that arose from my examination of the data have been added, and frequently multiple strategies will be observed in a single response. Indeed, Culpeper, Bousfield and Wichmann (2003: 1555) stress the preliminary nature of the framework, noting that they "make no claims about how the impoliteness superstrategies should be ordered for degree of offence, or about how hard-edged the distinctions are between them, and that it is evident that "some strategies can be mixed." This is apparent in Table 1, which summarizes the strategies used.

4.1   Positive impoliteness strategies

The most common positive impoliteness strategy that was found in the data was *make the other feel uncomfortable*. Frequently (n=41) interlocutors did this by ridiculing the joke-teller, the joke, or both. Culpeper (1996: 358) lists "condescend,

Table 1. Summary of impoliteness strategies

Positive Impoliteness Strategies (Total = 88)

- Make the other uncomfortable
  - Condescend, scorn or ridicule (S, the joke, or both): 41
  - Be silent: 12
  - Maintain excessive eye contact: 3
- Ignore, snub the other: 12
- Be disinterested, unconcerned, unsympathetic: 10
- Use taboo words: 7
- Disassociate from: 3

Negative Impoliteness Strategies (Total = 21)

- Challenge your interlocutor: 16
- Invade the other's space: 2
- Shout: 2
- Repeat: 1

Sarcasm/Mock Politeness: 11

Total strategies used: 120*

* This number exceeds the number of responses collected, as interlocutors frequently combined strategies.

scorn or ridicule" as a negative impoliteness strategy because he sees it as a way of emphasizing power differences between interlocutors. Here, however, in examples that were collected largely from family and friends, belittling the speaker could only result in humiliation (i.e., making him or her feel uncomfortable), rather than some real, physical consequence, therefore I have listed it as an example of this positive impoliteness strategy. The hearer could choose to ridicule the speaker, the joke, or both, as the following examples illustrate:

(1) Male friends, I (Investigator) = mid-30s, R (Respondent) = early 20s
     Response: hey! man. you're stupid.

(2) I = woman in her 40s; R = her mother, in her 80s
     Response: that is stupid!

(3) I = 21 year old male; R = his girlfriend, age 20
     Response: (hits investigator) THAT IS THE *WORST* JOKE! YOU *SUCK*! AHHH!

In Example 1, the teller is ridiculed as "stupid", while Example 2 ridicules the joke itself, using the same adjective. In the third example, both the joke and the teller are denigrated.

   Hearers can also make speakers uncomfortable by *being silent* (Culpeper 1996: 358). This occurred in 12 extracts, with two examples provided here. In the first, the only response is non-verbal:

(4)   I = male, early 20s; R = his wife, late 20s
        Response: (a very disapproving look)

Sometimes, too, the speaker could be made uncomfortable with silence which was eventually broken, here after a very long 10 seconds:

(5)   I = male, mid-20s; R = his wife, mid-20s
        Response: (10) that wasn't very good.

I see silence as different from 'snubbing', (see Examples 7 and 8 below), as the speaker is acknowledged in some way, usually through a facial expression or an eventual comment, rather than being completely ignored.

Culpeper (1996) lists the avoidance of eye contact as a negative impoliteness strategy, but does not mention the possibility of its opposite. In the data collected here, however, *excessive eye contact* emerged, in three instances, as another apparent means of making the other uncomfortable:

(6)   Male classmates, both in their 30s
        Response: helloooo! (staring at me!)

The discomfort this investigator felt is clear from the way that he recorded the response – with exclamation point! In all, the general strategy of making the other uncomfortable was employed 56 times.

The positive impoliteness strategy *ignore, snub the other* was found in 12 responses. The most common way that this was achieved was simply by looking away from the speaker:[2]

(7)   Female co-workers, both in their 20s
        Response: ugh. (looks away)

In this example, the respondent verbally expressed her disgust with the joke/teller before snubbing her. Sometimes, however, the speaker was not even addressed and more than once the interlocutor actually left the room:

(8)   Roommates, I = female, late 20s; R = male, early 30s
        Response: (turns head away and sighs, then walks away)

As noted by Hay (2001), not conveying recognition of a joke is a risky strategy for hearers, as lack of response might be equated with lack of understanding, and thus tends to be used only when the attempt at humor is very obvious, as is the case here.

---

2.   A few investigators also collected data during computer-mediated communication. Interestingly, this same effect was achieved through the use of emoticons:

Response: <.< (emote resembling a face looking away)

Some respondents (n=10) opted to *be disinterested, unconcerned, unsympathetic.* This was generally conveyed through minimal responses, such as the following:

(9)   Sorority sisters, early 20s
       Response: um, ok.

(10)   Classmates in their early 30s, I = female, R = male
       Response: oh. What are we doing after this?

These responses show some overlap with the previous strategy of snubbing, but their brief acknowledgement of the joke ensures that the teller knows that it has been heard, but not appreciated. In addition, the abrupt subject change in Example 10 further communicates the hearer's disinterest.

In seven instances respondents *use taboo words,* identified as a positive impoliteness strategy by Culpepper (1996: 358):

(11)   I = female, late 30s; R = her husband, mid-40s
       Response: oh shit.

(12)   Male friends in their early 20s
       Response: (punches me in the arm) fuck you.

In some cases the use of taboo words might be seen as an aggravator, available for use with any impoliteness strategy. In these examples, however, the absence of profanity would render these comments very benign (cf. "oh gosh.").

The final positive impoliteness strategy that occurred in this corpus was *disassociate from the other.* Culpeper (1996: 357) explains that this strategy might involve "deny[ing] association or common ground with the other." This may be an intention or result of some of the other strategies presented here, however below I provide one of the three instances in which this strategy was used explicitly:

(13)   Female friends, both 21
       Response: (shakes her head) what? Sometimes I think we have the same humor, but times like now I don't. Why was that supposed to be funny?

Here the respondent invokes a past feeling of closeness, but compares it to the present moment, clearly stating the distance she feels from the joke-teller. In addition, she challenges her interlocutor to explain why the joke was funny, a negative impoliteness strategy discussed in the next section.

4.2   Negative impoliteness strategies

The relative lack of negative politeness strategies in this corpus may be due to the egalitarian relationships that predominate. When both participants are on equal footing it is difficult for one to threaten the other with anything other than social exclusion, a positive impoliteness strategy. Still, some negative impoliteness strategies were employed by these interlocutors. The most common one (n=16), *challenge the other,* was added to the initial framework by Culpeper, Bousfield, and Wichmann (2003). In my data, as in theirs, challenges were done through the use of questions, often rhetorical questions, as seen in the previous example (13, above). In the next example the hearer pauses, employing a strategy to make the other uncomfortable, then implies uncertainty as to whether the punch line has been delivered:

> (14)   Male roommates in their early 20s
>   Response: (pause) is this where I laugh?

The next example manages to both challenge and ridicule the speaker, combining a positive and a negative impoliteness strategy in a single utterance:

> (15)   Sisters in their 20s
>   Response: why are you so stupid?

The impoliteness strategy *invade the other's space* occurred twice. In Examples (3) and (12) above, the investigator was punched by the hearer. Although this physical aggression did not result in injury, and likely had a playful element to it, in combination with the other strategies used it adds unmistakably to the rudeness of the response. Example (3) also illustrates an additional strategy noted in Culpeper (1996) as *shout*, and in Culpeper, Bousfield, and Wichmann (2003) as *invade auditory space*. This strategy was seen twice.

A final negative impoliteness strategy, *repetition* (from Culpeper, Bousfield and Wichmann 2003), occurred once in this data. In this extract the respondent imposes on the joke-teller's negative face by taking the floor and not allowing her to deliver her punch line – or at least not acknowledging it, thus also employing a snub:

> (16)   Friends in their 20s, I = female, R = male
>   I: what did the big cup say to the little cup?
>   R: (sarcastically) I'm bigger than you?
>   I: No. Nothing. Cups can't talk.
>   R: (completely ignoring I) I can hold more water than you?

On the surface, these responses suggest participation in the event, but, as the investigator noted, she perceived them as 'sarcastic' (see the section below). In providing clearly unfunny possible responses to the riddle, and in wresting the floor from the teller, this respondent shows just how little he cares to hear the answer to her joke and implicitly ridicules her for telling it. It is worth noting that this was a public venue (a party), so loss of face was potentially serious for both, as discussed above. Of course, the investigator deliberately told the joke hoping that it would fail in order to collect data; the unwitting respondent, however, undertakes aggressive moves to protect his own face needs and identity claims.

4.3   Sarcasm or mock politeness

I have maintained Culpeper's separation of this strategy, although it may well function as another way of making the speaker uncomfortable, the first positive impoliteness strategy discussed. Sarcasm and mock politeness were used in 11 instances, almost always in conjunction with other strategies. The first example, however, relies solely on mock politeness:

(17)   I = female, late 20s; R = her father, early 50s
       Response: uh-huh. That's a good one. (looks at I, shakes head to indicate 'no')

Note, though, that the respondent in (17) uses non-verbal signals in conjunction with mock politeness to ensure that the kind assessment of the humor is seen as false. The next example employs sarcasm:

(18)   Male friends in their early 20s
       Response: bravo. (returns to watching movie) that was pretty lame, Dave.

This example employs multiple strategies. The mock congratulatory statement is followed with a clearly negative assessment of the joke, an example of making the speaker feel uncomfortable. The statement also serves, like the head shake, above, to ensure that the sarcastic nature of the first comment is not overlooked. In addition, the quick return to the activity that the attempt at humor had interrupted shows the hearer's disinterest.

4.4   Offensive vs. defensive strategies

Overwhelmingly, the impolite responses in this data set were offensive, attacking the speaker, rather than defending the hearer. Such responses suggest that interlocutors perceived the telling of this joke as inappropriate and the speaker as in need of censure. Such an attempt at humor was, in short, an attackable offense for these interlocutors. Some offensive responses revealed more specific expectations on the part of the hearer. For example, twice sarcastic expressions of appreciation were used:

(19)   Male friends in their early 20s
       Response: thanks asshole.

Such a response suggests that, in telling a joke, the speaker could be seen as doing something nice for the hearer, that is, entertaining the hearer. When the joke was found to be dismally unfunny, the appreciation was expressed sarcastically. Similarly, the mock laudatory statement in Example (18) reveals an expectation of a performance (i.e., entertainment for the hearer) of which the speaker can normally be proud. The use of these offensive strategies suggests that something has gone awry, and that the fault is with the would-be humorist.

A few hearers, however, oriented to themselves, using potentially defensive strategies:

(20)   Female friends in their early 20s
       Response: um, why did you just tell me that?

(21)   I = Female, late 20s; R = her brother, late 30s
       Response: why do you do this to me? I shouldn't even call you anymore.

In one sense these questions can be seen as a challenge to the speaker, and thus as offensive moves, but they are also defensive in orientation, as the respondents imply that the speakers have some reason for sharing that joke with them, specifically. From this perspective, the hearers' challenge is also a query regarding which of their personal qualities suggested that they might be someone who would appreciate this kind of humor. Example (13) is similar, in that the hearer explicitly distances herself from her friend's joke, and defends her own sense of humor.

Another self-oriented, potentially defensive response is to frame the negative evaluation of the joke as a personal affront:

(22)   Female friends, 20
       Response: (stares) I hate that joke. (very curtly)

Both Beebe (1995) and Culpeper, Bousfield, and Wichmann (2003) emphasize the importance of intonation in perceptions of rudeness. This respondent's 'curt' tone implies that she is offended by the joke. Because of its benign content, it is unlikely that the joke itself has offended her, but rather it is her friend's having perceived her as an appropriate recipient of it that is offensive. Further evidence comes from her orientation to self, defending her sense of humor by descrying the joke as one she 'hates'.

These respondents follow the expected pattern of responses to failed humor, as discussed by Hay (2001), in that they manage to demonstrate recognition of the attempt at humor while also conveying their lack of appreciation. In this large subset of responses, however, polite laughter or noncommittal comments were not sufficient, and even those responses with defensive elements either openly or implicitly also attack the speaker. Failing at humor is often humiliating for a speaker, so why might these hearers of a bad joke exacerbate this misery by attacking the teller? It is to this question that we now turn.

5.   Discussion

There are at least four, somewhat overlapping reasons I propose as to why the respondents in this study greeted this joke with such aggression: the disruptive nature of humor, the expectations they held of the teller's behavior, the characteristics of the study participants, and the identity concerns or face claims of the hearer. I shall address each of these in turn.

5.1 Humor as disruptive

The types of responses that have been discussed here reveal a great deal about audience expectations for humor. As noted above, a canned joke, like the one used here, is one form of humor that can be viewed as rather high on the scale of aggression, as it tends to disrupt the flow of conversation. The audience normally tolerates, and even welcomes this, however, because of the payoff in entertainment. (Note the sarcastic expressions of congratulations or appreciation in Examples 18 and 19). Rather unsurprisingly, the hearers seem to anticipate that the telling of a joke will be pleasant for them. Because the teller has volunteered to make this performance, the audience may assume that he or she has considered their desires and also claims responsibility for the outcome. Indeed, other evidence supports this, such as the teller's need to apologize for the poor quality of a joke (e.g., Norrick 1993: 66). If the attempt at humor fails, the teller has not only disrupted the ongoing talk, but has also failed to entertain. This dual failure is apparently, under some conditions, worthy of attack.

5.2 Behavioral expectations

Context, of course, influences whether or not an attack is seen as appropriate or not, and behavioral expectations, as discussed by Spencer-Oatey (2005), play an important part in an interlocutor's judgments. In this case, imagine hearing this riddle from a child. The humor may still be lacking, but a verbal attack on the child would not, for most people, be considered an appropriate response. The aggressive responses seen in this corpus suggest that this type of verbal behavior is not only not expected of adults, but that it is not desirable and thus can be censured. Inappropriate humor may, in some cases, be a type of proscribed behavior: "people are obliged to avoid it and others have the right NOT to experience it" (emphasis in original, Spencer-Oatey 2005: 97–98). The telling of this joke appears to be in violation of Spencer-Oatey's (2005) association principle: The behavior of the joke-teller is not in keeping with the type of relationship that has been implicitly mutually agreed upon. In fact, the teller can be seen as lacking in both empathy and respect for her or his hearer, making the rebuke appropriate.

5.3 Interlocutor characteristics

Related to the issue of behavioral expectations is that of the characteristics of the participants. Nearly all of these examples of impolite responses were gathered between intimates: friends and family. In addition, most were close in age and quite young, usually in their early 20s. Culpeper (1996) suggests that among intimates not only might face attacks be more possible than in other relationships, due to participants' familiarity with each other's faults, but counter-attacks, as opposed to mitigating moves are a common response. Culpeper (1996: 355) notes that "equal relationships – by definition – lack a default mechanism by which one participant achieves the upper hand." In such situations, thus, perceptions of rudeness can beget more rudeness. Certainly, too, Wolfson's (1988) bulge theory of social inter-action suggests that when social distance is very low little speech elaboration will be necessary, as these relationships are fixed. In many cases this means that we can safely be rude to those closest to us. The strong tendency toward positive impo-liteness here can also be attributed to the egalitarian nature of the interlocutors' relationships. In such cases one participant cannot normally threaten the other – except with the threat of removal of intimacy, which then places us squarely back into the realm of positive impoliteness.

Another important aspect of intimate relationships is the long-term investment interlocutors have in them. Culpeper (1996) points out that impoliteness, even if it is momentarily damaging to a relationship, can be in an interlocutor's long-term interest. The aggressive responses by these participants made it clear that they did not want to have similar jokes repeated to them in the future, so much so that they were willing to risk hurting the teller's feelings to ensure that this behavior would end. Their responses then can be seen as an attempt at social regulation of the joke-teller's behavior.[3]

5.4   Identity concerns/face claims

Humor is well-understood as means of constructing identities. The decision to joke, as well as the types and content of jokes reveal a great deal about their teller (Tannen 1984; Norrick 2003: 1344). In responding to humor, the hearer indicates his or her willingness to share these views (Hay 2001). In the case of failed humor, hearers are typically portrayed as needing to respond in such a way as to indicate that they have understood the joke, but that they do not find it amusing, and in doing so they "signal that the problem lies not with them, but on the side of the teller" (Norrick 2003: 1345). The data here, however, sug-gests that sometimes the audience members will see the joke as an indication that the problem lies with on them, as well as with the teller, because it implies

---

3.   This interpretation is bolstered by the data collected between strangers, who tended to respond with polite comments or laughter. Not having a long-term investment in the relationship, they could afford to indulge a single inanity.

something about their own sense of humor: Why would you think I would enjoy that joke? Do you think my sense of humor is that bad? The joke, then, becomes a face-threatening act for individuals who want to claim 'good sense of humor' as a part of their face (cf. Spencer-Oatey 2007). In addition to this independent aspect, because face and identity are relational, there is also an interdependent aspect at least implicit in these responses. In attacking the joke-teller, the hearers not only communicate their individual concern ("why me?"), but also censure the teller for violating group norms, implicitly saying, "We don't joke like that."

6. Conclusion

This study has used the concepts of rapport management and impoliteness to examine the rude rejoinders that were collected in reaction to a failed attempt at humor, and has suggested that interlocutor characteristics, behavioral expectations, identity concerns/face claims, and the disruptive nature of humor all played a part in the hearers' decisions to respond with aggression. Failed humor, like impoliteness, has been an understudied phenomenon, and the use of recent theoretical developments, such as the concept of rapport management, in the study of politeness suggests similar directions for the continuing development of humor theory. Just as impoliteness has been recognized as integral to understanding politeness, so failed humor, as well as responses to (failed) humor will illuminate our understanding of the entire phenomenon.

Humor has often been conceptualized as utterances that are intended to amuse. Reworking Spencer-Oatey's (2005: 97) definition of (im)politeness slightly, we arrive instead at a discursive conception of humor as "the subjective judgments people make about the *humorousness* of verbal and non-verbal behavior." Such a view requires us to examine (failed) humor in a socially sensitive and context-dependent manner. It leads to questions involving how the success or failure of humor is constructed among interlocutors and its consequences. We are invited to examine when, where, how and with whom certain types of humor are likely to succeed or fail.

Despite not having been fully grounded in this view of humor, this preliminary investigation nonetheless demonstrates the importance of the study of failed humor for a broad theory of humor, by revealing behavioral expectations regarding the use of humor and showing how humor styles are constructed and regulated by different communities. As a preliminary investigation, it has raised, perhaps, more questions than it has answered. Although it was presented as if it were spontaneous, the humor here was not only prescripted, but could also be classified as children's humor. Do similar interlocutors respond with similar rudeness to failed spontaneous, adult humor? When less disruptive forms of humor, such as narratives (cf. Norrick 1993), fail, are they responded to less aggressively? Future research along these lines should also require data collectors to explicitly note their perceptions of the response in order to create a data set based on emic principles.

Although scholars recognize the many serious functions of humor, among lay people humor is generally considered as merely frivolous and fun, and this portrayal is easy to maintain when all goes well. However, as with a great deal of linguistic behavior, it is when expectations are not met that social norms are revealed. The responses presented here suggest that, under some conditions, humor is not at all frivolous – if this were the case, its failure would be of little consequence and certainly not worthy of some of the more vehement responses that were collected. It is apparent that there is much at stake in terms of face and identity for both conversational participants, making this an area of humor studies that warrants further investigation.

References

Arundale, Robert. 2006. "Face as relational and interactional: A communication framework for research on face, facework, and politeness." *Journal of Politeness Theory* 2(2): 193–216.

Attardo, Salvatore. 2005. "Humor." In *Handbook of Pragmatics* (2nd Edn), Jef Verschueren, Jan-Ola Ostman, Jan Blommaert & Chris Bulcaen (Eds), 1–18. Amsterdam: John Benjamins.

Basso, Keith. 1979. *Portraits of "The Whiteman": Linguistic Play and Cultural Symbols among the Western Apache*. Cambridge: Cambridge University Press.

Beebe, Leslie. 1995. "Polite fictions: Instrumental rudeness as pragmatic competence." In *Linguistics and the Education of Language Teachers: Ethnolinguistic, Psycholinguistic, and Sociolinguistic Aspects. Georgetown University Roundtable on Languages and Linguistics*, James E. Alatis, Carolyn A. Straehle, Brent Gallenberger & Maggie Ronkin (Eds), 154–168. Washington, D.C.: Georgetown University Press.

Bell, Nancy D. In press. "Responses to failed humor." *Journal of Pragmatics* (2008), doi:10.1016/j.pragma.2008.10.010.

Boxer, Diana & Cortés-Conde, Florencia. 1997. "From bonding to biting: Conversational joking and identity display." *Journal of Pragmatics* 27: 275–294.

Brown, Penelope & Levinson, Stephen C. 1987. *Politeness: Some Universals in Language Usage*. Cambridge: Cambridge University Press.

Chiaro, Delia. 1992. *The Language of Jokes: Analysing Verbal Play*. New York: Routledge.

Culpeper, Jonathon. 1996. "Towards an anatomy of impoliteness." *Journal of Pragmatics* 25: 349–367.

Culpeper, Jonathon, Bousfield, Derek & Wichmann, Anne. 2003. "Impoliteness revisited: With special reference to dynamic and prosodic aspects." *Journal of Pragmatics* 35: 1545–1579.

Eder, Donna. 1993. "'Go get ya a French!': Romantic and sexual teasing among adolescent girls." In *Gender and Conversational Interaction*, Deborah Tannen (Ed.), 17–31. New York: Oxford University Press.

Eelen, Gino. 2001. *A Critique of Politeness Theories*. Manchester: St. Jerome Publishing.

Eisterhold, Jodi. 2007. "Failed humor in American discourse." Paper presented at International Society for Humor Studies, Newport, RI, 2007.

Fraser, Bruce & Nolen, William. 1981. "The association of deference with linguistic form." *International Journal of the Sociology of Language* 27: 93–109.

Goldberg, David. 1997. "Joking in a multi-disciplinary team: Negotiating hierarchy and the allocation of 'cases.'" *Anthropology and Medicine* 4(3): 229–244.

Hay, Jennifer. 1994. "Jocular abuse patterns in mixed-group interaction." *Wellington Working Papers in Linguistics* 6: 26–55.

Hay, Jennifer. 2001. "The pragmatics of humor support." *Humor: International Journal of Humor Studies* 14(1): 55–82.

Holmes, Janet. 1995. *Women, Men and Politeness*. New York: Longman.

Holmes, Janet. 2000. "Politeness, power and provocation: How humour functions in the workplace." *Discourse Studies* 2(2): 159–185.

Holmes, Janet. 2007. "Humour and the construction of Maori leadership at work." *Leadership* 3(1): 5–27.

Holmes, Janet & Marra, Meredith. 2002. "Over the edge? Subversive humor between colleagues and friends." *Humor: International Journal of Humor Studies* 15(1): 65–87.

Holmes, Janet & Marra, Meredith. 2006. "Humor and leadership style." *Humor: International Journal of Humor Studies* 19(2): 119–138.

Jorgensen, Julia. 1996. "The functions of sarcastic irony in speech." *Journal of Pragmatics* 26: 613–634.

Kienpointner, Manfred. 1997. "Varieties of rudeness: Types and functions of impolite utterances." *Functions of Language* 4(2): 251–287.

Kotthoff, Helga. 1996. "Impoliteness and conversational joking: On relational politics." *Folia Linguistica* 30(3/4): 299–325.

Locher, Miriam. 2004. *Power and Politeness in Action: Disagreements in Oral Communication*. New York: Mouton de Gruyter.

Locher, Miriam & Watts, Richard. 2005. "Politeness theory and relational work." *Journal of Politeness Research* 1(1): 9–33.

Mills, Sara. 2005. "Gender and impoliteness." *Journal of Politeness Research* 1(2): 263–280.

Morreall, John. 1983. *Taking Laughter Seriously*. Albany: State University of New York Press.

Norrick, Neal. 1993. *Conversational Joking: Humor in Everyday Talk*. Bloomington: Indiana University Press.

Norrick, Neal. 2003. "Issues in conversational joking." *Journal of Pragmatics* 35: 1333–1359.

Palmer, Jerry. 1994. *Taking humour seriously*. New York: Routledge.

Sacks, Harvey. 1974. "An analysis of the course of a joke's telling." In *Explorations in the Ethnography of Speaking*, Richard Bauman & Joel Sherzer (Eds), 325–345. Cambridge: Cambridge University Press.

Sherzer, Joel. 1978. "Oh! That's a pun and I didn't mean it." *Semiotica* 22(3/4): 335–350.

Spencer-Oatey, Helen. 2000. "Rapport management: A framework for analysis." In *Culturally Speaking: Managing Rapport through Talk across Cultures*, Helen Spencer-Oatey (Ed.), 11–46. London: Continuum.

Spencer-Oatey, Helen. 2002. "Managing rapport in talk: Using rapport sensitive incidents to explore the motivational concerns underlying the management of relations." *Journal of Pragmatics* 34: 529–545.

Spencer-Oatey, Helen. 2005. "(Im)Politeness, face and perceptions of rapport: Unpackaging their bases and interrelationships." *Journal of Politeness Research* 1(1): 95–119.

Spencer-Oatey, Helen. 2007. "Theories of identity and the analysis of face." *Journal of Pragmatics* 39: 639–656.

Straehle, Carolyn. 1993. "'Samuel?' 'Yes, dear?' Teasing and conversational rapport." In *Framing in Discourse*, Deborah Tannen (Ed.), 210–230. New York: Oxford University Press.

Tannen, Deborah. 1984. *Conversational Style: Analyzing Talk Among Friends*. Norwood, NJ: Ablex.

Watts, Richard. 2003. *Politeness*. Cambridge: Cambridge University Press.

Wolfson, Nessa. 1988. "The bulge: A theory of speech behavior and social distance." In *Second Language Discourse: A Textbook of Current Research*, Jonathon Fine (Ed.), 21–38. Norwood, NJ: Ablex.

Yedes, Janet. 1996. "Playful teasing: Kiddin' on the square." *Discourse and Society* 7(3): 417–438.

Zajdman, Anat. 1995. "Humorous face-threatening acts: Humor as strategy." *Journal of Pragmatics* 23: 325–339.

Failed humor in conversation

A double voicing* analysis

Béatrice Priego-Valverde

While humor in everyday conversation has been acknowledged widely as an area of linguistic research, failed humor has not received much linguistic attention. This paper describes unperceived humor and rejected humor, analyzing several examples from a conversational corpus using the double voicing approach according to Bakhtin. Unperceived humor can quickly lead to misunderstandings such as a joke being understood as a verbal attack. Rejected humor, on the other hand, is perceived but purposely ignored by one or several of the listeners, for instance in order to continue the discourse as planned. In both cases, the difference in mode of speech (bona fide communication versus non-serious communication) can be considered a major reason for the failure of humor.

1.　Introduction

Humor is an omnipresent phenomenon within our everyday interactions and a main element of our conversations with family and friends. One of the reasons for this phenomenon is that in personal interaction, the people involved know each other particularly well. Thus, they do not hesitate to tell jokes and mock themselves or each other. In addition, humor favors the establishment and the maintenance of a mood for conviviality, lightness and play. However, despite these positive functions of humor and the fact that participants are often favorably disposed towards each other, humor can sometimes fail to fulfill its purpose. The topic of failed humor has received only scant attention in the literature on humor so far. Therefore, in this article, I will focus my attention on these failures with the intent of explaining them by using a double voicing approach.

After having defined the theoretical framework, the interactive frame of the everyday conversation, and after having specified the kind of humor we frequently encounter, I will analyze some examples of failed humor. Two cases will be examined: humor simply not perceived and humor perceived but rejected by the listener.

---

*In Bakhtin's sense. Or what I call in French 'double énonciation' (1998, 2003).

2.   Theoretical frame

2.1   Humor, a generic term

This study was carried out in the linguistic areas of pragmatic, interactionist and enunciative trends, according to which we should consider humor as it actually appears within our daily conversations. We observe it in order to explain how it works and how it influences the current interaction and the relationship between participants. We are confronted with various forms of humor; while it seems heterogeneous at first glance, we will observe that humor can be related to irony, mockery and sarcasm; these forms may be of questionable taste or more on the witty side. But what we are aiming at here is not to produce a gradation among humorous utterances nor even to attempt to classify them according to their types. Instead, we shall adopt the term 'humor' as a generic term, as the majority of researchers studying humor in interactions have chosen to do.

In my corpus, the term humor refers to a variety of types of utterances which have made the participants laugh and which, consequently, may be regarded by the participants as humorous, although this judgment may be correct or incorrect. However, if we define utterances which make the conversation's participants laugh as humorous, we are defining humor by way of the reaction. This poses the question of how to define utterances which do not provoke laughter? How can we even identify humor in such a case (Holmes 2000)? In this study, I took advantage of the recording conditions of my corpus. Since I was both an observer of and a participant in the conversations, I was able to understand, as the other participants were, the implicitness on which many of the examples analyzed here are based. Thus, I was able to discern supposedly humorous utterances as well. This is a distinct advantage of ethno-methodographical studies in humor.

2.2   Discussing the subject's uniqueness

In *Marxism and the Philosophy of Language* (1929), Bakhtin/Volochinov opposes the two theories in force at the time, namely those of 'individualistic subjectivism' and 'abstract objectivism', by claiming that verbal interaction is the central and founding element of language:

> The actual reality of language-speech is not the abstract system of linguistic forms, not the isolated monologic utterance, and not the psychological act of its implementation, but the social event of verbal interaction implemented in an utterance or utterances. Thus, verbal interaction is the basic reality of language. [...] Any utterance, no matter how weighty and complete in and of itself, is only a moment in the continuous process of verbal communication (1929 [1986]: 94–95).

Thus, the notion of 'dialogism' was conceived. In 1984, on the basis of Bakhtin's research, Ducrot elaborated a "polyphonic theory of the utterance" (1984: 171) and established the idea of the heterogeneous speaker by distinguishing the *speaker* (S) and the *enunciator* (E). S and E together constitute the subject or "empirical being" (1984: 199). In Ducrot's theory, S is in charge of the utterance and E (one or more than one enunciator) corresponds to various 'voices', that is the points of view speaking through S. In this case, when S is speaking, we can state that he or she is never speaking alone. This is why I follow Ducrot in saying that there is no uniqueness of the subject. Other voices speak through S. These other voices can be the hearer's voice ('diaphony', Roulet 1985) in the case of humor or irony for example, or a third person's voice. Additionally, the other voice can even be absent, as in reported speech, or another person's voice or S's own voice (by way of reformulation, for example). These various voices can be identifiable or not, recognizable or not, real or fictitious (in the case of humor, for example). Last but not least, they can correspond to the stance and beliefs of the speaker or not.

2.3   Definition of the interactive space

Through Ducrot's distinction between speaker and enunciator, the principle of 'enunciative staging' is founded. According to this principle, speakers stage their own discourse by letting other voices speak through them. On this basis, Vion (1995) establishes a frame with the aim of showing the enunciative staging of different voices and its effect on the participants' relationship(s). This frame permits the description of 'interactive space': the image of the interaction, as constructed by all of the participants:

> By the term interactive space we define [...] an image of the interaction construed by the subjects engaged in the management of this interaction. [It corresponds] to a plurality of connections of position. This interactive space is jointly construed by all of the subjects, even if each of them will strive to initiate a particular connection of position. (Vion 1995: 278–279).

Thus defined, the notion of interactive space aims to rethink the notion of relationship by showing its complexity and focusing simultaneously on the different types of relationships and on the reciprocal links which join them. In this way, Vion suggests two kinds of relationships: the social and interpersonal one and the interlocutive one. These two relationships involve five kinds of positions: *institutional* positioning, *modular, subjective, discursive* and *enunciative* positioning. Even if the first three positions are more linked to the social relationship and the two final are more linked to the interlocutive relationship, all of these positions are constantly in interconnection. In other words, when people are speaking with each other, the speaker must always position himself or herself in more than only one stance in regard to the listener(s). For example, during a medical consultation, a doctor speaks through the institutional position of 'doctor', the discursive position of 'prescriber of medicine', the subjective position of 'expert'. Therefore, generally speaking, the doctor has a higher position than the patient. But at the same time, if this doctor asks his or her patient, who is a cook, for a recipe, the hierarchy changes and the patient will occupy the higher position of the expert for several minutes. Thus, the interactive space is not a steady state defined in advance but is rather defined anew by each interaction.

When speakers produce a humorous utterance, they principally speak while occupying two kinds of positions. The first one is the subjective position, e.g., images of themselves and of others that they show through their discourse. The second one is the enunciative position, which concerns the manner of presentation and implication that the subject has produced through discourse. Indeed, it is not the same thing to say "so-and-so is like this" and "apparently, so-and-so is like this". In the second case, the speaker reports someone else's words.

2.4 A double voicing approach to humor

Considering humor as double voicing does not supplant the current theories of humor, but rather completes them. If we consider, for instance, the most widely used and accepted theory according to which humor is the opposition between two incompatible elements, which creates humorous incongruity, the double voicing theory facilitates the attribution of a kind of 'responsibility' to each different meaning of a humorous utterance, in addition to that of the speaker him/herself.

Thus, this approach emphasizes, on the one hand, the distance the speaker maintains from his or her own discourse, and on the other hand, the consequences of this attitude. Thus,

- By using other voice(s), the humorist speaker can create distance from the seriousness of language (play words), from the hearer, from the situation, from himself (self-disparaging humor), and in general, he/she can create distance from "serious reality" (Bange 1986).
- Double voicing is basically the *materialization* of a contrast between two modes of communication – one being serious and the other playful. This contrast creates humorous incongruity.
- Double voicing refers to a doubly-coded discourse. It involves, on the side of production, a speaker's ambiguous intention and an ambivalent utterance. On the side of the reception, this doubly-coded discourse forces a double interpretation which is not possible without a minimum of connivance, on the affective plane (accepting an absurd, illogical or indecent utterance) and on the cognitive plane.
- Double voicing must be at least partly playful. It is part of what secures humor as benevolent. In connection with the distance produced ("what I am saying

is not serious and maybe not even true"), it reduces or indeed cancels all of the possible aggressive, vexing, subversive or indecent literal meanings in a humorous utterance.

2.5 Double voicing approach to failed humor

Numerous factors can explain the failure of a humorous utterance. Jen Hay (1996) presents some of them and, in particular, the case, found in our corpus, that humor sometimes interrupts a serious conversation. But, contrary to Hay, in this article, I want to explain these failures with an enunciative approach and not a pragmatic one – although, of course, I know that both are always more or less linked.

When a speaker produces a humorous utterance, he or she appeals to two enunciators: E1 saying and E2 observing what he or she says, joking about him/herself, about the language he/she uses, about the situation, the other(s) … about everything he/she is mocking. This second enunciator or second voice makes the utterance into 'non bona fide communication' (Raskin 1985) and must be decoded by the listener in order to understand that what he/she is hearing should not be taken seriously. At the same time, however, it is precisely this second voice which is not easy to detect, at the risk of not perceiving the humorous intention of the utterance. Indeed, when a speaker produces a humorous utterance, the responsibility for this utterance devolves to the other enunciators. Therefore – and the double voicing approach permits the revelation of this fact – the humorist speaker attempts such complex play with the various voices he/she stages through him/herself that it is sometimes very difficult, or even impossible, to identify these other voices, or even to know if they correspond to the speaker or not. At that point, it is sometimes impossible for the listener to know who is really speaking and whether the speaker is being serious or not. In this case, the humor is not and cannot be perceived.

In another case, this speaker's game of hide-and-seek with all of these various voices can turn on him/her. This means that these other voices are, if not hidden, at least implicit, so that it is up to the listener to choose to recognize them, to hear them or not. Listeners can choose to proceed in conversation and pretend they did not perceive the humor and did not decode the humorous intention, even if they actually did.

3. The corpus

3.1 Presentation

My corpus consists of various everyday conversations recorded during evenings passed among friends. The participants are very well acquainted with each other. They are between twenty-five and thirty years old. The recordings were made with a visible microphone. Although the participants knew that they were being recorded, they did not know the real reason why. Except for the first few minutes during which some of the participants asked for the reasons of the recording, the relationships between the friends were so close and their encounters so frequent that the microphone was quickly forgotten. Thus, I believe that I have collected a corpus with quite spontaneous and undistorted speech (see Norrick 1993 on the effects of recording).

3.2   Nature of the interactive setting

We usually define conversation with the following criteria:

–   Symmetric positions between the participants. Theoretically, all of them have the same rights and the same duties, especially those who are alternately speaker and listener.
–   A degree of cooperation more important than the competitive one. The former is present, however, because we cannot reasonably think that no competition ever exists within conversation, even if the competition revolves merely around loss of face.
–   An *inward goal, centered on the contact* (Vion 1992), the maintenance of the relationship, the cohesion of the group where the only one goal acknowledged is the pleasure to be together and to talk.
–   A mood of conviviality, which is the consequence of the previous criterion.
–   An apparent informality which carries on into the discourse (to be able to speak about everything and nothing, in a spontaneous way, without a precise goal), and into the interaction itself. Indeed, as Schegloff and Sacks (1973) have shown, in a conversation, the are no explicit rules concerning the order of beginning to speak or the duration of a speaking turn – all this is defined by the group (SE déterminant).

Thus, conversations are so providential that it is natural that they are a preferential space for humor. It is all the more natural because the conversations of our corpus are familiar conversations between people who know each other very well. As Traverso says, they are the space of a "pre-eminence of the relational and of complicity, pointing out the importance of shared knowledge and experiences" (1996: 13).

3.3   Humor in everyday conversation

The affective tonality of conversational humor (or, at least, of the humor encountered in my corpus) is particular, even paradoxical. Indeed, the familiar conversations I have observed are clearly convivial because all of the participants wanted to be together and all of them wanted to spend an agreeable time together. With such conditions, on the one hand, familiar conversations should run well and humor should be frequent. But, on the other hand, because the participants are often close friends or members of the same family, the rules of politeness and other social rites are more flexible and less constraining than in other situations. Even if the danger of face loss is omnipresent (as it necessarily must be), much freedom can be taken with it. This explains the numerous humorous utterances with which speakers do not hesitate to mock their listeners or themselves. This leads to a particular sort of humor that interferes with all the existing typologies, a sort of humor in which benevolent humor and sour mockery lie close together. The high level of frequency of mockery and teasing within these conversations is explained by this fact, as well as the fact that it is not always possible to distinguish irony from less ostensibly aggressive forms of humor. Finally, this explains the fact that, sometimes, people who do not belong to the group may have difficulties understanding the humor in such conversations, because the humor applied is anchored within a 'conversational history' (Golopentja 1988) shared by all of the participants. It is based on the implicitness of details unknown to outsiders; the insiders, in contrast, can divine the presence of humor thanks to their great connivance.

On the contrary, this does not explain that the failure of humor exists. Even if we could believe that the knowledge the participants have of each other suffices to reveal the humorous intention, we will show that this knowledge does not succeed in counterbalancing the complexity of the enunciative staging set by the humorist speaker. In return, the complicity that links the participants – and that diminishes the danger of face loss – partly explicates the fact that listeners may take the liberty of rejecting humor.

4.   Analysis of the data

4.1   When humor is not perceived

(1)   *M2 does not have a driver's license. In this excerpt, he tells the others that sometimes F2, his girlfriend, shows him how to drive.*

156   F2:   non mais en fait j'crois que le mieux c'est que t'apprennes d'abord
              à::: + dans une auto-
157   école et puis après heu::
158   M2:   et ouais //
159   F1:   *(en riant)* ah oui c'est clair c'est l'idéal pour <u>passer le permis une</u>
              <u>auto-école</u> *(rires)*
160   M2:   <u>mais pas avec elle + pas avec elle</u>

161	F2:	ouais mais qu'il lui apprenne les rudiments heu::: + comment démarrer la bagnole et tout
162		et puis après on ira la conduire heu: ++ <u>sur un parking</u>=
163	F1:	⟨*voix souriante*⟩ on n'a rien <u>trouvé de mieux</u> pour le moment hein *(rires)*
164	F2:	*(rires)* + non parce qu'en fait c'est vachement dur d'apprendre à quelqu'un à: démarrer la
165		voitu:::re heu:: ++ tu vois= <u>+ c'est</u> dur d'expliquer
166	F1:	<u>ah ben ouais</u>

156	F2:	no but actually I think that it's best if you learn at first at::: + in a driving school and then
157		hum::
158	M2:	yeah //
159	F1:	*(laughing)* oh yes it's clear a driving school is ideal to <u>pass the driver's license test</u>
160		*(laugh)*
161	M2:	<u>but not with her + not with her</u>
162	F2:	yeah but for learning the basics hum + how to start a car and so on and afterwards we will
163		drive it hum: ++ <u>on a parking lot</u>=
164	F1:	⟨*smiling voice*⟩ we didn't <u>find anything better</u> at that time huh *(laugh)*
165	F2:	*(laugh)* no because actually it is damned hard to teach someone how to start the car:::
166		hum:: ++ you see= + <u>it's hard</u> to explain
167	F1:	<u>oh why yeah</u>

Just before this excerpt begins, M2 has been explaining that since he is thirty and he does not know how to drive a car yet, it will be difficult to learn, because learning takes longer, the older we get. This fact justifies F2's utterance in (156), proposing that he should begin learning to drive in a driving school. F2 is M2's girlfriend and she directs this utterance at him. The subjects are in a bona fide communication: M2 exposes his problem and F2 tries to find solutions.

F1 takes advantage of F2's hesitations to begin her sentence and attributes a meaning to F2's utterance which was not intended by F2. Thus, by way of 'diaphonic retaking' (Roulet 1985), (lines 159–160), F1 pretends that F2 has said merely that a driving school is a good place to learn how to drive. F1 ascribes the act of having said a platitude to F2 by pretending to believe it, to believe that F2 could have really said something so commonplace. Here, F1 plays three different enunciators: E1, corresponding to a fictitious F2 saying truisms; E2, corresponding to a fictitious F1 believing F2's false purposes, and E3, corresponding to a facetious F1 laughing about all this.

Thus, interfering in the serious dialogue between F2 and M2, F1 does not really laugh at F2, but at the image she gives her by the different enunciators she has given life to through her own discourse. Not only does she give F2 a particularly depreciated image – although fictitious – she also assumes the right to criticize, to belittle F1 and M2 by interrupting their discourse. She assumes a higher position with respect to him.

But F2 is still trying to find a solution for her boyfriend's lack of driving experience. She apparently does not perceive F1's joking intent. In fact, she is in a bona fide communication mode, explaining to M2 the easier way to learn driving ("at first", "and after"). It can be proven that she is very wrapped up in this bona fide communication because she expresses herself with difficulty and because she is searching for words. This is the reason why F2 does not or cannot identify the joking aspect of F1's utterance. Consequently, she does not perceive the way F1 has distanced herself from her own discourse. She does not know that F1 is joking and playing to give to her a fictitious image. Thus, F2 thinks that the goal of F1's sentence is to pick at her awkwardness and to laugh at F2 as speaker. In consequence, F2 tries to justify herself (162–163) although F1 has not asked for any justification.

The sort of misunderstanding here is due to the inadequacy between two modes of communication, the bona fide one, into which F2 confines herself, and the non bona fide other one, initiated by F1. The clash between the two modes leads to a failure on the relationship level because, as F2 is not able to switch into the non bona fide communication, she does not recognize the image F1 gives to her. Thus, she rejects it and, above all, she does not accept the dissymmetric relationship fixed by F1, because F2 cannot perceive and then identify all the different voices played by F1 in her discourse, voices which are the cause of this redefinition of their relationship. From that time, as F2 locks herself in the bona fide communication, F1's second attempt (164) to say to her she is joking has a sort of fierceness of which F2 is the clear victim.

But as F2 persists in her elucidation, it becomes increasingly difficult for her vis-à-vis someone (F1) who does not care about her explanation. Thus, in her last sentence (165–166), F2 tries in vain to persuade F1 by speaking directly to her ("actually", "you see"), while F1, who would like F2 to switch with her into a non bona fide communication, remains deaf to F2's arguments because they are useless to her.

At the end of this sort of conflict between F1 and F2, nobody wins, because neither of them has at any time made concessions to give up one of the two incompatible modes of communication. F2's laughing before she speaks her final sentence is not a rallying type of laughing. She still has not understood F1's 'real' intent and she does not understand precisely what F1 is laughing at. So, if F2 is effectively laughing, it is more a sort of concession to F1 because she perceives vaguely F1's humor without being able to perceive the distance between F1's and her own discourse. Consequently, she goes on believing that F1 is mocking her and not the fictitious image she has.

If the complicity between speakers is a necessary condition for humor to succeed, this excerpt shows its limits. Indeed, the nevertheless real complicity between F1 and F2 did not allow F2 to perceive the enunciative mechanisms of F1's humorous sentences. Several factors contribute to this failure of humor. On one hand, perhaps F1 did not give enough convincing clues. Maybe F2, locked too tightly within the bona fide communication with M2, was not able to perceive these clues. Finally, maybe F2 did not want to take them into account because at that time, she would have to react to F1's humor. And yet, insofar as F1 knowingly interrupted the dialogue between F2 and M2, a dialogue of which she was merely witness, F2 probably perceived F1's humor as a parasitic sentence. Consequently, she preferred not to understand it.

(2)   *In this excerpt, F2 points out her culinary talents with a certain pride.*

72   F2:   mais j'avais pensé tu sais faire un truc↑ + et acht / aller prendre un emballage ⟨*voix*

73   *souriante*⟩ à la boulangerie et vous le mettre dans l'emballage

74   F1:   (*rires*)

75   F2:   ⟨*voix enfantine*⟩ c'est moi qui l'ai fait ++ vous m'auriez JA-mais crue (*rires*)

76   F1:   (*rires*)

77   F1:   ⟨*voix souriante*⟩ ah non c'est clair (+) avec l'emballage ⟨*sérieuse*⟩+ eh bè dis donc↑

78   F2:   ⟨*fière*⟩ eh ouais +hein↑ j'ai fait de bons petits trucs hein j'ai fait le poulet

79   BASQUAI::SE + qu'est-ce que j'ai fait↑

80   F1:   (*de la cuisine*) le poulet basquaise↑

81   M1:   ⟨*air moqueur*⟩ le poulet basquaise↑

82   F2:   ⟨*ne perçoit pas le ton moqueur et continue*⟩ le poulet basquaise qu'est-ce que j'ai fait↑

83   M1:   ⟨*alors il insiste*⟩ c'est dur ça à faire hein

84   F2:   ⟨*toujours incompréhension*⟩ ouais hein↑ t'as vu↑

85   M1:   putain + moi je le rate tout le temps

86   F2:   (*rire*) ⟨*elle semble rire parce qu'elle le croit et non parce qu'elle a saisi le ton*

87   *moqueur*⟩

88   M1:   c'est:::: //

89   F2 :   ouais non c'est //

90   M2:   elle aussi hein↑

91   M1:   (*éclat de rire*)

92   F2:   oh dis:: c'est pas vrai parce que tu te régales

93   M2:   non c'est pas ⟨inaudible⟩

94   F2:   qu'est-ce que j'ai fait↑
95   F1:   *(elle est en train de préparer la raclette et parle à M1)* je coupe le
               fromage ⟨inaudible⟩
96   M1:   ouais= ouais= ouais
97   M2:   VOILÀ↑ tu fais //
98   ⟨inaudible⟩
99   M1:   BON ben RAclette ce soir

72   F2:   but I though you knew how to make something ↑ + and to buy / to go
               to get packaging
73   ⟨*smiling voice* ⟩ at the baker's shop and put it into the package
74   F1:   *(laugh)*
75   F2:   ⟨*childlike voice*⟩ I've done it ++ you would never have believe me
               (laugh)
76   F1:   *(laugh)*
77   F1:   ⟨*smiling voice*⟩ oh no it's clear + with the package ⟨*seriously*⟩ + oh
               isn't it ↑
78   F2:   ⟨*proud*⟩ oh yeah + eh ↑ I cooked some good little things eh I cooked
               the BASQUAI::SE
79   chicken + what did I cook ↑
80   F1:   *(from the kitchen)* the basquaise chicken ↑
81   M1:   ⟨*in a mocking way*⟩ the basquaise chicken ↑
82   F2:   ⟨*she does not perceive the mocking tone of voice and goes on listing all
               the meals she*
83   *cooked)* the basquaise chicken what did I cook ↑
84   M1:   ⟨*insisting in his mocking way*⟩ that's hard to cook eh
85   F2:   ⟨*still misunderstanding*⟩ yeah eh ↑ as you saw ↑
86   M1:   goddammit + I always make a mess of it
87   F2:   *(laugh)* ⟨*she seems to laugh because she believes him and not because
               she has perceived*
88   *the joke)*
89   M1:   it's::::: //
90   F2:   yeah no it's
91   M2:   so does she eh ↑
92   M1:   *(burst of laughter)*
93   F2:   oh it's not true because you have had a delicious meal
94   M2:   no it's not ⟨inaudible⟩
95   F2:   what did I cook ↑
96   F1:   *(preparing the raclette and talking to M1)* I'm cutting the cheese
               ⟨inaudible⟩
97   M1:   yeah= yeah= yeah
98   M2:   there ↑ you're cooking //
99   ⟨inaudible⟩
100   M1:   well raclette tonight

As her 'smiling voice' shows, at the beginning of this excerpt, F2 accepts that her culinary talents are potentially being mocked by her friends (72–73). But, from line 80 on, F2 is so proud of her new culinary competence that she wants to demonstrate it to her friends. Her pride can be seen, among other, thanks to her tone of voice (78). She is thinking aloud, without really listening to her friends' sentences and commentaries, probably without looking at them because she is entirely concentrated on remembering all the meals she has cooked recently (80). It is clear that F2 wants her talents to be appreciated at their true value. But F1 and M1 are not prepared to accept that and they want to stay within the non bona fide communication initiated from the line 80. For instance, in lines 81 and 82, F1 and M1 joke about the alleged difficulty of cooking chicken basquaise, but F2 does not perceive it. As F1 and M1 content themselves with repeating F2's words, she probably thinks that it is only feedback, a sort of invitation continue listing the meals she has cooked. So, she continues (83–84). With their humorous sentences, F1 and M1 are probably saying that is not really hard to cook chicken basquaise and thus, not worthy of pride. In consequence, they are laughing at F2's pride. With this mockery, F1 and M1 try to restore a non bona fide communication, which F2 rejects. But F2 does not perceive the mocking tone of voice. Several reasons can explain this failure of humor. At first, she does not want to perceive it because they are laughing at her and her culinary talents; she probably rejects it. Then, she is so trapped in her own pride and she is so taken up by remembering all the delicious meals she has cooked that she cannot perceive the humorous intent. Both reasons are probably valid. Consequently, F1 and M1's simple joke devolves into real and aggressive mockery.

One can believe that the misunderstanding between F2 and the others is linked to the fact that their humorous production is not sufficiently marked. M1 seems to think it is, because he goes on insisting and explicitly uses a mocking tone of voice: "That's hard to cook eh" (84). Here, M1 is playing with an implicit background that he believes to be common and shared by all of the participants i.e., that chicken basquaise is easy to cook. He probably thinks and maybe hopes that when F2 will recognize the implicitness of his utterance, she will also discover the humorous dimension of M1's utterance. But F2 does not seem to share M1's opinion about how easy it is to cook this meal. Thus, she cannot pick out the allusion. Because F2 does not share the same value scale as M1, she cannot perceive the distance M1 puts into his utterance and takes it very seriously. F2 does not perceive M1's signal, which he is making to initiate the switch into a non bona fide communication. Thus, a conflict between two modes of communication appears: M1's humorous one and F2's serious one. In other words, even if everything M1 says does not have to be taken seriously, it is taken seriously by F2. Thus, from line 81 onwards and even more so in lines 86 and 89, M1 uses a double voicing. The first voice has to be taken in a literal (and serious) way: chicken basquaise is difficult to cook. So, saying that, he is congratulating F2 for having cooked this plate. Here, M1 allows an enunciator to speak – an enunciator whose opinion does not correspond to his own, actual opinion. The second voice corresponds to the humorous sense of the utterance: he is teasing F2 and, as in an ironic utterance, it is the contrary which must be taken into account. In this second case, chicken basquaise is anything but a difficult meal. Not only does M1 not have any reason to congratulate F2 but he is also mocking her pride. And as we have shown, F2 takes M1's false congratulations seriously. Moreover, as she believes M1 when he is saying (in a humorous way) that he does not know how to cook this meal (86), the laughter she produces (87) is mocking laughter, albeit friendly.

F2 speaks in a bona fide communication. She only understands the literal meaning and not the humorous sense of M1's utterances. She does not perceive the humorous sense nor the distance M1 puts between what he says and what he is really thinking. So, she cannot adopt the same mode of communication as him and thus, she cannot play with him. From that moment onwards she is not in the same mode of communication as the other participants. She does not have the necessary tools *to rebuild* the second and ludicrous voice. This is the difficulty for the participants within the double voicing process of humor. Generally, the second voice is not explicit and must be rebuilt. But, like F2, we do not perceive the signals of a second possible voice, there is no possible rebuilding. Humor is not understood because it is not perceived. We do not see it. We *cannot* see it. Here, F2 is never capable of perceiving M1's humorous intention. Thus, all of M1's attempts to lead F2 in a non bona fide communication become *fierce* and the friendly humor of the beginning becomes increasingly aggressive because F2 does not react in the appropriate way. She becomes the victim of M1's humor and not a partner in play.

We have already said that F2 devolves from a possible partner in humor to the victim, all the more so since her boyfriend (M2) joins M1 and F1 in line 91 when he infers that F2 does not know how to cook chicken basquaise either. Here again, F2 does not see M2's second voice and humorous meaning. She understands M2's utterance as a real, disloyal and unjustified attack against her. She does not have another choice than to directly question M2's dishonesty (93). F2's intervention is another clue of the conflict existing between the two modes of communication because if it were not the case, F2 would have probably answered something, but not by putting forward a lie. Lies only make sense and only can exist within 'serious reality'. M2 has joined M1 and F2's position as a victim is reinforced because now she is the victim of a male coalition.[1]

---

1. Here, we can notice that if F1 excludes herself from the humorous coalition it is not by any sort of feminine solidarity but only because she leaves the room to cook.

4.2   Humor rejected

The two following excerpts show that sometimes humor fails not because it is not perceived but because, although it is perceived, it is purely and simply rejected.

(3)   *This interaction is between four participants who are students: M1 and M2 of dentistry, F1 of linguistics and F2 of pharmacy. The four participants are discussing potential collaborations to have a good dentistry office.*

235	M1:	c'est compliqué (+) faut voir heu::: //
236	F1:	et un linguiste ça vous intéresse pas↑
237	M1:	⟨*très sérieux*⟩ non::↑ non non
238	**tout le monde**:	*(éclat de rire)*
239	M2:	une fac privée heu:::
240	F1:	*(rires)*
241	M1:	⟨par contre ?⟩ un médecin
242	M2:	⟨qui te fasse ?⟩ les cours heu::::
243	F1:	*(rires)*
244	M1:	un médecin c'est bon (+) si i t'arrive un pépin ou quoi
245	F1:	⟨inaudible⟩ ⟨*le ton est très sérieux et laisse donc penser qu'elle s'est ralliée à M1*⟩
246	M2:	moi par exemple je vois::: on a / on a commencé à en parler en délirant avec mes
247		copains de l'armée là médecins ⟨inaudible⟩ ben moi je me sentirais tout à fait de:: / d'être
248		avec lui tu vois
235	M1:	It's complicated (+) we have to see uh::://
236	F1:	and you're not interested in having a linguist in it ↑
237	M1:	⟨*very seriously*⟩ no:: ↑ no no
238	**Everybody** :	*(roar of laughter)*
239	M2:	a private univ[ersity] uh:::
240	F1:	*(laughter)*
241	M1:	⟨on the other hand?⟩ a doctor
242	M2:	⟨who?⟩ to teach you uh::::
243	F1:	*(laughter)*
244	M1:	a doctor is good (+) if you have a problem or whatever
245	F1:	⟨inaudible⟩ ⟨*tone is very serious and lets you think that she joins M1*⟩
246	M2:	I for example I see::: we have / we have begun discussing it in a funny way with my
247		doctor friends from the army ⟨inaudible⟩ and I will completely agree to::/ to be with him you
248		know

When F1 produces her humorous and very incongruous utterance (236), the topic about the professional collaborations has been discussed for 9 minutes and

30 seconds. During all this time, F1 and F2's interventions were only sporadic. Two factors can explain this phenomenon. The first one is maybe the little interest F1 and F2 feel for this specific topic, above all when it is developed for such a long time. The second reason is a real lack of knowledge in dentistry to be able to participate actively. Even if M1 and M2 are necessarily aware of these gaps, they do not think they should have to interrupt the topic. The reason is probably because F1 and F2 are their girlfriends and thus, they are *de facto* interested in topics concerning their future lives.

F1 attempts to interfere in the conversation. She chooses the humorous mode, proposing her own services to participate in the creation of a dentistry office. In 236, F1's utterance is voluntarily incongruous. Her production is thus humorous because, asking such an unrealistic question, she already knows the answer. So, she is not asking a real question. In fact, this humorous utterance only has a meaning thanks to its functions, actually two functions: (i) the management of face, (ii) the hope that F1 will abandon the current topic.

Concerning the first factor, the laughter she obtains allows her to amend the affront M1 made to her a few minutes ago when he did not take her sporadic interventions into account. She tried to save her own face by way of producing humor. She succeeds because her intervention is finally taken into account by M2 (239, 242) and greeted with laughter by the group (238). Nevertheless, M1 goes on, ignoring her utterance and, even if he perceives its humorous dimension (he participates in the general laughter), he chooses to respond in a serious way ("no no no" 237). This language strategy is very clever because it allows M1 to respond to F1 and thus, to accomplish his pragmatic constraint, and to go on developing the current topic: "on the other hand a doctor" (241) and "a doctor is good" (244).

With her humorous utterance and voluntarily absurdity, F1 produces a double voicing. The first enunciator (E1) is obtuse and unable to see that a linguist is completely useless in a dental practice. The second enunciator (E2) is amused by the situation created by the previous one. He/she had the sufficient distance to make the conversation funnier and lighter. But the fictive aspect of E1 can be actualized only if we take the existence of E2 i.e., F1's intention to provoke laughter, into account. But, recognizing the existence of E2 is dangerous for M1 because it also recognize F1's desire to switch into a non bona fide communication. Such a switch could trigger a thematic digression, a digression that M1 does not want. M1 is thus obliged to react as if he believed that F1's production was serious. By taking this utterance seriously, M1 can answer that a linguist is useless and continue his topic of choice.

A humorous utterance is built by convoking different voices or enunciators behind which the speaker hides him/herself. Thus, such an utterance requires an effort from the listener to decode it. But insofar as these sorts of enunciators are hardly identifiable and mostly implicit, the listener is free not to see them, not to switch with him or them into a non bona fide communication if he/she does not want to. Humor, although perceived, is not validated because the listener may pretend *as if*, as if he/she does not hear the intended humor.

The second reason why F1 produces her humorous utterance is probably the hope she has to interrupt the current topic about professional collaborations in a dentistry office. This interruption would have probably succeeded if, as M2 did, the other participants would have cooperated to develop the humor F1 tried to include. But F1's attempt to switch into a non bona fide communication fails at M1's behest. F1, recognizing her failure, seems to join M1, as the serious tone she employs shows (245), even if her production is inaudible. All the participants thus are going on the current topic (246–248).

(4)   *This interaction was recorded during a skiing vacation. Six friends were sharing the same small apartment. This excerpt takes place during the evening, after a long day of skiing.*

154	M2:	eh ben écoutez je me suis vraiment (+) fait une super journée de ski aujourd'hui
155	M3:	moi aussi
156	M1:	sans trop forcer↑
157	M2:	hmm= pétard
158	F2:	il est encore chaud ce truc ça dure ad vitam eternam↑
159	M2:	ad qui ↑
160		(petit rire des autres)
161	M3:	oh tu parles latin toi oh
162	M2:	elle veut impressionner ⟨inaudible⟩
163	F3:	couramment
164	M1:	c'est une pharmacienne elle sait ⟨inaudible⟩
165	F2:	oh putain ⟨lâche-les ?⟩ (+) les pauvres (+) i sont cons comme des manches

154	M2:	hey listen I had a super ski day today
155	M3:	me too
156	M1:	without forcing too much
157	M2:	hm Goddammit
158	F2:	it is still hot this thing[2] it lasts ad vitam eternan ↑
159	M2:	ad who ↑
160		The others : (small laughter)
161	M3:	hey you speak Latin you hey

---

2.   A gel bag one puts on the muscles to reduce the pain.

162	**M2:**	she wants to impress ⟨inaudible⟩
163	**F3:**	fluently
164	**M1:**	she's a pharmacist she knows ⟨inaudible⟩
165	**F2:**	oh goddammit ⟨keep them away?⟩ (+) poor guys (+) they are so stupid

This excerpt takes place at the beginning of the evening. The six friends are back from a long day of skiing. It is the moment when everybody makes an appraisal of the day (154–157). The utterance with the humorous sequence is in line 159 and concerns a gel bag F2 is applying to her leg. She applied this bag a long time ago and it is still hot, as we can understand from her utterance. This sentence would have gone unnoticed if F2 had not added a Latin locution. This locution, although very frequent in French, is still Latin and consequently connotes a certain level of culturedness. But, in this very close group, F2 is known for her unculturedness. With such an utterance, she takes up the image of a well-cultured person, an image generally rejected her by the other participants. That is exactly what will happen here. This Latin locution will be noticed by the listeners and particularly by M2 (159) and M3 (161). They choose to turn it into derision, and thereby turn on F2.

In line 161, M3 underlines that F2 is speaking Latin. He proceeds by exaggerating: he pretends that using a Latin locution implies being able to speak the whole language. In line 162, M2 outbids M3 by denunciating – correctly or incorrectly – the effect F2 wants to make i.e., impress. M2 wants to give F2 the image of a pretentious person. Thus, he adds a possibly fictive enunciator to F2's discourse. F2 did not really want to convoke this enunciator i.e., the utterance was not meant pretentiously. In line 164, M1 outbids M3 and stresses F2's false pretension by emphasizing the fact that she is a pharmacist i.e., a person who has a certain social level. At this point, F2 is a victim of a kind of 'beating' – indeed humorous, but real too. Above all, at that moment she is alone against all of the others. She is all the more alone because this 'beating' is probably unjustified: the enunciator, the image of a pretentious person, is probably false. Whether this image of which she is the victim corresponds to reality or not, F2 decides to dissociate from it – probably because it is too heavy (line 165). To do so, she proceeds in two different ways. First, she chooses a vulgar language and second, she clearly dissociates from the other pharmacists ("they") because being a pharmacist is the basis of the humorous beating: it is because she is pharmacist that she has a certain culture and that she use Latin locutions. According to this logic, if F2 refuses to be compared to the other pharmacists, she rejects the humorous logic as well. Here, humor is presumably perceived, but rejected by F2.

In this excerpt, F2 rejects the humorous sequence in order to repudiate the seemingly false image the others want to give her. By taking this sequence seriously, everything M2 and M3 say becomes a series of reproaches and not at all funny. This is probably the reason why she decides to stay in a serious mode of communication: she needs to respond to the reproaches; she feels the need to justify herself even if it is not really necessary.

5. Conclusion

There are many reasons why humor can fail: it can shock (e.g., turned into derision by the topic, because it is not the moment to produce humor), it can be not understood etc.

In this paper, we described two kinds of humor failure. In the first case, humor is purely and simply not perceived. In the second case, it is perceived but rejected by the listener, thus becoming a victim and not a participant of the humorous sequence. From friendly at the beginning, the humorous sequence becomes aggressive.

In all of the cases described, we have chosen the double voicing theory to explain the failures. Double voicing theory is not of course exclusive. Many other factors (pragmatic, psychological etc.) can contribute to the failure of humor. When humor is not perceived, the explanation we suggest shows that sometimes, it is impossible for the hearer to know which enunciator, which voice is speaking. As a result, is completely legitimate for him/her to question who is really speaking and above all, whether the utterance is serious or humorous.

In the case in which humor is perceived but denied, the double voicing process does not bother not the listener, but rather the speaker him/herself. Indeed, as the different enunciators convoked are screened, the listener chooses not to take them into account. The humor does not come to life because it is taken seriously and so, denied. "Tel est pris qui croyait prendre." The biter has been bitten.

Transcription conventions

F/M	Feminine/masculine and same couple (F1, M1), (F2, M2)
:	Vocalic lengthening. Quantity of : is proportional to the duration
/	Self-interruption of the discourse
//	Interruption by another speaker
(+)	Pause. Quantity of + is proportional to the duration
↑	High intonation. After the concerned syllable
↓	Low intonation. After the concerned syllable
=	Fast speech. After the concerned word or syllable

( )	Into brackets: description of behavior (in italic)
⟨ton moqueur⟩	Observer's commentary or interpretation
⟨puisque ?⟩	Doubts about the interpretation
⟨avez / aviez ?⟩	Hesitation between two possible words
⟨inaudible⟩	Inaudible word or sequence
NON, BONjour	Increased word or syllabus
pas-du-tout	To speak haltingly
Underlined words:	overlaps

References

Attardo, Salvatore. 1994. *Linguistic Theories of Humor*. Berlin: Mouton de Gruyter.

Bakhtin, Mikhail & Volosinov, V.N. 1977. *Le marxisme et la philosophie du langage*. Paris: Ed. de Minuit.

Bange, Pierre. 1986. "Une modalité des interactions verbales: fiction dans la conversation." *DRLAV* 34–35: 215–232.

Bariaud Bateson, Gregory et al. 1956. "Toward a theory of schizophrenia." *Behavioral Science* 1: 251–264.

Bariaud Bateson, Françoise. 1983. *La genèse de l'humour chez l'enfant*. Paris: PUF.

Ducrot, Oswald. 1984. *Le dire et le dit*. Paris: Ed. de Minuit.

Goffman, Erving. 1974. *Les rites d'interaction*. Paris: Ed. de Minuit.

Golopentja, Sanda. 1988. "Interaction et histoire conversationnelles." In *Echanges sur la conversation*, Cosnier, Gelas et Kerbrat-Orecchioni (Eds), 69–81. Paris : Editions du CNRS.

Hay, Jen. 1996. "No laughing matter: gender and humour support strategies." *Wellington Working Papers in Linguistics* 8: 1–24.

Holmes, Janet. 2000. "Politeness, power and provocation: how humour functions in the workplace." *Discourse Studies* 2(2): 159–185.

Kerbrat-Orecchioni, Catherine. 1996. *La conversation*. Paris: Ed. du Seuil, Coll. Mémo.

Norrick, Neal R. 1993. *Conversational Joking*. Bloomington: Indiana University Press.

Priego-Valverde, Béatrice. 1998. "L'humour (noir) dans la conversation: jeux et enjeux." *Revue de Sémantique et de Pragmatique* 3: 123–144.

———. 1999. *L'humour dans les interactions conversationnelles: jeux et enjeux*. Université de Provence, unpublished dissertation.

———. 2001. "'C'est du lard ou du cochon?': lorsque l'humour opacifie la conversation familière." *Marges linguistiques* 2: 195–208. On-line review: http://www.marges-linguistiques.com

Raskin, Victor. 1985. *Semantic Mechanisms of Humor*. Dordrecht: Reidel.

Schegloff, Emanuel A. & Sacks, Harvey. 1973. "Opening up closings." *Semiotica* 8(4): 289–327.

Roulet, Eddy et al. 1985. *L'articulation du discours en français contemporain*. Berne: Peter Lang.

Traverso, Véronique. 1996. *La conversation familière. Analyse pragmatique des interactions*. Lyon: Presses Universitaires de Lyon.

Vion, Robert. 1992. *La communication verbale. Analyse des interactions*. Paris: Hachette Supérieur.

———. 1995. "La gestion pluridimensionnelle du dialogue." *Cahiers de Linguistique Française* 17: 179–203.

PART IV

Humor in bilingual interactions

Humor and interlanguage in a bilingual elementary school setting

Kristin Kersten

This article focuses on the relationship between humor and language acquisition in a bilingual immersion setting. Data stem from picture story narrations by 18 informants taking part in an English immersion program in Germany. The analysis concentrates on instances of laughter and smiling as they appear spontaneously during the child narrations. In an initial step, different categories of laughter are identified and subsequently analyzed with regard to their relation to humor and to (the second) language, respectively. A final step of analysis discusses the functions of these categories within the social interaction of interviewer and child. The results point to young language learners' use of humor (among other functions) as a mechanism to cope with the linguistic inadequacies of their interlanguage.

1. Introduction

Research in the field of second language acquisition (SLA) has not yet focused intensely on the phenomenon of humor in relation to the level of linguistic development in the second language (L2). This article connects linguistic observations in a second language classroom with results from humor research to argue that young L2 learners have an awareness of the collision between demands that arise in communicative situations and their limited language skills. More specifically, it will be discussed whether the awareness of an incongruity between classroom expectations and interlanguage lead children to use humor as a coping strategy, and which functions of humor can be observed in the child data. It is suggested that learners use mechanisms of humor to alleviate the communicative problems that arise from their incomplete mastery of the target language. The first part of the article gives an overview of previous findings in the field of child humor, which will be related to the results of this study in the second part.

2.   Previous findings

2.1   Child language acquisition and the cooperative principle

The phenomenon of humor within the field of SLA is determined by the fact that the interlanguage system of the child does not equal that of a native speaker. As is intuitively obvious and as experience from bilingual language programs shows, difficulties with the second language arise on all different linguistic levels, even for very young L2 learners. A few examples from bilingual preschools in Germany[1] may serve as an illustration:

<u>Phonology</u>

(1)   Child: Chat et canard [kʰaˈnɑː], *das reimt sich ja!*
                [Cat and duck (French: [ʃa] / [kaˈnaʁ]), they rhyme!]

<u>Lexicon/Morphology</u>

(2)   Adult: Show me the mouth!
       Child: *Die Maus ist nicht da.*
                [The mouse is not there.]

(3)   Adult: Oh, I missed it!
       Child: *Mist sagen wir nicht! Oder?*
                [We don't say 'darn'. Do we? (*Mist* – dung, infml.: mild swearword in German)]

Especially for young children, difficulties may also arise on a cognitive level: The next example shows a French-German bilingual child talking to an adult whom she only knows as speaker of English in her preschool. She does not realize that the adult now answers in (one of) the child's mother tongues, French. The example illustrates a violation of the person-language bond, which the child is incapable of transferring to the newly experienced situation.

<u>Cognition</u>

(4)   Child: *Tu es un mouton!* (provocatively, expects not to be understood)
       Adult: *Et toi, tu es une chèvre.* (grins)
       Child: *Non, et toi, tu ne me comprends pas, parce que moi, je parle français!*
                [You are a sheep!
                And you, you are a goat!
                No, and you, you don't understand me because I, I'm speaking French!]

---

1.   The two bilingual preschools (French-German in Rostock, English-German in Kiel-Altenholz, northern Germany) form part of a larger research project consisting of several immersion institutions. The examples are taken from Westphal (1998), Leibing (1999), Berger (1999) and Kersten (2002). See also Wode (2001, 2003) and Section 3.1.

These examples show that all kinds of difficulties with the second language arise as early as in preschool. Moreover, as research in the field of SLA has shown (except for the cognitive level) they even increase with age (cf. Ellis 1994 for an overview).

However, difficulties in L2 situations are not confined to these specific linguistic areas. They affect the system of social communication and interaction as a whole. In his Cooperative Principle, Grice (1975) specified a number of maxims for a successful conversation: the maxims of Quality, Quantity, Relevance, and Manner, which postulate that speakers are expected to talk sincerely, relevantly and clearly, while providing sufficient information. In other words, they should cooperate on all levels with the expectations of the listener. Second language learners, however, are compelled to violate these expectations in spite of themselves since their interlanguage system necessarily falls short of the required means of communication: their expression of thought is starkly restricted by a lack of vocabulary and other linguistic means.

Most common applications of the Gricean maxims refer to native speakers of a language (cf. Attardo 1994: 274f for an illustration; Shultz and Robillard 1980 for children). Table 1 illustrates that second language learners are prone to violate some of these principles as a result of their stage of interlanguage:

Table 1. Violations of the Cooperative Principle (Grice 1975) in SLA (excerpts from grade 1 picture story narrations by German children)

Maxim	Excerpt from the Data	Effect
Quality	Child 16A mmh the bag with the # flies [beehive] fa/is falling down	incorrect description
Quantity	Child 03B The dog he's hungry and # (turns several pages) Interviewer Mmh! You skip all the pages! (...) Child 03B *Diese beiden sind irgendwie so blöd.* [These two are so stupid, somehow.]	insufficient information
Manner	Child 07A The boy *klettert* [climbs] on *ein Scht/* [a stone] on one stone and *rufing* (...) the *Frosch* [frog] Child 18B And on the next morning # mh are s/ see the dog and the boy that the frog is # ehm the frog is # ehm outgo of the glass. (...) Ehm # eh mh mmh eh the boy and the dog is feeling up from the deer ehm in/ in the water	limited comprehensibility

– pause; / – hesitation; *italics* – L1 (German)

The necessity to search for adequate modes of expression when essential vocabulary and grammatical knowledge are lacking as illustrated in these examples makes a child aware that his/her interlanguage is somewhat inadequate to the task.

Language learners are able to adapt to this situation more or less creatively. One first grader commented on this in a surprisingly explicit metalinguistic way:

(5)   Child 11 A   *Weißt du was Frau P. mir auch beigebracht hat? Wenn ich was nicht weiß, dann sag ich einfach was so Ähnliches.* (laughs)
[Do you know what else Mrs. P. taught us? If there's something I don't know, I simply say something similar.]

As Shultz and Robillard (1980: 85) point out, "the violation of pragmatic rules appears to be a rich natural source of incongruity humour." The connection between the Cooperative Principle and the experience of humor in SLA is thus the concept of *incongruity*, i.e., the violation of expectations in communication.

2.2   Child humor: Developmental issues

Recent research in psychology has shown that young children are not only susceptible to humor but that they also actively produce humor themselves. Different types of humor and their evolution in child development have been identified within the last decades. Children's appreciation and use of humor start at a very early age, i.e., between 1–2 years (McGhee 1979; Bergen 1998); For a contrastive overview of humor development in different approaches of developmental psychology see Bönsch-Kauke (2003: 49ff).

Incongruity as one of the key factors in child humor has been defined as the simultaneous experience of normally incompatible elements (Bariaud 1989: 17). The complexity of the humor element, however, is related (among other aspects) to the child's cognitive development (McGhee 1971; Masten 1986). McGhee (1971: 125) asserts that the experience of such elements requires "the cognitive capacities necessary for [the child's] identification of incongruities." Children at the age of 6–7, the age of the subjects in this study, appear to undergo striking changes in the quality of their humor behavior because, McGhee (1971) argues, this is the time when they experience what Piaget calls the transition between preoperational and operational modes of thinking (e.g., 1950, 1962). At this time, comprehension of logical relationships replaces the former dominance of perceptual appearance. Bariaud (1989: 35), referring to McGhee's model, describes this phenomenon as follows:

> Thought, at this point, ceases to be dominated by perceptual appearances. The child can ... keep two things in mind at the same time. ... Instead of simply keeping in mind the perceptual features of the event, he is also able to mentally reconstruct the successive actions that led up to it. This makes it possible to understand an incongruity which is not immediately obvious (McGhee, 1971 a and b, 1972).

Other characteristics of humor behavior at this age are, for instance, the use of play languages or secret languages (Shultz & Robillard 1980; Apte 1985), the incipient use of sexual humor (Wolfenstein 1954; Bariaud 1989), and the comprehension of irony (Dews et al. 1996), the appreciation of verbal humor with double meanings, the capacity to explain a funny experience (Apte 1985; Bariaud 1989) and consequently the true appreciation of jokes (Bergen 1998).

Bergen (1998)[2] and Bönsch-Kauke (2003)[3] found the majority of children's humor behavior among playful and clownesque forms of humor, i.e., nonsense, incongruity humor (performance of incongruous actions, humor reactions to incongruous situations), and the expression of joy or cheerfulness. Most of these are non-aggressive forms of humor. Only in later years of elementary school (grades 4–6), Bönsch-Kauke finds increasingly verbal and aggressive forms of humor, together with forms of humor used to cover up inabilities.

Shultz and Robillard (1980) point out that the different fields of linguistics (phonology, morphology, semantics, syntax, and pragmatics) each provide grounds for the use of linguistic humor, which is "based on the child's developing metalinguistic knowledge; that is, awareness of language *qua* language" (1980: 60). They also indirectly relate the violation of conversational principles to this age: "indirect request forms based on conversational postulates are comprehended as young as two years, produced by four years, and made objects of *the child's awareness by about six years*" (1980: 84, italics added).[4]

2.3 Functions of child humor

Children's humor has an interactive function which facilitates an ongoing reciprocal adaptation of child and social environment in the process of socialization (Apte 1985; Masten 1986; Simons et al. 1986; McGhee 1989; Bönsch-Kauke 2003); see Attardo (1994: 322ff) on social functions of humor in general. Bönsch-Kauke (2003: 59) summarizes:

> Humor is best described as a developmental phenomenon, which mediates successful interaction between the individual and its cultural and social context. (2003: 59 [translation KK])

---

2. Bergen's (1998) study aims at finding different types of humor spontaneously initiated and appreciated by young children age 2–7.

3. Bönsch-Kauke (2003) develops a detailed taxonomy of categories relevant to child humor interactions on the basis of longitudinal observation in a class of elementary school children from grades 2 through 6 (age 7–12).

4. Apte (1985: 84) cautions that categories of humor as those cited above are to some extent expected to "overlap, and the boundaries between them may be subject to frequent shifting." Additionally, they may vary according to the socio-cultural background.

Thus, humor behavior contributes to the process in which children internalize behavioral norms and value systems through social learning and enculturation (Apte 1985).

Play, especially pretend play, during which the child mimics or re-enacts observed adult interactions, has proved to be a very important means for this process. Recent research has found striking similarities between the play frame and the humor frame (Bergen 2006). Not only are the cues for both frames similar in the adult-child interaction, such as "exaggerated facial expressions, higher-pitched voice, intense gaze, and smiles or open mouth (Stern, 1974)" (Bergen 2007: 30), but humor qualities in children have also been found to be related to the personality construct of 'playfulness' (for a review, see Bergen 2006: 145). As Bergen points out, the 'as-if' mode relates to both the recognition of humor incongruity and to the 'pretend' nature of children's play.

> From this theoretical perspective, children's ability to develop a good sense of humor is based on their early adult-child play experiences, because these experiences transmit the essential metacommunication "This is humor." The implication of this view is that the human capacity to become socially skilled users of humor depends on their incorporation of this message. (Bergen 2006: 147)

Several studies have outlined more specific functions of child humor. Often, terminological differences conceal overlaps in meaning. Table 2 is primarily based on McGhee's (1989) model of child humor, but other models include many of the same aspects. From the variety of functions McGhee (and other authors) present, the following ones were found to have a special relevance for the data under consideration:

Table 2. Functions of humor in social interaction (adapted from McGhee 1989; Bönsch-Kauke 2003)

	Humor Function	Description
1	Facilitation of Social Interaction	Use of humor to make communication easier
2	Positive Attention	Use of humor to receive acceptance and recognition
3	Hostility	Use of humor as a socially acceptable means to express aggression
4	Amusement	Use of humor and funniness for its own sake
5	Saving Face	Use of humor to defuse tension in a difficult situation

Functions 1, 2, and 5 are cooperative functions of humor (Bönsch-Kauke 2003). Humor as Facilitation of Social Interaction establishes a feeling of bonding and group cohesiveness among the participants (Attardo 1994: 324f). Positive Attention, the use of humor to receive social integration, corresponds at least in part to 'ingratiation' and the display of 'cleverness' as cited in Attardo (1994: 324).[5] Hostility or exclusion from the mutual bond (Attardo 1994: 325) represents a competitive function incorporating socially acceptable forms of aggression and dominance (Bönsch-Kauke 2003). McGhee's list lacks Bönsch-Kauke's category of genuine Amusement (4), i.e., fun for its own sake, expressed by cheerfulness or joy. Finally, the function of Saving Face or Repair has been defined as "unpleasant situations [which] may be defused by humorous comments, connoting positive attitude" (Attardo 1994: 324). It will become important in the context of an interlanguage phenomenon (Section 4.4).

3. Method

Data elicitation: Data were obtained from a partial immersion elementary school in northern Germany, where all subjects are taught in English except for German as a subject.[6] A longitudinal study using picture story narrations was conducted to collect fluent, semi-spontaneous L2 speech samples; the data elicitation method was partly adapted from Housen and Pallotti (1999) and Pallotti (personal communication); see also Housen (2002). The story used for data elicitation has become known, in linguistic circles, as the so-called *Frog Story* (*Frog, where are you?*, Mayer 1969), a story of a little boy and his dog who go on an adventure trip through the woods in search of their pet frog. The story is rich in events which occur both simultaneously and chronologically as the plot unfolds.

The children were interviewed alone by adults previously acquainted to them. They were able to look at the pictures before the interview started. Each interview consisted of two parts. During the first part (A) the children told the story in English to an interviewer known to be a speaker of German. In this way, they could familiarize themselves with the story and ask for unknown vocabulary. In this part, the pictures were visible both to the child and the interviewer. In the second part (B) the children were supposed to tell the story again without interruption to a second interviewer whom they knew as a speaker of the L2 not capable of understanding their L1. In this part, the interviewer was not allowed to see the pictures, so she

---

5. Bönsch-Kauke (2003) differentiates between motives ('Why?') and functions ('What for?'). 1 includes Bönsch-Kauke's motives 'sociability' and 'cheerfulness', 2 incorporates all motives and functions relevant to social integration, i.e., acceptance, appreciation, attractiveness, prestige, contact and flirt. (All translations of the humor categories used by Bönsch-Kauke are provided by myself and will henceforth not be indicated anymore.)

6. The elementary school in Kiel-Altenholz, Germany, is one of several immersion institutions initiated and supervised by Henning Wode and his research group from the Linguistics Department of Kiel University (Wode 1998, 1999, 2001, 2003).

had to rely entirely on the children's capacity of making themselves understood in English. Except for signs of encouragement the interviewer did not interfere with the story-telling and the children were not able to ask questions. Each interview was audio- and video-taped. Data from both parts (A and B) are analyzed in this study (see also Lauer & Hansen 2001; Kersten et al. 2002).

Subjects: Data from 18 first graders (age 6–7), which constitute the first segment of data elicitation within the longitudinal study, serve as the basis for the analysis. The subjects were tested after 10 months of language input in school. Although this time span provides the children with enough L2 capacity to tackle the task, they were obviously unable to express themselves as freely as in their L1. However, their having to communicate with a person who, for all they knew, understood only English, called for other, creative solutions of expression.

Research Question and Expectations:

The research focus of this study is on the following questions:

1. Does the awareness of an incongruity between classroom expectations and interlanguage lead children in an L2 context to use humor as a coping strategy?
2. If so, what are the different categories and functions of humor as used spontaneously by the children?

According to findings of previous research, humor is one expected response among several others to the L2 context. Other reactions may include a non-humorous form of awareness, leading to a feeling of embarrassment. Categories of humor are expected to be found within the range of forms of humor that were described in previous research for the respective age range (cf. Section 2), and especially among the categories of clowning and cheerfulness or joy, amusement through incongruities (of all kinds), and verbal humor. Functions of humor are predicted to be manifold but with a distinct emphasis on social aspects.

Methodological Approach and Analysis: This analysis uses a descriptive approach to the L2 picture story narrations in that the data were not approached with certain predetermined humor categories in mind. Where applicable, the classifications outlined in Section 2.2 were used as reference points. In order to identify instances of humor in the child narrations, each turn was analyzed in which either the child or the interviewer displayed laughter or smiles on the video-recordings. Instances of laughter and smiling were understood as indicators of humor but were not identified with it since it would be wrong to assume a one-to-one relationship between laughter and humor (Apte 1985; Attardo 1994, cf. Section 4.2). Thus, the data were first subsumed under different *categories of laughter and smiling.* Subsequently it was quantified and analyzed with regard to their inherent *humor value*. The categories were then related to the *interlanguage context*. Finally, the *function* of the laughter categories was discussed. Only those turns were taken into consideration in which the classification seemed unambiguous to the author as an objective observer. All other instances were excluded from the analysis.[7]

4.   Results and discussion

4.1   Categories of laughter

279 tokens of laughter and smiling were identified in the interaction between children and interviewer in the data. They were categorized according to the following classification (Table 3):

Table 3. Categories of laughter and smiling identified in the L2 picture story narrations

	L2 Category of Laughter	Description
1	Joy	Child expresses joy, relief, or pride in connection with mastery of the narration
2	Embarrassment	Child expresses embarrassment in connection with perceived inadequacies in the narration
3	Narrative/Behavioral Incongruity	Unexpected change in narrative style or behavior
4	Meta-Linguistic Incongruity	Intentional use of unexpected verbal elements (comments, repetitions, Germanisms, inadequate words, etc.)
5	Clowning	Exaggerated, attention-seeking, coquettish behavior, exaggerated 'acting out' of scenes within the story
6	Deprecation	Child laughs or jokes at the expense of someone else
7	Self-Disparagement	Child laughs at own mistake
8	Pictorial Incongruity	Child laughs about picture in picture story booklet
9	Involuntary Incongruity	Child's wording of narration or event depiction is involuntarily funny to the interviewer/listener
10	Encouragement	Interviewer laughs encouragingly, admiringly, or rewardingly at the child

Categories 1–8 in Table 3 describe humor actions or reactions on the part of the children. Most of them are accompanied by a laugh or smile on the part of the interviewer. Categories 9–10 focus on the interviewer who actively interacts with the child. The interviewer used laughter either to encourage the child to go on with

---

7.   To increase the reliability of the analysis, future research may use several coders for the identification of humor and laughter categories. Unfortunately, this was beyond the scope of this study.

the story, or as spontaneous reaction to a child's involuntary comical use of words.[8] These situations usually triggered the child's laughter, as well. The categories of laughter display the following distribution in the data:

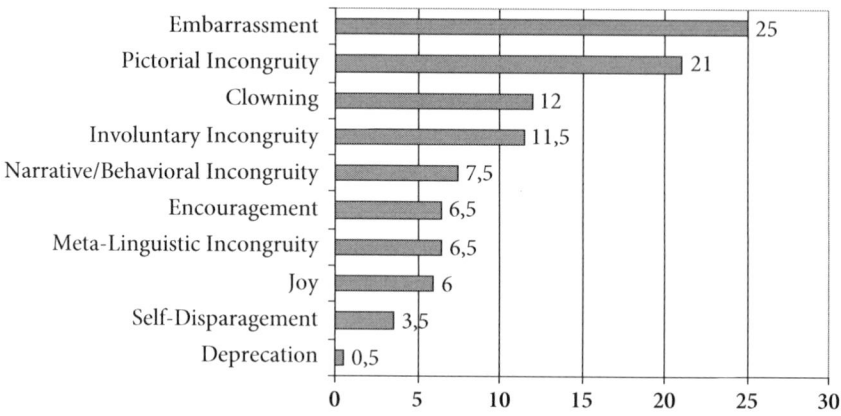

Figure 1. Distribution of categories of laughter/smiling (%)

Embarrassment (25%) and Pictorial Incongruity (21%) represent the two types of situations which most often elicit laughter and/or smiling in the interaction. Clowning (12%) and Involuntary Incongruities (11.5%) followed. The relatively high amount of the latter is mostly due to the L2 context in which the children were not aware that what they said was funny. Fewer instances, more or less evenly distributed, are found within the group made up of Narrative/Behavioral (7.5%), Meta-Linguistic Incongruities (6.5%) and Encouragement (6.5%), and the expression of Joy (6%). The least were found in the two categories of Deprecation; laughing at the own mistakes (Self-Disparagement 3.5%) occurring more frequently. Deprecation (0.5%) was so minor that it is henceforth neglected in the analysis.

As predicted, Embarrassment as well as Clowning and enjoying Pictorial Incongruity form a large part of the children's interaction, in contrast to a small amount of aggressive forms of humor (Deprecation and Self-Disparagement). These findings are basically in line with the anticipated results and correspond to those of other studies (Bergen 1998; Bönsch-Kauke 2003). The amount of Joy and Narrative or Behavioral Incongruity is not as great as expected. This can be explained by two factors: In contrast to other studies, these children were in a test situation (in spite

---

8.   Apte (1985: 99) describes the reaction of adults to the children's humor behavior: They laugh about children or "are amused because they see an incongruity in the children's acts between outward appearance and implications that are beyond the children's comprehension." See also Bönsch-Kauke (2003: 33), with reference to Röhrich (1977).

of all efforts on the part of the interviewers to relax the atmosphere) and the L2 context naturally contributed to a sense of insecurity for those children susceptible to it. This view is supported by the high amount of Embarrassment representing another, non-humorous reaction to the interlanguage situation. The amount of linguistic humor does not meet the expectations, either.[9] Its use is, however, all the more surprising, since the children in this study use their *second* language to make humorous comments on language, which requires a much higher linguistic awareness than in the L1. Table 4 compares the categories identified in the data with those established in previous research (cf. Section 2):

Table 4. Comparative categorization of laughter/smiling and humor categories from other studies (Apte 1985; Bergen 1998; Bönsch-Kauke 2003; Shultz & Robillard 1980)

	L2 Category of Laughter	Child Humor Category	Author
1	Joy	Cheerfulness/Amusement (Expressed joy in mastery (...))	Bönsch-Kauke Bergen
2	Embarrassment	Embarrassment/Shame	Bönsch-Kauke
3	Narrative/Behavioral Incongruity	Performing incongruous actions (Nonsense)	Bergen Bönsch-Kauke
4	Meta-linguistic Incongruity	Linguistic humour Linguistic humor Word play (Jargon)/(Games)	Shultz and Robillard Apte Bergen Bönsch-Kauke
5	Clowning	Humor in play Clowning Nonsense/Clownesque form	Apte Bergen Bönsch-Kauke
6	Deprecation	Mockery/Scorn/Teasing (Verbal or behavioral teasing)	Bönsch-Kauke Bergen
7	Self-Disparagement	Self-disparagement	Bergen
8	Pictorial Incongruity	Discovering incongruous objects, actions, events	Bergen
9	Involuntary Incongruity	(Humor of socialization)	Apte
10	Encouragement	–	–

( ) description includes only part of meaning of L2 category of laughter

Several categories identified in the data do not correspond entirely to categories suggested by other authors. This may partly be due to the different task in this study, i.e., the picture story narration related to linguistic performance. Nevertheless, the categories are included in the list for the sake of completeness and indicated by brackets.

---

9. The category of Meta-Linguistic Incongruity is more in line with Bösch-Kauke's study (Jargon [2.8%] and Games [5.2%] including puns and word play) than with Bergen's study, who finds word play in over 24% of her records.

4.2 What's so funny? – The laughter categories and their relation to humor

The categories described in Section 4.1 represent a compilation of all instances of laughter and smiling in the data. As already stated above, when analyzing humor categories, it is important not to fall into the trap of equating laughter with humor (Apte 1985). Already in 1956, Edmund Bergler criticized then popular theories of laughter, which claimed that "one laughs when and because something is funny, and something is funny because and when one laughs" (p. vii). As has often been pointed out since, neither can it be claimed that humor is a necessary criterion for laughter nor vice versa (overview of literature cf. Attardo 1994: 10ff). Rather, laughter and smiling are denoted as polysemic in meaning in that "they may derive from varied types of emotional experiences" (Bariaud 1989: 16). However, smiles and laughter can indisputably function as indicators of humor or, to put it in Austin's (1962) terminology, laughter is a perlocutionary effect of humor, i.e., the causal effect which the speaker intentionally wants to create (cf. Attardo 1994).

To distinguish instances of laughter related to the experience of humor from other kinds of situations, a set of criteria applicable to children and humor in a second language context had to be developed for this study. The point of departure is the focus on the child's experience of funniness irrespective of an adult's reaction to or perspective of it (Bergen 1998: 336). Additionally, it is important to differentiate between humor initiation and humor response as both categories require different criteria. Humor initiation is an active effort on the part of the child to say something funny, whereas humor response is the child's reaction to a funny stimulus. The criteria used for the humor classification are:

a. *incongruity* in the situation
b. the child's *awareness* of incongruity (cf. Bariaud 1989)[10]
c. the child's experience of *funniness* (cf. Bergen 1998)
d. the child's *intention* to amuse (cf. Bariaud 1989)

The last criterion (d) is necessary for humor *initiations*, the remaining criteria for both humor *initiation* and humor *response*. The following table (Table 5) describes the distribution of laughter categories with respect to these criteria:

---

10. Unlike Bariaud (1989), who focuses on humorous interaction, I do not require a dual awareness (of both participants) since the object of investigation is solely the child's humor competence. The same restriction is also valid for the child's experience of funniness (c), where Bergen (1998) explicitly excludes the feelings of the adult communication partner.

Table 5. Distribution of humor (initiation and response) in categories of laughter/smiling

Humor initiation	%	Criteria
Clowning	12.0	incongruity, awareness, funniness, intention to amuse
Narrative/Behavioral Incongruity	7.5	
Meta-Linguistic Incongruity	6.5	
Self-Disparagement	3.5	
Humor response		
Pictorial Incongruity	21.0	incongruity, awareness, funniness
Non-humor forms of laughter		
Embarrassment	25.0	no funniness
Joy	6.0	no incongruity
Interviewer reaction		
Involuntary Incongruity	11.5	no awareness
Encouragement	6.5	None

The categories of humor initiation are Clowning, Narrative and Meta-Linguistic Incongruity, and Self-Disparagement. They fulfill the set of criteria for humor, i.e., incongruity, awareness, the experience of funniness and the intention to make the interactor laugh. Since it lacks the intention to amuse, Pictorial Incongruity, i.e., laughter about a funny picture, is the only humor response. The rest of the laughter categories all lack one or another criterion for humor classification and are thus not included in the humor categories. Figure 2 shows that the presence of humor

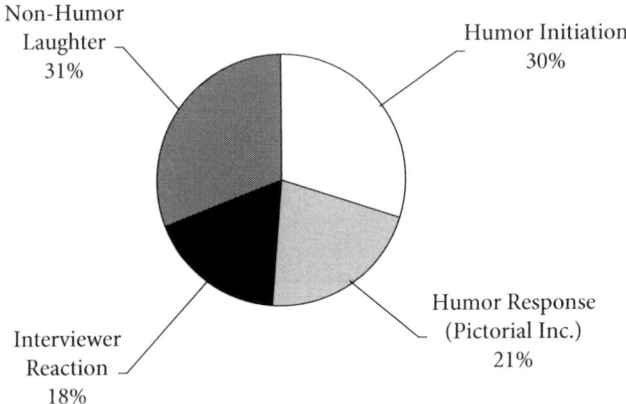

Figure 2. Distribution of humor categories and non-humor categories among instances of laughter/smiling (%, rounded up)

(initiation + response) amounts to about 50% of all instances of laughter and smiling. All other instances of laughter are either unrelated to humor (Embarrassment and Joy) or are only displayed by the interviewer (Involuntary Incongruity and Encouragement). Figure 2 summarizes the humor/non-humor classification in the categories of laughter and smiling.

4.3   Humor and language

The initial hypothesis held that children's use of humor in a second language context may be related to the violation of communicative principles, i.e., to a perceived incongruity between expectations and the child's linguistic performance. In order to make a statement about this, those instances of humor need to be identified, where the child is aware of an incongruity related to language. The examples in Table 6 serve as illustrations:

Table 6. Language-related use of humor

	Excerpt from the Data	Humor Category
1	Child 11B And the bees coming and will *pieks* the dog. (laughs, squirms) IE (laughs) Child 11B *Ich wußte das nicht mehr.* [I didn't know that (the word for 'sting') any more]	Meta-Linguistic Incongruity
2	Child 11A And then (laughing) *oh, schon wieder hab ich Hirsch vergessen.* [oh, I forgot 'deer' again]	Self-Disparagement
3	Child 12A The dog # stand on a *Baum* (shakes her head) eh on a tree. (smiles) I (laughs)	Self-Disparagement
4	Child 16A 'Nd there is a # a *Bambi.* (looks to I, smiles, laughs) I (laughs) Very good!	Meta-Linguistic Incongruity

I – German-speaking interviewer; IE – English-speaking interviewer; # – pause; *italics* – L1 (German)

In all of these examples, laughter is related to some sort of linguistic inadequacy experienced by the children. Obviously, not all humor situations are examples of this. On the contrary, the children employ humor very creatively for different purposes if they feel at ease with the situation and the language. Therefore, it was necessary to identify those instances of humor solely related to the second language context of the children. This kind of humor is henceforth referred to as 'language-related use of humor'. Its distribution within the humor categories is displayed in Figure 3:

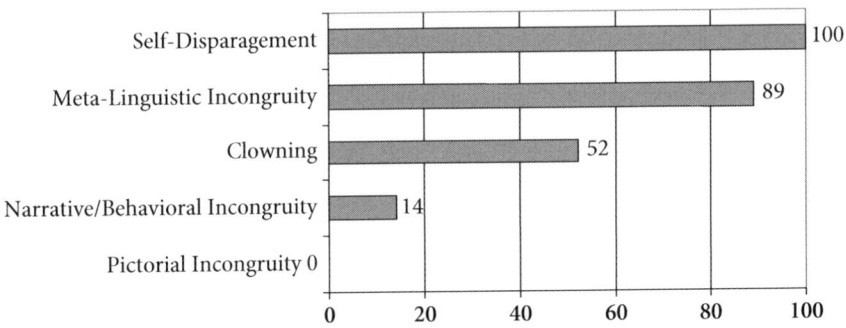

Figure 3. Distribution of language-related humor (%) among categories of humor

According to Figure 3, all tokens of Self-Disparaging humor relate to language, roughly 90% of all instances of Meta-Linguistic Incongruity and over 50% of Clowning relate to language, etc. Pictorial Incongruity never related to language, but this category is a humor *response* to a stimulus in the pictures. Thus, it is not relevant to the L2 context and the children's own initiation of humor. Leaving this category of humor response aside, language-related instances of humor amount to 55% of all humor initiation categories.

Unsurprisingly, in a second language situation like this, the other non-humor categories of laughter also display a connection with linguistic inadequacy. This is shown in the next graph (Figure 4):

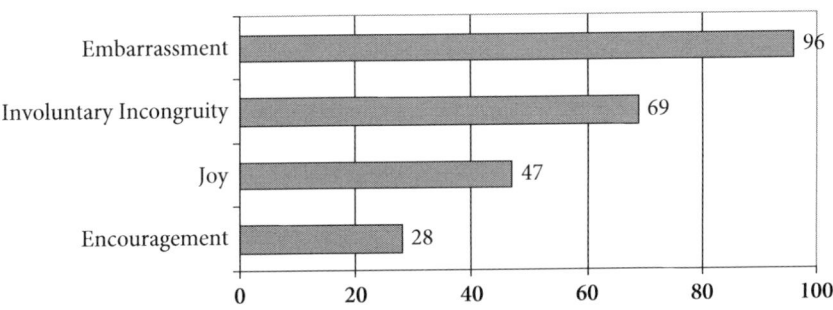

Figure 4. Distribution of language-related laughter/smiling (%) among non-humor categories

In 96% of instances of Embarrassment and half of all situations displaying Joy children laugh and smile about their use of language without any relation to humor. Involuntary Incongruity (28%) and Encouragement (69%) are the interviewer's reactions to the children's linguistic performance. Although they also represent instances of laughter in the data, they have to be excluded since the child is unaware of the reasons for it. 86% of the remaining non-humor tokens (i.e., of Embarrassment and Joy) are language-related. Table 7 illustrates the different relations of humor and language analyzed in this section:

Table 7. Relationship of humor categories and non-humor categories to L2 context (%, rd – rounded up)

L2 Category of Laughter	%	Classification of Humor and Non-Humor	% (rd.)	Related to Language %
Clowning	12.0	Humor initiation	30	55
Narrative/Behavioral Incongruity	7.5			
Meta-Linguistic Incongruity	6.5			
Self-Disparagement	3.5			
Pictorial Incongruity	21.0	Humor response	21	0
Embarrassment	25.0	Non-humor laughter	31	86
Joy	6.0			
Involuntary Incongruity	11.5	Interviewer reaction	18	(excluded)
Encouragement	6.5			

4.4 Motives and functions

This final section of analysis discusses the possible functions of the humor categories with regard to the interaction between child and interviewer. The categories established here are first discussed in the light of previously described functions of humor and then analyzed with respect to the observations in the data. Section 2.3 outlined the following humor functions as relevant to the data (cf. Table 2):

1. Facilitation of Social Interaction
2. Positive Attention
3. Hostility
4. Amusement
5. Saving Face

Humor as Facilitation of Social Interaction is a very broad function that can be applied to almost every category of child humor identified in this study except Deprecation. Even the category of Self-Disparagement can be used to create a mutual positive feeling in the interaction. The humor category observed in the data best described by Positive Attention is Clowning, defined as attention-seeking behavior. Yet, Positive Attention certainly also plays a role in Incongruous Behavior and Deprecation of others in order to elevate one's own status. Hostility represents another function of Deprecation and also includes Self-Disparagement. However, as already stated, aggressive forms of humor like this are barely found in the data at all. The function of Amusement relates Pictorial Incongruity and, partly, to Joy. Finally, the function of Saving Face or Repair is very important in the context of an interlanguage phenomenon. It can be used to cover up inabilities or embarrassment (Bönsch-Kauke 2003: 139, 137). This is illustrated by McGhee (1989: 129), who claims that "a skilled humorist can use a joke or playful remark to replace embarrassment ... with laughter." In her research, Bariaud (1989: 32f) observes a similar phenomenon:

> A young child who makes a mistake in formulating a word ... sometimes deliberately exploits the situation to provoke laughter. ... His attention is at first centered on his speech but shifts to the expectation of others and to the amusement produced by not conforming. The initial mistake is thus transformed into a farce.

Bariaud's description precisely illustrates those instances of humor initiations in the data, which follow inadequate linguistic performance in an L2 situation. Table 8 displays two examples from the data (Example 4 is repeated from Table 6). Child 16 describes the same picture, the sudden appearance of a deer, in the first and the second part of the test. In the first one (A), the interviewer is a native speaker of German. The situation becomes most revealing when the child repeats the story to the English-speaking interviewer in the second part (B). Example 5 shows how she exploits this situation in the second interview.

In 5, the uncertainty of the first interview is consciously transformed into a little dramatic performance to recreate the positive reaction the child experienced in the first interview. More abstractly, the child is aware of her linguistic limitations. As research on this age-group has demonstrated (McGhee 1971, Shultz and Robillard 1980), she has the necessary cognitive capacities to understand the incongruity arising from the expectation to cooperate with the interviewer (who she believes does not speak German) and her own language capacity. However, she also has the ability to very creatively defuse this uncomfortable situation by making a humorous comment, *Bambi*, a reference to a mutual association with the object, *deer*. This is the very definition of the function of Repair.

As shown in 4.3, 55% percent of children's humor initiations took place in language-related contexts in which the children were aware of the incongruity resulting from their interlanguage. Thus, the data suggest that it is the function of Saving Face/Repair which is most exploited in the language-related humor categories (Self-Disparagement, Meta-Linguistic Incongruity, Clowning, and, in part, Narrative/Behavioral Incongruity). Additionally, as Example 5 made clear, it also plays a major

Table 8. The function of Repair

	Excerpt from the Data	Humor Category
4	Child 16A 'Nd there is a # a *Bambi*. (looks to I, smiles, laughs) I (laughs) Very good!	Meta-Linguistic Incongruity
5	Child 16B There's a / (smiles embarrassedly, laughs, throws herself on the table) there's a # IE A what? Child 16B (laughs, preparing the punch-line) *Ich weiß gar nicht* [I don't know] XXX IE You forgot/ Child 16B A *Bambi* (looks challengingly and smiling to I) *sag ich dann eben!* [that's what I'll say then!] (looks enquiringly to P, laughs)	Meta-Linguistic Incongruity, Clowning, Embarrassment

I – German-speaking interviewer; IE – English-speaking interviewer; / – hesitation; # – pause,
XXX – incomprehesible; P – observer (present in both interviews); *italics* – L1 (German)

role in the category of Embarrassement, which, while not humor-related, is almost exclusively language-related (Figure 4). This outcome deviates somewhat from the study conducted by Bönsch-Kauke (2003). Her results indicate that children mainly use humor to amuse and have fun, to establish contact with others and create a sense of belonging, and to distance themselves from others in order to create and establish their own identity. Her categories relevant for Repair represent only a very small amount of her motive- and function-categories.[11] On the contrary, the use of humor to cover up inabilities appears only much later in her study, i.e., in grade 6 (age 11–12). Therefore, the data suggest that the large proportion of Repair-related humor in this study relates to the specific L2 context in which the children find themselves, which is distinct from common experience of elementary school environment.

There is no one-to-one relationship between a specific humor category and its social function in the interaction. The last example illustrates this very clearly. Not only is it impossible from an outsider's perspective to determine the immanent

---

11. Her categories "covering up embarrassment", "covering up inabilities", and "shame and fear of embarrassment" represent only 2.5%, 2.3%, and 0.8% of her motives/functions, respectively.

goal of a child's utterance, but it is safe to assume that in many cases more than one function is involved of which the child is not consciously aware at the moment of the utterance, let alone which the child him/herself could identify.[12] In many cases, one function sticks out as a more relevant – but not the only – one in a particular situation. However, this is not generally the case. For this reason, this analysis refrains from the attempt to map forms of humor directly onto distinct functions.

4.5 Issues of variation

Ruch and Köhler (1998) differentiate between Humor Traits, i.e., habitual individual differences in humor behavior, and Humor States, the actual dispositions for humor, which vary over time. The complex distribution of factors influencing humor behavior leads to great variation, intra- and interindividual, respectively. A person may be more apt to use or appreciate humor in one situation than in another and a different person will use it in a different manner, frequency etc. Studies on child humor confirm this result (Bergen 1998; Bönsch-Kauke 2003; Brodzinsky and Rightmyer 1980).

The same finding applies to the data in this study, especially with regard to interindividual variation. Some children are strongly inclined to use humor to relate to the interviewer during the narration and those who do so usually also display different forms of humor, whereas the data of other children do not show a single instance of smiling let alone humor. Rather, these children are prone to exhibit forms of embarrassment. Variation ranges from transcripts without a single incident of smiling or laughter to 43 instances of laughter distributed over 9 different categories. Overall 83%, i.e., 15 of 18 children, used humor in their narratives, and only two children (11%) did not exhibit humor nor smiles throughout both interviews. However, a detailed analysis of this kind of variation is beyond the scope of this article.

5. Conclusion

This study on the interface between humor and SLA has shown that young second language learners do indeed use humor in the context of a second language situation and that they use it in a variety of forms and functions. In answer to the research

---

12. Bönsch-Kauke (2003:132) speaks of "mixed-motive interactions" and emphasizes that only "an *aggregation* of functions helps us to see more comprehensively the functions which humor interactions fulfill in the life of a child" (p. 268f, italics added, [translation KK]).

questions, ten different categories of laughter and smiling have been identified inductively in the picture story narrations of the informants. Five of these categories relate to humor according to the criteria of incongruity, an awareness thereof, and the experience of funniness on the part of the child. The categories are Clowning, Narrative/Behavioral Incongruity, Meta-linguistic Incongruity, Self-disparagement and Pictorial Incongruity. Apart from the latter, all of these categories are instances of children's initiations of humor, which meet the additional criterion of the child's intention to amuse. Taken together, the humor categories constitute 50% of the laughter and smiles displayed in the narrations. They meet the predictions about the age range of the children (6–7) in that they predominantly represent non-aggressive humor forms, above all the exploitation of incongruities of all kinds, including verbal humor, and clowning. Only a very small number of children did not use humor throughout their interview.

The most prominent categories of non-humor-related laughter in the data are the expression of Embarrassment and Joy. Additionally, two categories of laughter have been identified in the interacting adult's response to the child's performance, namely Encouragement and a reaction to the child's Involuntary Incongruity, which is only funny for the adult. These must be distinguished from the child's own experience of funniness. Altogether, these categories represent the other half of laughter situations.

Most of these categories are in line with those presented in previous research on child humor (Apte 1985; Bergen 1998; Bönsch-Kauke 2003; Shultz and Robillard 1980), although some of them may be located differently in the respective classification system or may overlap in content. It seems likely, however, that the spontaneous use of some forms of humor is restricted by the test situation in which the child tells the story. Presumably, this leads to lower frequencies in the categories Joy, Narrative-Behavioral and Meta-Linguistic Incongruities than reported in other studies. At the same time, the amount of laughter generated by Embarrassment exceeds the results of the previous studies.

The L2-dominated environment may be another reason for these deviations. More than half of the children's humor initiations were clearly related to the linguistic context, as were 86% of the non-humor related instances of laughter or smiling, especially the category of Embarrassment and, less so, the expression of Joy about the mastery of the language. This confirms the initial hypothesis that children are aware of the inadequacy of their own interlanguage system with regard to the expectations of a cooperative social interaction and that they feel the need to respond to this incongruity. Embarrassment is an automatic reaction triggered by this awareness, whereas humor and some other strategies have to be actively initiated. However, these strategies display a high degree of intra- and interindividual variation, which was reported but not quantified in the analysis.

The laughter categories serve a range of different functions within the context of social interaction. Five functions identified by McGhee (1989) and Bönsch-Kauke (2003) could be related to the data, i.e., Facilitation of Social Interaction, Positive Attention, Hostility, Amusement, and Saving Face, also called Repair (Attardo 1994). The data suggest that the function of Repair in order to save face is the most important function with regard to the perceived inadequacy of the interlanguage system. Since this function is usually characteristic of an older age group, one might assume that the L2 context enhances the bilingual children's cognitive development and linguistic awareness. Similar findings of cognitive advantages over monolingual children have been reported repeatedly with respect to different cognitive tasks (e.g., Bialystok 2001). In order to test this assumption, it might be interesting to conduct a follow-up study with a larger number of informants and a monolingual control group to compare the amount and the quality of humor behavior in the L1 and the L2.

It has to be taken into account, however, that not all children exhibit the use of these different categories in the same way. For future studies, it might be a valuable contribution to carry out a detailed individual analysis of the humor/laughter instances of each informant and relate them to different personality factors such as shyness or aggressivity, as e.g., pointed out in the research of Bergen (1998, 2007) and Ruch (1998). According to these approaches, it can be assumed that especially the instances of humor initiation found in the data could be correlated with a specific personality dimension.[13] Unfortunately, a detailed individual analysis is out of the scope of this paper.

The findings of the present analysis basically correspond to the cognitive development of children in the first years of elementary school. Based on Piaget's work, McGhee (1971) and Shultz and Robillard (1980) postulate a shift toward logical thinking which enables the child to become aware of social roles and expectations as well as conversational principles (Grice 1975). This new experience may lead to tension in situations when the expected performance cannot be achieved, e.g., the imperfect use of an unfamiliar communication tool. Thus, in addition to its social function, the use of humor may have a cathartic effect, relaxing a tense or awkward atmosphere of a test situation in an L2 classroom. It is impressive to observe how young children are able to react to this kind of social pressure with surprising ease even in their *interlanguage*. In this sense, it can indeed be concluded that first graders use humor as a strategy in second language contexts to cope with violations of the Cooperative Principle.

---

13.   I am grateful to Doris Bergen for bringing this point to my attention.

Expanding on this train of thought, these findings lead to the question of whether the children's use of humor to facilitate aspects of their second language acquisition process could be actively enhanced through the role of the educator or teacher. Experience shows that humor is not always perceived as an educational goal ranking high among teaching priorities. As Bergen (2006, 2007) observes, the use and tolerance of humor seems to decrease from preschool and kindergarten to elementary school. She argues, however, that "[i]n early childhood, ... helping children to learn how to interpret and use humor effectively is an important part of the educator's role" (2007: 34) as it facilitates social interaction. With reference to the subject discussed in this paper, this holds true for the interaction within the second language classroom and, by extension, for the interaction in actual social encounters in which the second language will be the speaker's only means of communication. Once trained in humor tecniques in the classroom environment, the children will find it easier to lower their perceived level of risk-taking in the L2 and use such strategies to their advantage in real-life situations.

The learning environment for such mechanisms and strategies has to be a safe situation in which children can try, test and expand their skills (Bergen 2006). It has been argued that the humor frame does not differ essentially from the play frame in that the communicative signals are similar. Since teachers shape and control communication in a classroom, it is up to them to create such a safe environment to introduce and manage the cues for the use of humor strategies in the learning process, and to serve as a model to the children (Bergen 2006). Since humor techniques are not conveyed in the same way in all families, as Bergen points out in her study, it is even more desirable for teachers to take on this task because humor is generally seen as a facilitator of social competence. As a byproduct and an additional benefit, children will be exposed to different humor behaviors and learn to react to or use them appropriately. Since it has been found that a lack of humor competence may be detrimental to children at elementary age (Masten 1986), such social shortcomings might successfully be remedied by the teacher's deliberate use and ecouragement of humor as a means to cope with the acquisition of a second language.

References

Apte, Mahadev L. 1985. *Humor and Laughter*. Ithaca, London: Cornell University Press.
Attardo, Salvatore. 1994. *Linguistic Theories of Humor*. Berlin, New York: Mouton de Gruyter.
Austin, John L. 1962. *How to Do Things with Words*. Oxford: Oxford University Press.
Bariaud, Françoise. 1989. "Age differences in children's humor." In *Humor and Children's Development: A Guide to Practical Applications*, Paul E. McGhee (Ed.), 15–45. New York: Haworth Press.

Bergen, Doris. 1998. "Development of the sense of humor." In *The Sense of Humor: Explorations of a Personality Characteristic*, Willibald Ruch (Ed.), 329–358. Berlin: Mouton de Gruyter.

Bergen, Doris. 2006. "Play as a Context for Humor Development." In *Play from Birth to Twelve*, Doris P. Fromberg & Doris Bergen (Eds), 141–155. New York: Routledge.

Bergen, Doris. 2007. "Humor as a Facilitator of Social Competence in Early Childhood." In *Contemporary Perspectives in Early Childhood Education*, Olivia N. Saracho & Bernard Spodek (Eds), 19–38. Charlotte, NC: IAP.

Berger, Claudia. 1999. "Pilotuntersuchungen zum Lauterwerb des Englischen in bilingualen Kindergärten am Beispiel der "Roten Gruppe" in der AWO-Kindertagesstätte Altenholz." Staatsexamen Thesis, University of Kiel, Germany.

Bergler, Edmund. 1956. *Laughter and the Sense of Humor*. New York: Intercontinental Medical Book.

Bialystok, Ellen. 2001. *Bilingualism in Development: Language, Literacy, and Cognition*. Cambridge: Cambridge University Press.

Bönsch-Kauke, Marion. 2003. *Psychologie des Kinderhumors: Schulkinder unter sich*. Opladen: Leske & Budrich.

Brodzinsky, David M. & Rightmyer, Jonathan. 1980. "Individual differences in children's humor development." In *Children's Humor*, Paul E. McGhee & Antony J. Chapman (Eds), 181–212. Chichester: Wiley

Dews, Shelly, Winner, Ellen, Kaplan, Joan, Rosenblatt, Elizabeth, Hunt, Malia, Lim, Karen, McGovern, Angela, Qualter, Alison & Smarsh, Bonnie. 1996. "Children's understanding of the meaning and functions of verbal irony." *Child Development* 67(6): 3071–3085.

Ellis, Rod. 1994. *The Study of Second Language Acquisition*. Oxford: Oxford University Press.

Grice, Herbert P. 1975. "Logic and conversation." In *Syntax and Semantics. Vol. 3: Speech Acts*, Peter Cole & Jerry L. Morgan (Eds), 41–58. New York: Academic Press.

Housen, Alex & Pallotti, Gabriele. 1999. "The teaching of foreign languages in European primary schools." Paper presented at *Euroconference III*, 1999, San Sebastian, Sept. 26 – Oct. 2.

Housen, Alex. 2002. "Second language achievement in the European School system of multilingual education." In *Education and Society in Plurilingual Contexts*, Daniel W.C. So & Gary M. Jones (Eds), 96–128. Brussel: VUB Press.

Kersten, Kristin. 2002. "Äquivalenzklassifizierungen im Zweitspracherwerb in bilingualen Kindertagesstätten." MA Thesis, University of Kiel, Germany.

Kersten, Kristin, Imhoff, Christine & Sauer, Bianca. 2002. "The acquisition of English verbs in an elementary school immersion program in Germany." In *An Integrated View of Language Development: Papers in Honor of Henning Wode*, Petra Burmeister, Thorsten Piske & Andreas Rohde (Eds), 473–497. Trier: WVT.

Lauer, Kristin & Hansen, Nadine. 2001. "Second language English verb morphology with German Students in a grade 1 immersion class: some preliminary findings." In *Language as a Tool – Immersion Research and Practices*, Siv Björklund (Ed.), 272–285. University of Vaasa: Proceedings of the University of Vaasa, Reports.

Leibing, Christine. 1999. "Die Entwicklung des Wortschatzes der Fremdsprache in einem deutsch-englisch bilingualen Kindergarten." MA Thesis, University of Kiel, Germany.

Masten, Ann S. 1986. "Humor and competence in school-aged children." *Child Development* 57(2): 461–73.

Mayer, Mercer. 1969. *Frog, where are you?* New York: Pied Piper.

McGhee, Paul E. 1971. "Cognitive development and children's comprehension of humor." *Child Development* 41 (1): 123–138.

McGhee, Paul E. 1979. *Humor. Its origin and development*. San Francisco: Freeman.

McGhee, Paul E. 1989. "The contribution of humor to children's social development." In *Humor and Children's Development: A Guide to Practical Applications*, Paul E. McGhee (Ed.), 119–134. New York, London: Haworth Press.

Piaget, Jean. 1950. *Psychology of Intelligence*. London: Routledge & Kegan Paul.

Piaget, Jean. 1962. *Play, Dreams and Imitations in Childhood*. New York: Norton.

Röhrich, Lutz. 1977. *Der Witz: Figuren, Formen, Funktionen*. Stuttgart: Metzler.

Ruch, Willibald (Ed.). 1998. *The Sense of Humor: Explorations of a Personality Characteristic*. Berlin: Mouton de Gruyter.

Ruch, Willibald & Köhler, Gabriele. 1998. "A temperament approach to humor." In *The Sense of Humor: Explorations of a Personality Characteristic*, Willibald Ruch (Ed.), 203–228. Berlin: Mouton de Gruyter.

Shultz, Thomas R. & Robillard, Judith. 1980. "The development of linguistic humor in children: Incongruity through rule violation." In *Children's Humor*, Paul E. McGhee & Antony Chapman (Eds), 59–90. Chichester: Wiley.

Simons, C.J.R., McCluskey-Fawcett, Kathleen A. & Papini, Dennis R. 1986. "Theoretical and functional perspectives on the development of humor during infancy, childhood, and adolescence." In *Humor and Aging*, Lucille Nahemow, Kathleen A. McCluskey-Fawcett & Paul E. McGhee (Eds), 53–80. Orlando: Academic Press.

Stern, Daniel N. 1974. "Mother and infant at play: The dyadic interaction involving facial, vocal, and gaze behaviors." In *The Effect of the Infant on its Caregiver*, Michael M. Lewis & Leonard A. Rosenblum (Eds), 187–213. New York: Wiley.

Westphal, Katrin. 1998. "Pilotuntersuchungen zum L2-Erwerb in bilingualen Kindergärten: Bericht zum deutsch- französisch bilingualen Kindergarten 'Rappelkiste' in Rostock." Staatsexamen Thesis, University of Kiel, Germany.

Wode, Henning. 1998. "A European perspective on immersion teaching: The German scenario." In *Els Programes d'imersió: una Perspectiva Europea – Immersion Programs: a European Perspective*, Joaquim Arnau & Josep M. Artigal (Eds), 43–65. Barcelona, Spain: Universitat de Barcelona.

Wode, Henning. 1999. "Incidental vocabulary learning in the foreign language classroom." *Studies in Second Language Acquisition* 21: 243–258.

Wode, Henning. 2001. "Multilingual Education in Europe: What can preschools contribute?" In *Language as a Tool – Immersion Research and Practices*, Siv Björklund (Ed.), 424–446. University of Vaasa: Proceedings of the University of Vaasa, Reports.

Wode, Henning. 2003. "'Young age' in L2 acquisition: the age issue in reverse in phonology." In *La fonologia dell'interlingua. Principi e metodi d'analisi*, Lidia Costamagna & Stefania Giannini (Eds), Milano: FrancoAngeli, Materiali Linguistici, 71–92. Università di Pavia.

Wolfenstein, Martha. 1954. *Children's Humor: A Psychological Analysis*. Glencoe, IL: Free Press.

Cultural divide or unifying factor?

Humorous talk in the interaction of bilingual, cross-cultural couples

Delia Chiaro

This essay sets out to explore a positive aspect of bilingual cross-cultural couples in long term relationships, namely the occurrence of what is considered a harmonious factor: humour. The results of a purpose-built questionnaire completed by 59 couples sheds light on a series of socio and psycholinguistic aspects of their daily relationship including language choice and attitudes in the domain of the couples' ludic interaction, such as when they joke with each other verbally and their use of humorous talk. This essay reports the findings of the processed data that emerged from the questionnaires as well as qualitative data deriving from a series of semi-structured interviews.

> I love you, I love you , I love you, that's all I want to say,
> until I find a way,
> I will say the only words I know that you'll understand, my Michelle.
> (Lennon-McCartney)

1. Introduction

The notion of romance between two people who do not share the same language has attracted the imagination of numerous film directors over the years. The cinema offers several examples of bilingual cross-cultural dyads, such as American mercenary Captain Nathan Algren (Tom Cruise) who falls in love with a Japanese widow in *The Last Samurai* (USA; Edward Zwick, 2003) and the unrequited passion between English writer Jamie Bennett (Colin Firth) and Aurelia (Lucia Moniz), his Portuguese housekeeper, in Richard Curtis's blockbuster *Love Actually* (UK; 2003) in a sub-plot interestingly entitled "love as a second language". The cinematic convention in such stories appears to promote a series of cross-linguistic comic misunderstandings which inevitably result in a happy ending. But how different are real life situations from what happens on celluloid? Do couples really use gesture to communicate at the start of their relationship as we are so often led to believe at the movies? And surely the speed at which cinematic couples manage to communicate efficiently requires audiences to equip themselves with a substantial amount of suspension of disbelief as presumably such proficiency in real life would take many years to acquire. Piller (2000: 2) quotes Ervin-Tripp's study of American-Japanese couples who possessed no pivot language, yet reported to speak to each other in "the language of the eyes" (1968: 202) and also reports two cases of North American men who establish solid relationships with Russian women without the help of a common language, concluding that "…a romantic attachment may transcend linguistic confines not only in fiction…but also in real life." But, are such relationships as happy-go-lucky and packed with witty repartee as portrayed by fiction?

Thus, instead of focusing on misunderstandings which have most often been taken as the central category of studies in intercultural communication, Piller's study of bilingual cross-cultural communication in married couples (2002) is an attempt to pinpoint such people as successful rather than ineffective communicators. In fact, arguing that findings in social psychology show that problems in communication are the main reason for marital difficulties and failure (Fitzpatrick 1990; Sternberg 1988), Piller claims that it should follow that stable intercultural couples must be good communicators as they are obviously able to communicate successfully despite basic language impediments. And Piller's observations tie in well with studies in humor research that show that couples concur on the notion that the occurrence of humor enhances their relationship (Ziv 1988); and that a partner's propensity to create humor is linked to marital satisfaction (Ziv and Gadish 1989). Furthermore, the field of positive psychology generally promotes positive attitudes, highlighting virtues such as optimism, sense of humor and a happy disposition. Although a positive attitude does not make people live longer, it would appear from research in various fields of medicine and psychology, that by helping to cope with stressful situations (Lefcourt and Thomas 1998) optimism might make them live better:

> …though more humorous and cheerful people may not live longer, they may enjoy a better quality of life and greater overall life satisfaction. It also remains possible that different types of humor may affect different aspects of health in different ways. Although a cheerful sense of humor might contribute to earlier mortality by causing people to take less care of themselves overall, it remains possible that mirth could produce biochemical changes having some health implications, or that the use of certain styles of humor could facilitate coping with stress or enhance intimate relationships, indirectly producing some health benefits. (Martin 2007: 332).

In particular, the present study pursues the line of thought established by Coates (2007) in which she argues that "humorous talk" is a form of collaboration between speakers that reinforces group solidarity and intimacy. Presumably cross-cultural, bilingual couples have more obstacles to overcome than those who share both language and culture. I would like to argue that humorous talk within such relationships may act as a special bonding agent that helps such couples maintain solidarity over and above objective difficulties. Nevertheless, we should not lose track of the fact that, as well as being a bonding factor, humor may also be biting and thus a dividing element. While I would not like to suggest that oral communication in bilingual, cross-cultural relationships is always idyllic, I do set out to explore how such couples balance the fine line between laughing *with* each other as opposed to laughing *against* one another. Furthermore, I shall also touch upon the concept of comity within the couple and how those outside this nucleus may misunderstand the humorous interaction that takes place within it.

2. The study

2.1   Cross-cultural, bilingual couples

The concepts of 'intercultural communication' and 'intercultural couples' are extremely fuzzy. Naturally, the conurbations in which we live divide speech communities in terms of gender, regional and national origin, ethnicity, social class, education, religion, sexual orientation as well as interests that could range from sociolinguistics to knitting and, to quote Suzanne Romaine, there is indeed "…a sense in which all communication is cross-cultural". However, without wishing to enter into a discussion regarding where intra-cultural communication ends and intercultural communication begins, and taking it as given that cultural or national identity may be constructed by the self or co-constructed by others at different points of interaction, the data upon which the results of this study are based was collected from self-identified cross-cultural, bilingual couples. In fact, the couples involved in the study were contacted via two Web portals respectively called "The Bilingual Couples Page" and "The Bilingual Families' Web Page".

On "The Bilingual Couples Page", self-identified couples decide to appear publicly, advertising their hybrid union with photographs, explanatory texts, contact addresses, phone numbers and e-mail addresses, thus underscoring both their desire to identify themselves as such and their wish to contact other similar couples. Each member of the couples appearing on the site was born and raised in a country which was different from his/her partner's place of birth. The "Bilingual Families Web Page" is different from the latter in that it mainly focuses on how to raise children bilingually. Parents are invited to post problems and queries on a server list, and these are subsequently sent to members who are free to reply, recounting their experiences and generally giving advice. By picking respondents from users of these two sites, we could be certain that all identified themselves as part of a cross-cultural, bilingual relationship. Six traditional face-to-face interviews were also carried out involving couples identified via social networking in Karlsruhe, Germany.

2.2 Humorous talk

I have chosen to adopt the term 'humorous talk' in this essay to pursue the line in which Coates operates (2007) and thus embrace the entire area of talk as play within a 'play frame' (Bateson 1953). This allows me not only to focus on the couples' use of speech acts such as jokes or making puns, but also upon the kind of playful interactive banter which escapes categorization. In other words, while jokes, puns and the use of irony are a part of humorous talk, they are not the only way of creating verbally expressed humor. A joke more often than not disrupts the conversational flow (Chiaro 1992). Furthermore, a joke's independence from the conversation in which it may have occurred can allow it to be recited outside the context in which it first appeared. On the other hand, humorous talk may be sparked off by any element within the context of the here and now of a conversation and cannot be understood once divorced from that context. For example, Dutch speaking Geert[1] wrote to me saying:

> My wife has learnt to speak Dutch quite well, so the kind of humour related to language I can think of are the typical word jokes – a Swedish word that resembles a Dutch word which is funny in the original context (often a normal Swedish word resembling a naughty Dutch word :-) this is especially funny with other people around who do not understand this.) (Dutch speaking Geert, male, with Swedish partner)

Geert speaks of "typical word jokes" that are particularly funny when others do not understand what he and his wife are laughing about. They have created a form of play which only they understand and that constitutes an "interactive pact" (McCarthy and Carter 2004: 172) between two participants who know they are indulging in play. This kind of playful banter, like the repartee reported by Coates, creates solidarity and harmony, and above all a sense of exclusive intimacy. And Geert's perception that "this is especially funny with other people around who do not understand this" consolidates this sense of unity through the exclusion of others.

2.3 Tools and methods

Two different and complementary methods were used to investigate interaction in bilingual cross-cultural couples. Firstly, a self-reporting questionnaire was elaborated to gather quantitative data to be processed statistically. Secondly, further qualitative data were obtained both by means of six, semi-structured, face-to-face interviews

---

1. For reasons of privacy, the names of all the informants have been changed.

and through the elicitation of responses from cross-cultural, bilingual informants to a request to recount relevant experiences via an Internet posting.

2.3.1   *The questionnaire*

The questionnaire consisted of four blocks in which a first section gathered socio-demographic data concerning the couple (i.e., age, education, employment, etc.) and information regarding language choices over time; a second section elicited information regarding language choice within the couple according to different domestic domains; and a third section elicited information regarding attitudes towards the languages adopted within the relationship. This instrument included specific questions regarding respondents' use of humorous talk.

After creating a number of mailing lists from addresses gathered on the Bilingual Couples Page (2.1), a letter was prepared which invited recipients to take part in the survey by filling in and subsequently returning, the attached questionnaire. The questionnaire was sent out via e-mail to roughly 300 couples worldwide.

2.3.2   *The interviews*

Six traditional, face-to-face, semi-structured interviews were carried out with cross-cultural bilingual couples identified via social networking in the city of Karlsruhe, Germany.[2] In order to enlarge the sample, more volunteers were sought via a posting on "The Bilingual Families' Web Page". People willing to respond were specifically asked to comment on the languages they adopted for humorous talk with their partner and subsequently, they were invited to remark freely on their use of verbal humor in the two languages within their relationship and to recount any episode that came to mind exemplifying this kind of interaction.

3.   Results

3.1   The questionnaire

3.1.1   *The sample*

Mailings resulted in 59 valid returns mainly from couples living in Europe, the USA and Canada with a total of 24 language combinations.[3] Not surprisingly, in

---

2.   I would like to thank Elena Marchese for having conducted, and subsequently transcribed, the six interviews.

3.   The languages involved in the study were: Albanian; Amharic; Arabic; Croatian; Czech; Danish; Dutch; English; Estonian; Filipino; Finnish; French; German; Greek; Malay; Japanese; Polish; Portuguese; Russian; Shona; Spanish; Tagalog and Turkish.

view of the chosen method of data collection, the sample consists of highly educated couples, many of whom possess doctorates. The shortcomings of the sample are self-evident. The entire sample comprised graduate Internet users, frequently with their own home pages and domains, who are unlikely to reflect the average cross-cultural, bilingual couple. Furthermore, most of the respondents were extremely eager to respond, many offering to be interviewed and keen to put forward unsolicited information regarding the linguistic habits of their entire family. The Bilingual Couples gateway in itself is couched in English and the vast majority of couples present themselves in proficient English, with a few doing so in French or German. Many respondents were academics who requested a copy of the finished research. This sample is, of course, clearly skewed towards the highly educated. But then perhaps this was quite inevitable as academics tend to be internet *habitués*. Not only, but presumably academia is a profession in which cross-cultural relationships flourish and hence it should come as no surprise that so many academics responded positively to the survey.

The sample consisted of 39 female and 20 male respondents who had a mean age of 37 and had been together with their partners for an average of ten years. This high proportion of female respondents is surely linked with the fact that women are still the main family gatekeepers despite the major involvement of men in matters of childrearing over the past fifty years. Thus it should come as no surprise that females outnumbered males in the websites involved in the survey, as it is likely that it is still the female who is more involved in matters of schooling and language acquisition with respect to her male partner.

3.1.2   *Humorous talk and language choice*

Respondents were questioned on the language adopted in a variety of domestic and social domains. They were asked to report the language they used, *as a couple*, in the presence of their own relatives, of their partner's relatives, with mutual friends, at work, at prayer and for worship. They were also asked to report on language choice, within the couple's interaction, for arguing, for when they talked about food, about money, in intimacy and for humorous talk.[4]

Significantly, while for most domains respondents' choices tended to clearly position themselves in one direction or another, i.e., according to the domain, they

---

4.   Informants had to choose from the following options: Only Language A; Mostly Language A; Language A and B equally; Only Language B; Mostly Language B or Another language, in which Language A represented the respondent's mother tongue and B, their partner's. The raw data was processed after collapsing scores so that responses to Language A and Mostly Language A became a single item. Responses to Language B and Mostly Language B were also collapsed so as to obtain a single item too.

either exclusively or mainly adopted their own language or that of their partner's; the scores for talk used in play were more widely spread across the three options (Table 1). In other words, in the domain of humorous interaction, respondents tend to adopt all three options, i.e., either one of the two languages or both, to a fairly equal extent. In contrast, the majority of respondents prefer to use their mother tongue (MT) in dominions involving numeric skills; (73.7% of the sample count in their MT and 87.7% calculate and do sums in MT). Counting and math are generally introspective, cerebral activities, so it follows that MT would be the natural choice in bilinguals. This claim is supported by a study that shows that proficient bilingual interpreters display significant MT interference when translating numbers Mazza (2001). Again, in the presence of their partner's relatives, there is a predictable swing of 81.8%, towards the use of their partner's MT while in the presence of their own parents and relatives, 84.9% prefer to use their own MT. This can be explained by the notion that it is commonly considered to be bad manners to speak a different language in the presence of someone who may not understand it.

The language choice for humorous interaction, tends to correlate with the language chosen in intimacy (*sigma tau*[5] = 688; N=53; p=0.0001), for arguing (sigma tau = 685; N=52; p=0.0001) and to talk about money (sigma tau = 615; N=52; p=0.0001). However, in these three domains, only a few respondents claimed that they used both languages indifferently (see Table 1), although most opted for either Language A or B. On the other hand, scores pertaining to language used to talk about food (sigma tau = 712; N=55; p=0.0001), and language used in play are spread fairly evenly across the three choices. This correlation can be explained by the perception that the consumption of food is linked to conviviality. Planning meals, shopping for food and cooking in somebody's company, and above all, the relaxed, warm atmosphere of eating together may be more likely to trigger humorous talk than a discussion regarding finances, or during an argument.[5]

Furthermore, our qualitative data displays a propensity for couples to play with both languages, to the extent of creating humorous amalgams (3.2.2ii). Partners appear to be keen both to teach and learn reciprocal humor styles. Such give and take may explain the evenness in the spread of the scores in the domain of humorous interaction.

---

5. Kendall's tau-b is a nonparametric measure of association for categorical variables that take ties into account. The sign of the coefficient indicates the direction of the relationship, and its absolute value indicates the strength, with larger absolute values indicating stronger relationships. Possible values range from –1 to 1, but a value of –1 or +1 can only be obtained from square tables.

Table 1. Language choice in domestic and social domains.

Language Choice / Dominion	Language A	Both languages	Language B
With respondent's relatives (N=53)	45 (84.9%)	1 (1.9%)	7 (13.2%)
With partner's relatives (N=55)	9 (16.4%)	1 (1.8%)	45 (81.8%)
With mutual friends (N=55)	14 (25.5%)	22 (40.0%)	19 (34.5%)
At the workplace (N=47)	22 (46.8%)	5 (10.6%)	20 (42.6%)
For arguing (N=52)	22 (42.3%)	7 (13.5%)	23 (44.2%)
To talk about money and finances (N=53)	22 (41.5%)	6 (11.3%)	25 (47.2%)
To talk about food (N=55)	18 (32.7%)	13 (23.6%)	24 (43.6%)
In intimacy (N=53)	18 (34.0%)	9 (17.0%)	26 (49.1%)
For humorous interaction (N=55)	18 (32.7%)	21 (38.2%)	16 (29.1%)
For counting (N=57)	42 (73.7%)	11 (19.3%)	4 (7.0%)
For doing sums and calculating (N=55)	50 (87.7%)	4 (7.0%)	3 (5.3%)
In prayer and worship (N=42)	34 (81%)	5 (11.9%)	3 (7.1%)
For swearing and using taboo language (N=54)	31 (57.4%)	15 (27.8%)	8 (14.8%)
For talking to oneself (N=58)	42 (72.4%)	12 (20.3%)	4 (6.9%)

N is the size of the sample.

3.1.3   *Attitudes towards language use within the couple*

The third section of the questionnaire attempts to understand respondents' attitudes towards the use of one another's languages within their interaction as a couple. Respondents were asked to rate six statements on a graphic rating scale numbered from 1 to 10 in which 10 expressed total agreement and 1 total disagreement. This reflects points of view on the statements, i.e., the highest score was given to generally positive attitudes towards the bilingual quality of interaction in the relationship.

Results show that couples are generally happy to make an effort to use their partner's language and, similarly, are pleased when their partner uses theirs. They also feel at ease within the frame of play and are happy to tell and receive jokes in their partner's language. Conversely, they tend to feel annoyed if their partner does not make an effort to speak their language. They also feel excluded when their partner uses his or her own language to partake in humorous talk with fellow native speakers. A factor analysis with varimax rotation was performed in order to advance the analysis by condensing the variables into fewer underlying dimensions.

The Principal Component Analysis produced three components which have eigen values greater than 1 and which explain nearly 65% of total variance. The variables are summarized into three main factors illustrated in Table 2. These factors should help us understand attitudes towards language choice within the couple. The first factor was strongly influenced by the following statements:

> "I am happy when my partner makes an effort to speak to me in my language."
> "I am happy to make an effort to speak my partner's language."
> "I am happy to speak to my partner in either language."

As a result, Factor 1 has been labeled the 'Effort Component'. The second factor was strongly influenced by the statements:

> "I am able to tell jokes and make others laugh in my partner's language."
> "I feel like an outsider when my partner is able to laugh at jokes in his/her language."

The second factor was labeled the 'Comity Component'. The third factor was strongly influenced by the statement:

> "I am annoyed that my partner does not make an effort to speak to me in my language."

Factor 3 has been labeled the 'Annoyance Component'.

Table 2. Rotated component matrix

	Component		
	EFFORT	COMITY	ANNOYANCE
MY EFFORT	0.774	−0.177	−0.242
PARTNER EFFORT	0.745	0.374	0.000
EITHER	0.658	−0.000	0.189
MY JOKES	0.193	**0.858**	0.193
OUTSIDER	−0.137	**0.848**	−0.260
ANNOYED	0.000	−0.004	**0.963**

Extraction method: Principal component analysis.
Rotation method: Varimax with kaiser normalization.

These three components highlight that in bilingual couples there is a process of evolution within interaction that leans towards a switching mode. In fact, the Effort Component shows the willingness of both partners to learn and to use the language of the others. This is also confirmed by the positive score of the Annoyance Component where it emerges that partners get annoyed or perhaps frustrated when there is no effort to communicate in their language. The positive scores of the Comity Component underline the role of humorous talk in this process of convergence towards the use of both languages.

3.1.3 i   *The Effort Component*   The score of 0.774 of the MY EFFORT variable (I am happy to make an effort to speak my partner's language); 0.745 of PARTNER EFFORT (I am happy when my partner makes an effort to speak to me in my language) and 0.658 of EITHER (I am happy to speak to my partner in either language), groups the three variables and creates the Effort Component. Respondents are happy to adopt their partner's language and are equally happy that their partners make an effort to adopt theirs. They are also equally at ease switching from one language to another. Thus the notion of relaxed interaction emerges, through couples who are at ease communicating in either language.

3.1.3 ii   *The Comity Component*   Feeling at ease telling jokes and laughing in their partner's language (MY JOKES 0.858) is paired with the variable OUTSIDER (I feel like an outsider when my partner is able to laugh at jokes in his/her language) which scored 0.848. Humorous talk in either language is well accepted by respondents, yet the negative notion of feeling excluded from the play frame of others is also present. This could be explained by the fact that while joking and laughing together as a couple is perceived constructively despite directionality of humorous talk, once the respondent is excluded from the interaction, joking is understandably perceived negatively. These attitudes are sustained in much of the qualitative data that emerged from interviews, in which several respondents felt the negative attitude of outsiders to their attempts at joking (see 3.2.2).

3.1.3 iii   *The Annoyance Component*   The variable ANNOYED (I am annoyed that my partner does not make an effort to speak to me in my language) stands out alone with a score of 0.963. It is this component that seems to highlight a switch in attitude with respect to the other two components. We may assume that respondents become irritated at less than perfect language produced by their partner and may feel that communication could be more effective in their partner's language.

3.2   The interviews

3.2.1   *The sample*

Traditional, semi-structured interviews were carried out on six bilingual couples that had been contacted via social networking in Karlsruhe, Germany. Other information was collected by means of a posting on the "Bilingual Family Web Page" inviting readers to comment and express their attitudes towards verbal humor in cross-cultural, bilingual relationships. In the examples that follow, information extracted from traditional, face-to-face interviews is labeled FFI and information gathered via the Internet are labeled WI. Female respondents are labeled F, and male respondents M.

3.2.2   *Results*

While the face-to-face interviews were carried out with both partners present, responses from the web posting came from individuals. The majority of these web respondents were female (see 3.1.1). Moreover, respondents from the web posting tended also to supply heartfelt answers that were frequently emotionally loaded too. This fervor, however, in itself underscores the importance of the issue in questions to informants. In addition, several informants displayed a tendency for humorous talk within their responses.

Respondents generally agreed that humor is an important part of a relationship:

(1)   Humour is such a key thing in a relationship (Sandra F; British English with Italian partner; W)

(2)   I mean you grow together and you...then you laugh more or less about the same jokes or you make the same jokes… (Holger M; German with British English partner, FFI)

(3)   ...it [humorous talk] means you're making an effort, it's good. (Colm M; Irish English with Italian partner FFI)

Moreover, informants were also quite aware of the complexity of the creation of humor in interaction with their partner. This awareness surfaces in the frequent voicing of uncertainty regarding whether a partner's use or non-use of humorous talk depends upon the linguistic difficulty involved in producing and appreciating humor in a language other than one's own, or on their personality. Furthermore, respondents seemed to be highly conscious of the cultural dimension of humorous talk and the difficulties that transposing socio-cultural elements may involve.

3.2.2i   *Sense of humor*   The issue of whether the notion of sense of humor is culture specific is a complex one which has not as yet been resolved by research communities. While some studies suggest that definitions of sense of humor do exist between (and within) cultures (Ziv 1998; Kuipers 2007), studies in personality

research seem to show that sense of humor has more to do with characteristic traits and momentary mood than culture (Ruch 1998). Furthermore, studies in sociology reveal that certain joke typologies (e.g., the underdog, the skinflint etc.) exist in all cultures (Davies 1998), and the 'Semantic Script Theory' (Raskin 1985), later to be expanded and developed into the 'General Theory of Verbal Humor' (Attardo & Raskin 1991), shows certain mechanisms in jokes (i.e., overlap and opposition) to be common across languages, yet, at the same time, require a number of 'knowledge resources' in order to be understood (Attardo 1994). Nevertheless, language itself is an undeniable barrier in the transmission of humor, and the perception that different language speakers have a different sense of humor clearly emerges from the interviews. Significantly, it would appear that when there is an English speaker within the couple, it is he or she who will tend to perceive themselves as having a 'better' sense of humor than their foreign partner. Marchese (2007: 101) reports the following exchange between English husband Jim, and Italian wife Anna Maria:

Interviewer:	"Do you sense differences in your sense of humour?"
Anna Maria:	"Yes."
Jim:	"Mine's better!"

From the present data, British English speaker Sandra with an Italian husband claims that

(4)   British humour is particularly hard for Italians to get, especially the difference between sarcasm and irony and as for understatement...they are just totally unknown concepts here (W)

American Geena with Hebrew speaking husband responded to this comment as follows:

(5)   OK, I'm not British, but still I had to laugh in recognition when I read this. Maybe it's Anglophone to Mediterranean? Anyway, my Israeli husband (and no, I don't have any others) used to look at me as if I'd fallen from the moon when I made ironic or sarcastic statements. At this point, he not only understands, but joins in. I suppose his family thinks I've corrupted him – as they still don't get any of that sort of thing. Numerous Israelis correct my 'faulty' Hebrew when I think I'm just speaking colourfully. Understatement is not in the Israeli lexicon (Geena F; US English with Israeli [Hebrew] partner, W)

It would appear that when one partner is a native speaker of English, that person perceives their sense of humor to be in some way better or superior than that of their partner's. Both Sandra and Geena imply that their Italian and Israeli partners have a less subtle appreciation of humor than they do. And both extend such lack of subtlety to their partner's ethnicity as a whole e.g., "…sarcasm and irony and as for understatement...they are just totally unknown concepts here [i.e., in Italy]"; "Understatement is not in the Israeli lexicon". Thus, it would appear that the use of tropes such as irony, sarcasm and understatement are considered in some way to be more sophisticated than other types of humor. Furthermore 'English humor' is frequently taken as a (positive) benchmark of what humor should be. Anyone who does not understand it is seen to have a 'problem':

(6)   There's a big difference with the Danish humour, which is similar to English humour, which is very sarcastic at times. This sometimes could give problems because many people can't understand that kind of humour. The Italians have a bit of a problem with that... (Henrik M; Danish with Italian partner, FFI)

Not having a similar sense of humor seems to be a somewhat negative trait in a partner. Yet from partner, respondents go further and extend such 'non-sameness' to their partner's entire culture. In other words, the humor of a partner is seen to correspond to that of the whole nation. However, alongside the use of a 'better' humor style, such as one that includes irony and understatement, the concept of 'dry' humor also arises as a desirable type of humor to possess.

(7)   He prefers the juicy kind of humour, whereas I like mine as dry as possible. (Sophie F; British English with German partner, W)

The idea of dry humor as being characteristic of English humor leads one respondent to claim:

(8)   My sense of humour is quite dry, even drier than the natives... (Danuta F, Polish with British English partner, W)

suggesting that humor which is drier still than that of the autochthonous Brits must be very sophisticated and thus in some way 'better'. However, partners of English speakers are initially confused by their dry, sarcastic humor and often mistake it for rudeness:

(9)   I must say that it really took me a while to get used to my English partner's sense of humour!! He is very ironic and sarcastic and initially I really used to get upset at his kind of comments. After a few years now I manage to laugh and even to make use of some his kind of sarcasm and 'English sense of humour'. I must admit though that occasionally I still look at him in disbelief at some of his jokes. (Amália F, Hungarian with English partner, W)

Nonetheless, respondents are also aware of the fact that sense of humor is not only simply language/culture dependant:

(10) It would be nice if Will was able to make me laugh out loud more often, but I'm not sure it would make any difference if we usually spoke his language! (Sophie F; British English with German partner, W)

Notably Sophie is an English speaker who seems to perceive herself, and is likely to be stereotypically perceived, as belonging to a group of holders of a 'good/positive/desirable' sense of humor, (i.e., English humor). Her partner is German and thus belongs to a group of people stereotypically renowned for their lack of humor. However, not all couples abide by the cliché:

> (11) I occasionally tell a German joke but you tell English jokes more frequently [...] well there are moments when yes it's different, but I don't think that's anything to do with culture I think it's character based really... (Mary F; British English with German partner, FFI)

Conversely, Italian Sergio claims his English wife Corrine has a different sense of humor because "She likes American sitcoms. I don't find them funny." (Marchese 2007: 89), while English speaking Stacey says that

> (12) I can enjoy both British and German comedy programmes. Although I am not particularly fond of the German 'Karneval', but then again, there are LOTS of Germans who aren't either. (Stacey F; British English with German partner, W)

Of course in the above examples in which one speaker is often a native speaker of English, English is likely to be the most used language in the couple. Undeniably, at present, the English language has acquired social dominance as *the* global language and we may safely presume that within bilingual couples it is chosen as the principal language of communication if one partner is an English native speaker for reasons that go beyond the merely practical (e.g., social prestige; educational plus for English speaking offspring, etc.). If the English of the non-native speaker lags behind, this could explain the negative image that English speakers tend to have of their partner's humor.

Significantly too, the females in this sample are acting contrary to the typical belief that humor production is more of a male domain. Traditionally, women are expected to show their sense of humor by laughing at men's jokes. However, the female respondents involved in this study appear to be actively creating humor and are sensitive to their partner's humorous reactions and needs. Of course, the fact that these respondents are highly educated may also influence this sensitivity towards humor talk, and possibly also their assertiveness. In addition, many females in the sample tend to be English speakers (Geena Sophie, Mary, Stacey) or else have adopted English as the couples' language (Danuta). Could we speculate that the social strength of English may have empowered these females to adopt a role that is generally seen as more traditionally masculine in terms of humor style?

3.2.2ii *Willingness to laugh together* The willingness of couples to learn to laugh together emerged from the interviews. Typically, either one partner would 'teach' the other how to understand his or her own humor or else they themselves would try to somehow access the partner's humor in a sort of attempt at 'self-access learning'.

(13)   My husband is well trained to recognise my puns...and now even makes a few himself in both languages....(Sandra)

(14)   Many years ago, when we still lived in Finland, we used to tape some comedy shows and I would interpret more or less simultaneously, pausing when a longer explanation was needed. That was a good way to get him started on appreciating the Finnish brand of humour... (Carita F; Finnish with Bengali speaking partner, W)

These comments fit well with the data that emerge from the factor analysis labeled the 'Effort Component' (3.1.3i). Teaching (and learning) certainly require effort, and partners appear to be 'trained' and initiated ("I got him started") into the understanding and appreciation of the other partner's humor and, over and above the linguistic barrier, it would seem that couples try to make a special effort to encourage humorous comity. Again comments triangulate well with our quantitative data (3.1.3ii) and the 'Comity Component'. However, several couples mention a type of bilingual play which only exists within domestic walls and is only understood by family members:

(15)   A lot of our internal humour is definitely situational and a comment inserted in another language brings out laughs but would not be understood by outsiders. (Carita)

(16)   One great source of amusement in this house is also translating names....last night's was Cassius Clay (*Cassio Argilla*)....(hubby not me); others are ones like, Joe Green (*Giuseppe Verdi*) etc. My husband gets the word play jokes in both languages. I don't often do puns in Italian with other Italians as they tend to leap in to correct your Italian if they are not linguists (Sandra)

This is the kind of repartee described by Geert (2.2) and illustrates Coates' vision of collaborative play and "manifestation of intimacy" (2007: 33). Conversely, outsiders are not game to such play and mark their non-participation through the use of correcting the 'foreigner's' attempts at play. The issue of being corrected when trying to joke is picked up by Geena:

(17)   Numerous Israelis correct my 'faulty' Hebrew when I think I'm just speaking colourfully. I've never even considered telling a joke in Hebrew!

Notably, both Sandra (16) and Geena are corrected by "other Italians" and "numerous Israeli", in other words, people outside the domestic domain. Markedly, Carita (15) uses the term "internal humour" for verbally expressed humor *within* the family unit and refers to 'outsiders' who cannot understand it. In fact, it would appear that while it is acceptable, and indeed auspicial, to play with one's partner's language as part of domestic interaction, once outside familiar boundaries, attempts at verbal humor may be misinterpreted. Could it be that being able to include humorous talk (i.e., make jokes, play with words, etc.) in interaction in a language other than one's own can only be 'permitted' when a person is fully accepted as a member of that group? Or, is it simply the case that verbally expressed humor is pervasive in more linguistic environments in certain countries and not in others? Yet the notion of 'exclusion' works in both directions. Just as one partner may be reprimanded for her attempts at adopting humorous talk and thus, to a certain extent, is excluded from the dominant group, the couple can exclude others by means of creating their own brand of linguistically exclusive humor:

(18)   …a Swedish word that resembles a Dutch word which is funny in the original
        context (often a normal Swedish word resembling a naughty Dutch word :-)
        this is especially funny with other people around who do not understand this.)
        (my italics; Geert, Dutch M; Danish Partner, W)

Thus, apparent exclusion of others heightens the humorous effect of such verbal play. However, even in the domain of laughing together, it would appear that once more the English speakers underscore their perception of their humor being somehow better than that of others:

(19)   …luckily he's not into the typical Italian comedies so I don't have to sit through
        them…not sure I would laugh even in company. (Sandra)

(20)   We watch quite a lot of UK comedy on DVD, and my husband can understand
        a lot of the humour, but misses things when it gets complicated or there are a lot
        of UK references, of course. Sometimes he falls asleep: most irritating. […]After
        15 years in Germany I can now watch some modern German comedy shows and
        even find them almost as funny as British ones! I still dislike a lot of the older/
        traditional German humour, though, and like to spoil my husband's enjoyment
        by telling him what is wrong with the jokes. (Anne F; English with German
        partner, W)

(21)   I'm still faster at humour in English. In German, though, I'm happy to say I can
        now make light-hearted, offhand remarks to lighten up a situation where every-
        one would otherwise be silent or serious, or to make someone feel less embar-
        rassed if they have done something stupid. I'd say it took at least 10 years before I
        could start doing that. Actually, I think I can now do that better than my German
        husband can do it in English. He does come over as more serious in English: he
        has an excellent accent and vocab, but doesn't play about with the language that
        much, probably as we've never spent more than a couple of weeks in the UK.
        When we are in the UK and he tries to make jokes in front of my mother, she
        sometimes misunderstands and gets a bit ratty with him, thinking he's criticising

her or something. Partly because it's hard for him to joke AND watch out that he doesn't accidentally offend her (she gets offended easily, and he's good at putting his foot in it). (Sophie)

Several contradictory issues emerge from these narrations. Sandra and Anne both respectively express aversion to Italian and German comedy, with Sandra feeling "lucky" at not having to "sit through" any, while Anne conveys her "dislike" of German ones. British humor superiority raises its head once more as Anne enjoys spoiling her husband's enjoyment of German humor by criticizing it. But just as each informant desires that the humor of her culture be accepted by her partner, her own attempts at humor may be perceived as being faulty. Just as Geena (17) complains of being corrected on occasions in which she is not attempting to be funny, Sophie's mother misunderstands the attempts at humor made by her German son-in-law (20). Being able to use humorous talk may well be a final frontier of cross-cultural social acceptance, with total approval of the foreigner in the host culture being the acquiescence to joke freely outside the safety of domesticity. And domesticity here appears to be restricted to the couple's family unit. Sophie's mother 'misunderstands' her son-in-law and Geena suspects her husband's family "think[s] I've corrupted him" (5). Humor talk outside the domain of the couple's immediate family unit appears to be falling flat.

These last data colligate with the quantitative data and the component of the factor analysis labeled 'The Annoyance Component' (3.1.3 iii). It would appear that there is a certain tension where senses of humor and/or tastes in humor do not match. And this is especially true with regard to speakers of English. It appears that accusing someone of not having a sense of humor or not having good taste in humor simply underscores the fact that that person does not have the same sense of humor as we do.

3.2.2iii *Humorous talk, language and culture*   Several respondents appear to link humorous talk in their partner's language with translating a joke from their own language into the target language. Marchese, reports Irish born Deidre married to Italian Gianni:

> ...it's [humour] very hard to translate. Sometimes jokes don't come out well in the other language. And sometimes English people wanted me to explain the political situation there, which is quite complicated and it's not easy because the English have a completely different idea of politics...I mean it's much more simpler. (2007: 74).

Interestingly, the notion of translating from Language A into Language B occurs frequently in interviews, implying that when they joke verbally, couples perceive that they translate mentally before speaking.

(22)   …when I explain a joke to him, or if he translates an Iranian joke to me, we both think them funny – but the funniest thing about a joke is that you catch the clue fastly, (sic.) and that we miss. So I think our humour is rather the same, and maybe we choose each other because we have things like this in common, but the languages provide some barriers to catch the other language's humour well. (Giselinde F; Dutch with Iranian [Farsi] partner, W)

(23)   Claudia: [translation] it's always a disaster.
       Colm: Oh yes…but you have to be careful, because sometimes you lose the complete meaning if you don't translate well. (FFI)

Many informants tended to link cultural knowledge to television and/or cinematic knowledge. Having the same sense of humor seemed to be often reduced to appreciating the same sitcoms, more often than, for example, laughing at common experiences, or even simply playing with language.

(24)   There are some English sitcoms that I never watched until I saw my husband laughing at them.…the fact that he likes them has made me a bit more willing to try and see the funny side…I never watch these on my own but in the company of hubby I'll watch things like "Keeping up Appearances"…and laugh when he laughs…I think it must be because I like the fact that he gets the jokes. (Sandra)

(25)   I manage to make jokes, just. It took me ages to get to this point, as I find a lot is based on references to TV programmes, celebrities, etc. (Danuta)

(26)   I guess I just don't get Israeli comedy. To be fair, my husband doesn't get Seinfeld, et alia either. So we meet halfway at Mr. Bean, who doesn't speak and is funny to both of us. One thing that's always intrigued me is why he likes Fawlty Towers. Now *I* can easily understand why it's funny, but he must miss all those little throw-away lines, plays on words and small things like the "Fawlty Towers" sign outside that morphs into anagrams or almost-anagrams like "Watery Fowls". (Geena)

(27)   I find that I enjoy a good American comedy (not the slapsticky kind – I honestly loathe that kind of stumble/trip/hit-her-head/how hilarious from any country) and somehow accept much of it unthinkingly as part of my culture. The question I cannot answer is, of course, whether that's just because I lived in the States for quite some time, or whether this is the influence of American imported culture. All I know is that my mother and her friends prefer watching German TV, but do laugh at American movies if they see them. My teen babysitters wouldn't be caught dead watching German comedy shows. So there is also the aspect of age. I remember showing my American friends a German comedy called "Der bewegte Mann" – don't remember the English title. They found it very unfunny indeed, while I was rolling on the floor crying with mirth… (Wilma F; German with US English partner, W)

References to English language sitcoms are understandably frequent if one partner is a native speaker of English, yet it would appear that the power of the media is such that US/UK-made sitcoms epitomize taste in humor over and above geographical and cultural barriers:

(28)   …likes to tell bedtime stories turning German words into really strange Japanese expressions which has my sons groaning...before giggling. Both kids (me too) are really into British style humour as well, they like Monty Python and Douglas Adams, and a recent big favourite are DVDs of the BBC show "Goodness Gracious Me" which mixes weird British Asian situations with dry British humour. Their English isn't that advanced, but the shows are so funny they enjoy them nevertheless. (Christine German; F with Japanese partner, W)

(29)   I do enjoy the humour in Bengali comedies, I can understand most of it without needing explanations, and I enjoy Bollywood movies also now that we get them with English subtitles. My husband does enjoy Finnish and Swedish humour in movies and TV series, but won't get it all without English subtitles or my explanations. (Carita)

Undoubtedly, a quest for comity emerges. Sandra (23) claims that she "laugh[s] when he laughs...I think it must be because I like the fact that he gets the jokes." And Christine (27) "likes" her Japanese partner's hilarious attempts at translating German into his language. Similarly, Carita and partner "enjoy" Bengali, Finnish and Swedish humor through English. What surfaces is a sense of almost effortless effort. Effortless, because it is enjoyable, but at the same time, a large effort must surely be made to undertake the far from simple task of learning the humor of a partner's culture.

4. Conclusions

Data regarding language chosen for interaction in different domains was collected from a small sample of bilingual, cross-cultural couples by means of a purpose-built questionnaire. Particular attention was paid to data resulting from questions focusing specifically on the use of verbally expressed humor in the couples' interaction. As well as statistics, qualitative data was collected from six face-to-face, semi-structured interviews and from open responses gathered via the Internet.

Processed data emerging from the questionnaires show that couples used both languages for humorous talk quite indifferently. Furthermore, while they felt at ease creating verbally expressed humor in their partners' language, they also felt excluded if and when their partner partook in humorous discourse in his/her own language with fellow citizens. Results show that humorous talk does indeed act as a bonding agent in cross-cultural, bilingual couples, with partners often making a special effort to teach their own brand of humor to their mate and vice versa, and to learn to appreciate and to use the humor of their partner's culture. All this appears to be undertaken in order to create some kind of humorous comity. Respondents had positive attitudes towards their partner's (culture's) sense of humor, even if, in some cases, hostility was felt by outsiders when informants attempted to play with a language that was not their own. Furthermore, it emerged that native speakers of English seemed to harbor a sense of superiority regarding their native sense of humor and seemed to look down upon their partner's more naïve variety of humor.

The sample of both questionnaire and interview studies were skewed. The respondents from the questionnaire were all highly educated internet users. They were also mainly female. Similarly, informants who responded to the Web posting were also highly educated and mainly female. Nevertheless, what was especially significant of the latter sample was the way each response triggered off other connected responses. Furthermore, interviewees themselves (both face-to-face and via Web) made frequent use of humorous talk in their responses. One of the chats triggered off by the request for information was a long list of "silly children's jokes" which generated requests to explain or even translate the jokes into a number of languages. Couples interviewed face-to-face frequently teased each other throughout, and in many of the web responses, examples of humor are evident (see Geena and Alison). Thus, as well as being highly educated, mainly female and internet *habitués*, this small group of respondents also possessed a good sense of humor.

In conclusion, humorous interaction in cross-cultural, bilingual couples, may well be an important bonding agent to help overcome the myriad of intercultural difficulties such relationships inevitably face. Coates borrows a metaphor from music to describe humorous talk (2007: 32). Comparing it to jazz in which players improvise and co-construct new melodies, so do participants in humorous talk create harmony. Cross-cultural, bilingual couples, with their diverse 'instrumental' repertoires must collaborate even harder to create harmony by means of what to some ears must appear like syncopated musical clashes. Yet to the members of the band, the couple themselves and their immediate family, the syncopated rhythm of cross-cultural, bilingual humorous talk may well be tantamount to harmony.

References

Attardo, Salvatore & Raskin, Victor. 1991. "Script theory revis(it)ed: joke similarity and joke representation model." *Humor* 4(3): 293–347.
Attardo, Salvatore. 1994. *Linguistic Theories of Humor*. Berlin: Mouton de Gruyter.

Bateson, Gregory. 1953. "The position of humour in human communication." In *Cybernetics*, Ninth Conference, Foerster, H. (Ed.), 1–47. New York: Josiah Macey Jr. Foundation.

Chiaro, Delia. 1992. *The Language of Jokes: analyzing verbal play*. London: Routledge.

Coates, Jennifer. 2007. "Talk in a play frame: More on laughter and intimacy." *Journal of Pragmatics* 39: 29–49.

Davies, Christie. 1998. *Jokes and their Relation to Society*. Berlin: Mouton de Gruyter.

Ervin-Tripp, Susan. 1968. "An analysis of the interaction of language, topic and listener." In *Readings in the sociology of language*, J. Fishman (Ed.), 192–211. The Hague: Mouton.

Fitzpatrick, Mary Anne. 1990. "Models of marital interaction." In *Handbook of Language and Social Psychology*, H. Giles & W.P. Robinson (Eds), 433–450. Chichester: Wiley.

Kuipers, Giselinde. 2007. *Good Humor, Bad Taste*. Berlin: de Gruyter.

La Fave, Lawrence, Hadda, Jay & Maessens, William A. 1976. "Superiority, enhanced self-esteem an perceived incongruity humour theory" In *Humour and laughter: Theory, research, and applications*, A.G. Chapman & H.C. Foot (Eds), 63–91. New York: Wiley.

Lefcourt, Herbert M. & Thomas, Stacy. 1998. "Humor and Stress Revisited" In *The Sense of Humor: explorations of a personality characteristic*, W. Ruch (Ed.), 179–202. Berlin: Mouton de Gruyter.

Marchese, Elena. 2007. *Anglo-Italian Couples: Bilingualism, Identity and Culture*. Unpublished degree dissertation, Advanced School in Modern Languages for Interpreters and Translators, University of Bologna, Italy.

Martin, Rod A. 2007. *The psychology of humor: An integrative approach*. Burlington, MA: Elsevier.

Martin, Rod A. 1989. "Humor and the Mastery of Living: Using Humor with the Daily Stresses of Growing Up." In *Humor and Children's Development*, P. McGhee (Ed.), 135–154. New York: Haworth.

McCarthy, Michael & Carter, Ronald. 2004. "'There's millions of them': Hyperbole in everyday conversation." *Journal of Pragmatics* 36: 149–184.

Mazza, Cristina. 2001. "Numbers in simultaneous interpretation." *The Interpreters' Newsletter* 11: 87–104.

Piller, Ingrid. 2000. "Language choice in bilingual, cross-cultural interpersonal communication." *Linguistik Online* 5(1) at http://www.linguistik-online.com/1_00/index.html

Piller, Ingrid. 2002. *Bilingual Couples Talk*. Amsterdam: Benjamins.

Raskin, Victor. 1985. *Semantic mechanisms of humour*. Dordrecht: Reidel.

Ruch, Willibald (Ed.). 1998. *The Sense of Humor: explorations of a personality characteristic*. Berlin: Mouton de Gruyter.

Sternberg, Robert J. 1988. "A triangular theory of love." *Psychological Review* 93: 119–135.

Ziv, Avner (Ed.). 1988. *National Styles of Humor*. Westport, CT: Greenwood.

Ziv, Avner & Gadish, Orit. 1989. "Humor and marital satisfaction." *The Journal of Social Psychology* 129: 759–768.

Name index

Subject index